Unity Virtual Reality Projects

Explore the world of virtual reality by building immersive and fun VR projects using Unity 3D

Jonathan Linowes

PACKT PUBLISHING

open source
community experience distilled

BIRMINGHAM - MUMBAI

D1455362

Unity Virtual Reality Projects

First published: August 2015

Production reference: 1280815

Published by Packt Publishing Ltd.
Livery Place
35 Livery Street
Birmingham B3 2PB, UK.

ISBN 978-1-78398-855-6

www.packtpub.com

Credits

Author
Jonathan Linowes

Reviewers
Krystian Babilinski
Arindam Ashim Bose
Rongkai Guo
Arun Kulshreshth
Robin de Lange
Samuel Mosley

Commissioning Editor
Neil Alexander

Acquisition Editor
Reshma Raman

Content Development Editor
Mamata Walkar

Technical Editor
Gaurav Suri

Copy Editor
Vedangi Narvekar

Project Coordinator
Sanjeet Rao

Proofreader
Safis Editing

Indexer
Priya Sane

Production Coordinator
Shantanu N. Zagade

Cover Work
Shantanu N. Zagade

About the Author

Jonathan Linowes is the owner of Parkerhill Reality Labs, a start-up VR/AR consultancy firm. He is a veritable VR and 3D graphics enthusiast, full-stack web developer, software engineer, successful entrepreneur, and teacher. He has a fine arts degree from Syracuse University and a master's degree from the MIT Media Lab. He has founded several successful start-ups and held technical leadership positions at major corporations, including Autodesk Inc.

This book is dedicated to Lisa—my wife, best friend, and soul mate—and the amazing family we created together: Rayna, Jarrett, Steven, and Shira who know in their hearts that the future is theirs to embrace.

About the Reviewers

Krystian Babilinski began working with Unity and Blender when he was in middle school. Since high school, he and his brother, Adrian, taught via Google's Helpouts service. Through teaching, he exposed himself to a new assortment of problem sets, which he then experienced firsthand. Slowly, he began getting involved in large-scale projects and freelance work. With a growing portfolio and knowledge of Unity 3D along with platform optimizations, he and his brother started their own creative firm in 2014. They began developing assets for Unity's Asset Store and worked for larger clients, such as The Hasley Group and Beach Consulting. These successes wouldn't have been possible without their loyal customers.

Arindam Ashim Bose, as of 2015, is pursuing his master's degree in computer science at the Georgia Institute of Technology in Atlanta. He is interested in computer graphics, virtual and augmented reality, and game development.

He was born in Mumbai and has been fascinated by computers and technology, especially computer games, since a very young age. He would spend countless hours during his vacations and weekends playing games and tinkering with them to modify them. It was this habit of tinkering and modding that got him into computer programming.

He is currently trying to break into the games industry as a programmer while pursing his master's degree.

Rongkai Guo is an assistant professor in the department of computer software engineering and game design and development at Kennesaw State University. His research interests are serious gaming, computer/mobile gaming, and virtual reality (VR). He has been conducting research on a VR for rehabilitation project for more than 4 years. He has conducted his first basic research study, IN THE WORLD, which formally investigated how VR impacts persons with mobility impairments.

Arun Kulshreshth is a researcher in the department of computer science at the University of Central Florida. His research interests include 3D user interfaces, human-computer interactions (HCI), games, and virtual reality. He received his master of technology (an integrated 5-year program) in mathematics and computing from the Indian Institute of Technology, Delhi, in 2005. He received a master of science in computer science in 2012 and a PhD in computer science in 2015 from the University of Central Florida.

He is the author of several publications that are related to his research work pertaining to utilizing 3D user interface technologies (such as stereoscopic 3D, head tracking, gestural interfaces, and so on) for video games. He is a professional member of the Association for Computing Machinery (ACM) and Institute of Electrical and Electronics Engineers (IEEE). In the past, he has conducted research at several international locations, including Spain, Denmark, and USA. One of his papers was awarded an honorable-mention award in a leading HCI conference (CHI 2014). In 2014, his name was featured in a Reuters article, and one of his projects was featured on Discovery News.

Robin de Lange is a researcher, lecturer, and entrepreneur with a focus on virtual reality and education.

Robin has an MSc degree in media technology from Leiden University and a bachelor's degree in physics and philosophy from the same university. He conducts part-time PhD research at the media technology research group of Leiden University under the supervision of Dr. Bas Haring. For his research, he is exploring the potential of augmented and virtual reality to understand and solve complex problems. Part of this research is an elective course, where Robin leads a group of students to create virtual reality prototypes for the field of education.

Besides his academic career, Robin has started many different initiatives. He is the director of a homework guidance company and the founder of Lyceo CodeWeken, a unique program for high-school students that teaches how to code.

Samuel Mosley is a game designer. He studied programming and game design at the University of Texas in Dallas. Showing an interest in both programming and games, he hopes to play an important role in both fields. He is currently working as a game designer for Bohemia Interactive Simulations.

www.PacktPub.com

Support files, eBooks, discount offers, and more

For support files and downloads related to your book, please visit www.PacktPub.com.

Did you know that Packt offers eBook versions of every book published, with PDF and ePub files available? You can upgrade to the eBook version at www.PacktPub.com and as a print book customer, you are entitled to a discount on the eBook copy. Get in touch with us at service@packtpub.com for more details.

At www.PacktPub.com, you can also read a collection of free technical articles, sign up for a range of free newsletters and receive exclusive discounts and offers on Packt books and eBooks.

https://www2.packtpub.com/books/subscription/packtlib

Do you need instant solutions to your IT questions? PacktLib is Packt's online digital book library. Here, you can search, access, and read Packt's entire library of books.

Why subscribe?

- Fully searchable across every book published by Packt
- Copy and paste, print, and bookmark content
- On demand and accessible via a web browser

Free access for Packt account holders

If you have an account with Packt at www.PacktPub.com, you can use this to access PacktLib today and view 9 entirely free books. Simply use your login credentials for immediate access.

Table of Contents

Preface

Today, we are witnesses to the burgeoning of virtual reality (VR), an exciting new technology that promises to transform in a fundamental way how we interact with our information, friends, and the world at large.

What is consumer virtual reality? By wearing a head-mounted display (such as goggles), you can view stereoscopic 3D scenes. You can look around by moving your head and walk around by using hand controls or motion sensors. You can engage in a fully immersive experience. It's like you're really in some other virtual world.

This book takes a practical, project-based approach to teach you the specifics of virtual reality development with the Unity 3D game engine. We walk through a series of hands-on projects, step-by-step tutorials, and in-depth discussions using Unity 5 and other free or open source software. While VR technology is rapidly advancing, we'll try to capture the basic principles and techniques that you can use to make your VR games and applications immersive and comfortable.

You will learn how to use Unity to develop VR applications that can be experienced with devices such as the Oculus Rift or Google Cardboard. We'll cover technical considerations that are especially important and possibly unique to VR. By the end of this book, you will be equipped to develop rich, interactive virtual reality experiences using Unity.

What this book covers

Chapter 1, *Virtually Everything for Everyone*, is an introduction to the new technologies and opportunities in consumer virtual reality (VR) as regards games and non-gaming applications.

Chapter 2, *Objects and Scale*, discusses how you can build a simple diorama scene. It introduces the Unity 3D game engine as well as Blender for 3D modeling and explores the issues of world coordinates and scale.

Chapter 3, VR Build and Run, helps you configure your project to run on a VR headset, such as the Oculus Rift and Google Cardboard (Android or iOS). Then, we go into detail about how the VR hardware and software works.

Chapter 4, Gaze-based Control, explores the relationship between the VR camera and objects in the scene, including 3D cursors and gaze-based ray guns. This chapter also introduces Unity scripting in the C# programming language.

Chapter 5, World Space UI, implements many examples of user interface (UI) for VR, which includes a heads-up display (HUD), info-bubbles, and in-game objects with a lot of code and explanations.

Chapter 6, First-person Character, dissects the Unity character objects and components, which are used to build our own first-person character with gaze-based navigation. Then, we'll explore the experience of having a first-person virtual body and consider the issue of motion sickness.

Chapter 7, Physics and the Environment, dives into the Unity physics engine, components, and materials as we learn to work with forces and gravity in a number of VR project examples and games.

Chapter 8, Walk-throughs and Rendering, helps us build a 3D architectural space and implement a virtual walk-through. We also talk about rendering in Unity and performance optimizations.

Chapter 9, Using All 360 Degrees, uses 360-degree media in a variety of projects, including globes, panoramas, and photospheres. We also have a discussion on how it all works.

Chapter 10, Social VR Metaverse, explores the multiplayer implementations with VR using the Unity 5 networking components. We also have a look at VRChat as an example of an extensible platform for social VR.

Chapter 11, What's Next?, in this chapter the author comments about the potential of this exciting technology.

What you need for this book

Before we get started, there are a few things that you'll need. Grab a snack, a bottle of water, or a cup of coffee. Besides this, you'll need a PC (Windows or Mac) with the Unity 3D game engine installed.

You don't need a superpowerful rig. While Unity can be a beast that can render complex scenes and Oculus has published recommended specifications for PC hardware, you can get by with less. Even a laptop will do for the projects in this book.

To get Unity, go to `https://unity3d.com/get-unity/`, select the version that you want, click on Download Installer, and continue following the instructions. The free Personal Edition version of Unity is fine.

We can also optionally use the Blender open source project for 3D modeling. This book isn't about Blender, but we'll use it if you want. To get Blender, go to `http://www.blender.org/download/` and follow the instructions for your platform.

Access to a virtual reality head-mounted display (HMD) is recommended in order to try out your builds and get first-hand experience of the projects developed in this book. It's entirely possible to build and run all the projects on a desktop monitor, but where's the fun in that? This book addresses the details of both Google Cardboard and Oculus Rift.

Google Cardboard is an example of Mobile VR, where you use your smartphone to run the VR apps. If you have an Android smartphone, you'll also need the Android development tools from Google. If you have an iOS device, you'll also need the Xcode development tools (and license) from Apple. The details are covered in *Chapter 3, VR Build and Run*.

Oculus Rift is an example of Desktop VR. Presently, Unity has built-in support for the Rift. However, if you have a different head-mounted display (HMD), you may also need to download a Unity interface package from the device manufacturer. Again, the details are covered in *Chapter 3, VR Build and Run*.

This should just about do it—a PC, the Unity software, a HMD, and we're good to go!

Who this book is for

If you are interested in virtual reality, want to learn how it works, or want to create your own VR experiences, this book is for you. Whether you're a nonprogrammer and are unfamiliar with 3D computer graphics, or experienced in both but new to virtual reality, you will benefit from this book. It is not a fresh start with Unity, but you do not need to be an expert either. Nevertheless, if you're new to Unity, you can pick up this book as long as you realize that you'll need to adapt to the pace of the book.

Game developers may already be familiar with the concepts in the book, reapplied to the VR projects while learning many other ideas specific to VR. Mobile and 2D game designers who already know how to use Unity will discover another dimension! Engineers and 3D designers may understand many of the 3D concepts, but they may learn to use the game engine for VR. Application developers may appreciate the potential nongaming uses of VR and want to learn the tools that can make this happen.

Conventions

In this book, you will find a number of text styles that distinguish between different kinds of information. Here are some examples of these styles and an explanation of their meaning.

Code words in text, database table names, folder names, filenames, file extensions, pathnames, dummy URLs, user input, and Twitter handles are shown as follows: "Modify the `AvatarMultiplayer.cs` script."

A block of code is set as follows:

```
using UnityEngine;
using System.Collections;

public class RandomPosition : MonoBehaviour {
  // Use this for initialization
  void Start () {
  }
  // Update is called once per frame
  void Update () {
  }
}
```

When we wish to draw your attention to a particular part of a code block, the relevant lines or items are set in bold:

```
public class ButtonExecute : MonoBehaviour {
  public float timeToSelect = 2.0f;
  private float countDown;
  private GameObject currentButton;
  private clicker = new Clicker ();
```

Any command-line input or output is written as follows:

```
moveDirection *= moveDirection * velocity * Time.deltaTime;
transform.position += transform.position  + moveDirection;
```

New terms and important words are shown in bold. Words that you see on the screen, for example, in menus or dialog boxes, appear in the text like this: "Click on the **Create a Room** button."

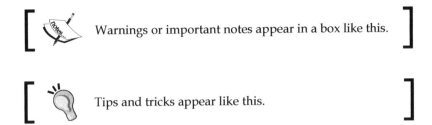

Warnings or important notes appear in a box like this.

Tips and tricks appear like this.

Reader feedback

Feedback from our readers is always welcome. Let us know what you think about this book—what you liked or disliked. Reader feedback is important for us as it helps us develop titles that you will really get the most out of.

To send us general feedback, simply e-mail feedback@packtpub.com, and mention the book's title in the subject of your message.

If there is a topic that you have expertise in and you are interested in either writing or contributing to a book, see our author guide at www.packtpub.com/authors.

Customer support

Now that you are the proud owner of a Packt book, we have a number of things to help you to get the most from your purchase.

Downloading the example code

You can download the example code files from your account at http://www.packtpub.com for all the Packt Publishing books you have purchased. If you purchased this book elsewhere, you can visit http://www.packtpub.com/support and register to have the files e-mailed directly to you.

Downloading the color images of this book

We also provide you with a PDF file that has color images of the screenshots/ diagrams used in this book. The color images will help you better understand the changes in the output. You can download this file from http://www.packtpub.com/ sites/default/files/downloads/ 8556OS_ColorImages.pdf.

Errata

Although we have taken every care to ensure the accuracy of our content, mistakes do happen. If you find a mistake in one of our books — maybe a mistake in the text or the code — we would be grateful if you could report this to us. By doing so, you can save other readers from frustration and help us improve subsequent versions of this book. If you find any errata, please report them by visiting http://www.packtpub. com/submit-errata, selecting your book, clicking on the **Errata Submission Form** link, and entering the details of your errata. Once your errata are verified, your submission will be accepted and the errata will be uploaded to our website or added to any list of existing errata under the Errata section of that title.

To view the previously submitted errata, go to https://www.packtpub.com/books/ content/support and enter the name of the book in the search field. The required information will appear under the **Errata** section.

Piracy

Piracy of copyrighted material on the Internet is an ongoing problem across all media. At Packt, we take the protection of our copyright and licenses very seriously. If you come across any illegal copies of our works in any form on the Internet, please provide us with the location address or website name immediately so that we can pursue a remedy.

Please contact us at copyright@packtpub.com with a link to the suspected pirated material.

We appreciate your help in protecting our authors and our ability to bring you valuable content.

Questions

If you have a problem with any aspect of this book, you can contact us at
questions@packtpub.com, and we will do our best to address the problem.

Image credit

Images in this book are created by the author or covered by Creative
Commons License.

1
Virtually Everything for Everyone

This virtual reality thing calls into question, what does it mean to "be somewhere"?

Before cell phones, you would call someone and it would make no sense to say, "Hey, where are you?" You know where they are, you called their house, that's where they are.

So then cell phones come around and you start to hear people say, "Hello. Oh, I'm at Starbucks," because the person on the other end wouldn't necessarily know where you are, because you became un-tethered from your house for voice communications.

So when I saw a VR demo, I had this vision of coming home and my wife has got the kids settled down, she has a couple minutes to herself, and she's on the couch wearing goggles on her face. I come over and tap her on the shoulder, and I'm like, "Hey, where are you?"

It's super weird. The person's sitting right in front of you, but you don't know where they are.

-Jonathan Stark, mobile expert and podcaster

Welcome to virtual reality! In this book, we will explore what it takes to create virtual reality experiences on our own. We will take a walk through a series of hands-on projects, step-by-step tutorials, and in-depth discussions using the **Unity 5** 3D game engine and other free or open source software. Though the virtual reality technology is rapidly advancing, we'll try to capture the basic principles and techniques that you can use to make your VR games and applications feel immersive and comfortable.

In this first chapter, we will define virtual reality and illustrate how it can be applied not only to games but also many other areas of interest and productivity. This chapter discusses the following topics:

- What is virtual reality?
- Differences between **virtual reality (VR)** and **augmented reality (AR)**
- How VR applications may differ from VR games
- Types of VR experiences
- Technical skills that are necessary for the development of VR

What is virtual reality to you?

Today, we are witnesses to the burgeoning consumer virtual reality, an exciting technology that promises to transform in a fundamental way how we interact with information, our friends, and the world at large.

What is virtual reality? In general, VR is the computer-generated simulation of a 3D environment, which seems very real to the person experiencing it, using special electronic equipment. The objective is to achieve a strong sense of being present in the virtual environment.

Today's consumer tech VR involves wearing a head-mounted display (such as goggles) to view stereoscopic 3D scenes. You can look around by moving your head, and walk around by using hand controls or motion sensors. You are engaged in a fully immersive experience. It's as if you're really there in some other virtual world. The following image shows a guy experiencing an **Oculus Rift Development Kit 2 (DK2)**:

Virtual reality is not new. It's been here for decades, albeit hidden away in academic research labs and high-end industrial and military facilities. It was big, clunky, and expensive. Ivan Sutherland invented the first head-mounted display in 1966, which is shown in the following image. It was tethered to the ceiling! In the past, several failed attempts have been made to bring consumer-level virtual reality products to the market.

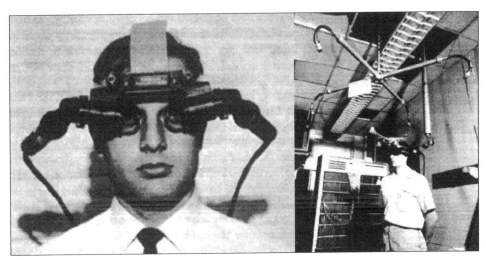

"The Ultimate Display", Ivan Sutherland, 1965

In 2012, Palmer Luckey, the founder of Oculus VR LLC, gave a demonstration of a makeshift head-mounted VR display to John Carmack, the famed developer of Doom, Wolfenstein 3D, and Quake classic video games. Together, they ran a successful **Kickstarter** campaign and released a developer kit called Oculus Rift Development Kit 1 (DK1) to an enthusiastic community. This caught the attention of investors as well as Mark Zuckerberg, and in March 2014, Facebook bought the company for $2 billion. With no product, no customers, and an infinite promise, the money and attention that it attracted has helped fuel a new category of consumer products. Others have followed suit, including Google, Sony, Samsung, and Steam. New innovations and devices that enhance the VR experience continue to be introduced.

Most of the basic research has already been done and the technology is now affordable thanks in large part to the mass adoption of devices that work on mobile technology. There is a huge community of developers with experience in building 3D games and mobile apps. Creative content producers are joining in and the media is talking it up. At last, virtual reality is real!

Say what? *Virtual reality is real?* Ha! If it's virtual, how can it be... Oh, never mind.

Eventually, we will get past the focus on the emerging hardware devices and recognize that *content is king*. The current generation of 3D development software (commercial, free, and open source) that has spawned a plethora of indie, or independent, game developers can also be used to build non-game VR applications.

Though VR finds most of its enthusiasts in the gaming community, the potential applications reach well beyond that. Any business that presently uses 3D modeling and computer graphics will be more effective if it uses VR technology. The sense of immersive presence that is afforded by VR can enhance all common online experiences today, which includes engineering, social networking, shopping, marketing, entertainment, and business development. In the near future, viewing 3D websites with a VR headset may be as common as visiting ordinary flat websites today.

Types of head-mounted displays

Presently, there are two basic categories of head-mounted displays for virtual reality—**desktop VR** and **mobile VR**.

Desktop VR

With desktop VR (and console VR), your headset is a peripheral to a more powerful computer that processes the heavy graphics. The computer may be a Windows PC, Mac, Linux, or a game console. Most likely, the headset is connected to the computer with wires. The game runs on the remote machine and the **head-mounted display** (**HMD**) is a peripheral display device with a motion sensing input. The term *desktop* is an unfortunate misnomer since it's just as likely to be stationed in either a living room or a den.

The **Oculus Rift** (https://www.oculus.com/) is an example of a device where the goggles have an integrated display and sensors. The games run on a separate PC. Other desktop headsets include **HTC/Valve Vive** and Sony's project **Morpheus** for PlayStation.

The Oculus Rift is tethered to a desktop computer via video and USB cables, and generally, the more **graphics processing unit** (**GPU**) power, the better. However, for the purpose of this book, we won't have any heavy rendering in our projects, and you can get by even with a laptop (provided it has two USB ports and one HDMI port available).

Mobile VR

Mobile VR, exemplified by **Google Cardboard** (http://www.google.com/get/cardboard/), is a simple housing (device) for two lenses and a slot for your mobile phone. The phone's display is used to show the twin stereographic views. It has rotational head tracking, but it has no positional tracking. Cardboard also provides the user with the ability to click or *tap* its side to make selections in a game. The complexity of the imagery is limited because it uses your phone's processor for rendering the views on the phone display screen. Other mobile VR headsets include Samsung **Gear VR** and Zeiss **VR One**, among others.

Google provides the open source specifications, and other manufacturers have developed ready-made models for purchase, with prices for the same as low as $15. If you want to find one, just Google it! There are versions of Cardboard-compatible headsets that are available for all sizes of phones—both Android and iOS.

Although the quality of the VR experience with a Cardboard device is limited (some even say that it is inadequate) and it's probably a "starter" device that will just be *quaint* in a couple of years, Cardboard is fine for the small projects in this book, and we'll revisit its limitations from time to time.

The difference between virtual reality and augmented reality

It's probably worthwhile clarifying what virtual reality is not.

A sister technology to VR is augmented reality (AR), which superimposes **computer generated imagery (CGI)** over views of the real world. Limited uses of AR can be found on smart phones, tablets, handheld gaming systems such as the Nintendo 3DS, and even in some science museum exhibits, which overlay the CGI on top of live video from a camera.

The latest innovations in AR are the AR headsets, such as Microsoft **HoloLens** and **Magic Leap**, which show the computer graphics directly in your field of view; the graphics are not mixed into a video image. If the VR headsets are like closed goggles, the AR headsets are like translucent sunglasses that employ a technology called **light fields** to combine the real-world light rays with CGI. A challenge for AR is ensuring that the CGI is consistently aligned with and mapped onto the objects in the real-world space and eliminate latency while moving about so that they (the CGI and objects in real-world space) stay aligned.

AR holds as much promise as VR for future applications, but it's different. Though AR intends to engage the user within their current surroundings, virtual reality is fully immersive. In AR, you may open your hand and see a log cabin resting in your palm, but in VR, you're transported directly inside the log cabin and you can walk around inside it.

We can also expect to see hybrid devices that somehow either combine VR and AR, or let you switch between modes.

Applications versus games

The consumer-level virtual reality starts with gaming. Video gamers are already accustomed to being engaged in highly interactive hyper-realistic 3D environments. VR just ups the ante.

Gamers are early adopters of high-end graphics technology. Mass production of gaming consoles and PC-based components in the tens of millions and competition between vendors leads to lower prices and higher performance. Game developers follow suit, often pushing the state-of-the-art, squeezing every ounce of performance out of hardware and software. Gamers are a very demanding bunch, and the market has consistently stepped up to keep them satisfied. It's no surprise that many, if not most, of the current wave of the VR hardware and software companies are first targeting the video gaming industry. A majority of the demos and downloads that are available on **Oculus Share** (https://share.oculus.com/) and **Google Play** for the Cardboard app (https://play.google.com/store/search?q=cardboard&c=apps) are games. Gamers are the most enthusiastic VR advocates and seriously appreciate its potential.

Game developers know that the core of a game is the **game mechanics**, or the rules, which are largely independent of the *skin*, or the thematic topic of the game. Gameplay mechanics can include puzzles, chance, strategy, timing, or muscle memory (*twitch*). VR games can have the same mechanic elements but might need to be adjusted for the virtual environment. For example, a first-person character walking in a console video game is probably going about 1.5 times faster than their actual pace in real life. If this wasn't the case, the player would feel that the game is too slow and boring. Put the same character in a VR scene and they will feel that it is too fast; it could likely make the player feel nauseous. In VR, you will want your characters to walk a normal, earthly pace. Not all video games will map well to VR; it may not be fun to be in the middle of a war zone when you're actually there.

That said, virtual reality is also being applied in areas other than gaming. Though games will remain important, non-gaming apps will eventually overshadow them. These applications may differ from games in a number of ways, with the most significant having much less emphasis on game mechanics and more emphasis on either the experience itself or application-specific goals. Of course, this doesn't preclude some game mechanics. For example, the application may be specifically designed to train the user at a specific skill. Sometimes, the **gamification** of a business or personal application makes it more fun and effective in driving the desired behavior through competition.

 In general, non-gaming VR applications are less about winning and more about the experience itself.

Here are a few examples of the kinds of non-gaming applications that people are working on:

- **Travel and tourism**: Visit faraway places without leaving your home. Visit art museums in Paris, New York, and Tokyo in one afternoon. Take a walk on Mars. You can even enjoy Holi, the spring festival of colors, in India while sitting in your wintery cabin in Vermont.

- **Mechanical engineering and industrial design**: Computer-aided design software such as AutoCAD and SOLIDWORKS pioneered three-dimensional modeling, simulation, and visualization. With VR, engineers and designers can directly experience the hands-on end product before it's actually built and play with what-if scenarios at a very low cost. Consider iterating a new automobile design. How does it look? How does it perform? How does it appear sitting in the driver's seat?

- **Architecture and civil engineering**: Architects and engineers have always constructed scale models of their designs, if only to pitch the ideas to clients and investors, or more importantly, to validate the many assumptions about the design. Presently, modeling and rendering software is commonly used to build virtual models from architectural plans. With VR, the conversation with stakeholders can be so much more confident. Other personnel, such as the interior designers, HVAC, and electrical engineers, can be brought into the process sooner.

- **Real estate**: Real estate agents have been quick adopters of the Internet and visualization technology to attract buyers and close sales. Real estate search websites were some of the first successful uses of the Web. Online panoramic video walk-throughs of for-sale properties are commonplace today. With VR, I can be in New York and find a place to live in Los Angeles. This will become even easier with mobile 3D-sensing technologies such as **Google Project Tango** (`https://www.google.com/atap/projecttango`), which performs a 3D scan of a room using a smartphone and automatically builds a model of the space.

- **Medicine**: The potential of VR for health and medicine may literally be a matter of life and death. Every day, hospitals use MRI and other scanning devices to produce models of our bones and organs that are used for medical diagnosis and possibly pre-operative planning. Using VR to enhance visualization and measurement will provide a more intuitive analysis. Virtual reality is also being used for the simulation of surgery to train medical students.

- **Mental health**: Virtual reality experiences have been shown to be effective in a therapeutic context for the treatment of **post traumatic stress disorder (PTSD)** in what's called **exposure therapy**, where the patient, guided by a trained therapist, confronts their traumatic memories through the retelling of the experience. Similarly, VR is being used to treat arachnophobia (spiders) and the fear of flying.

- **Education**: The educational opportunities for VR are almost too obvious to mention. One of the first successful VR experiences is **Titans of Space**, which lets you explore the solar system first hand. Science, history, arts, and mathematics—VR will help students of all ages because, as they say, field trips are much more effective than textbooks.

- **Training**: Toyota has demonstrated a VR simulation of drivers' education to teach teenagers about the risks of distracted driving. In another project, vocational students got to experience the operating of cranes and other heavy construction equipment. Training for first responders, police, and the fire and rescue workers can be enhanced with VR by presenting highly risky situations and alternative virtual scenarios. The NFL is looking to VR for athletic training.

- **Entertainment and journalism**: Virtually attend rock concerts and sporting events. Watch music videos. Erotica. Re-experience news events as if you were personally present. Enjoy 360-degree cinematic experiences. The art of storytelling will be transformed by virtual reality.

Wow, that's quite a list! This is just the low-hanging fruit.

The purpose of this book is not to dive too deeply into any of these applications. Rather, I hope that this survey helps stimulate your thinking and provides a perspective towards how virtual reality has the potential to be virtually anything for everyone.

What this book covers

This book takes a practical, project-based approach to teach the specifics of virtual reality development using the Unity 3D game development engine. You'll learn how to use Unity 5 to develop VR applications, which can be experienced with devices such as the Oculus Rift or Google Cardboard.

However, we have a slight problem here—the technology is advancing very rapidly. Of course, this is a good problem to have. Actually, it's an awesome problem to have, unless you're a developer in the middle of a project or an author of a book on this technology! How does one write a book that does not have obsolete content the day it's published?

Throughout the book, I have tried to distill some universal principles that should outlive any near-term advances in virtual reality technology, that includes the following:

- Categorization of different types of VR experiences with example projects
- Important technical ideas and skills, especially the ones relevant to the building of VR applications
- General explanations on how VR devices and software works
- Strategies to ensure user comfort and avoid VR motion sickness
- Instructions on using the Unity game engine to build VR experiences

Once VR becomes mainstream, many of these lessons will perhaps be obvious rather than obsolete, just like the explanations from the 1980's on *how to use a mouse* would just be silly today.

Who are you?

If you are interested in virtual reality, want to learn how it works, or want to create VR experiences yourself, this book is for you. We will walk you through a series of hands-on projects, step-by-step tutorials, and in-depth discussions using the Unity 3D game engine.

Whether you're a non-programmer who is unfamiliar with 3D computer graphics, or a person with experience in both but new to virtual reality, you will benefit from this book. It is not a cold start with Unity, but you do not need to be an expert either. Still, if you're new to Unity, you can pick up this book as long as you realize that you'll need to adapt to the pace of the book.

Game developers may already be familiar with the concepts in the book, which are reapplied to the VR projects while learning many other ideas that are specific to VR. Engineers and 3D designers may understand many of the 3D concepts, but they may wish to learn to use the game engine for VR. Application developers may appreciate the potential non-gaming uses of VR and want to learn the tools that can make this happen.

Whoever you are, we're going to turn you into a *3D Software VR Ninja*. Well, OK, this may be a stretch goal for this little book, but we'll try to set you on the way.

Types of VR experiences

There is not just one kind of virtual reality experience. In fact, there are many. Consider the following types of virtual reality experiences:

- **Diorama**: In the simplest case, we build a 3D scene. You're observing from a third-person perspective. Your eye is the camera. Actually, each eye is a separate camera that gives you a stereographic view. You can look around.

- **First-person experience**: This time, you're immersed in the scene as a freely moving avatar. Using an input controller (keyboard, game controller, or some other technique), you can walk around and explore the virtual scene.

- **Interactive virtual environment**: This is like the first-person experience, but it has an additional feature—while you are in the scene, you can interact with the objects in it. Physics is at play. Objects may respond to you. You may be given specific goals to achieve and challenges with the game mechanics. You might even earn points and keep score.

- **Riding on rails**: In this kind of experience, you're seated and being transported through the environment (or, the environment changes around you). For example, you can ride a roller coaster via this virtual reality experience. However, it may not necessarily be an extreme thrill ride. It can be a simple real estate walk-through or even a slow, easy, and meditative experience.

- **360-degree media**: Think panoramic images taken with **GoPro®** on steroids that are projected on the inside of a sphere. You're positioned at the center of the sphere and can look all around. Some purists don't consider this "real" virtual reality, because you're seeing a projection and not a model rendering. However, it can provide an effective sense of presence.

- **Social VR**: When multiple players enter the same VR space and can see and speak with each other's avatars, it becomes a remarkable social experience.

In this book, we will implement a number of projects that demonstrate how to build each of these types of VR experience. For brevity, we'll need to keep it pure and simple, with suggestions for areas for further investigation.

Technical skills that are important to VR

Each chapter of the book introduces new technical skills and concepts that are important if you wish to build your own virtual reality applications. You will learn about the following in this book:

- **World scale**: When building for a VR experience, attention to the 3D space and scale is important. One unit in Unity is usually equal to one meter in the virtual world.

- **First-person controls**: There are various techniques that can be used to control the movement of your avatar (first-person camera), gaze-based selection, game controllers, and head movements.

- **User interface controls**: Unlike conventional video (and mobile) games, all user interface components are in world coordinates in VR, not screen coordinates. We'll explore ways to present notices, buttons, selectors, and other **User interface (UI)** controls to the users so that they can interact and make selections.

- **Physics and gravity**: Critical to the sense of presence and immersion in VR is the physics and gravity of the world. We'll use the Unity physics engine to our advantage.

- **Animations**: Moving objects within the scene is called "animation" (duh!) It can either be along predefined paths, or it may use AI (artificial intelligence) scripting that follows a logical algorithm in response to events in the environment.

- **Multiuser services**: Real-time networking and multiuser games are not easy to implement, but online services make it easy without you having to be a computer engineer.

- **Build and run**: Different HMDs use different developer kits (SDK) and assets to build applications that target a specific devise. We'll consider techniques that let you use a single interface for multiple devices.

We will write scripts in the C# language and use features of Unity as and when they are needed to get things done.

However, there are technical areas that we will not cover, such as realistic rendering, shaders, materials, and lighting. We will not go into modeling techniques, terrains, or humanoid animations. Effective use of advanced input devices and hand and body tracking is proving to be critical to VR, but we won't have a chance to get into it here either. We also won't discuss game mechanics, dynamics, and strategies. We will talk about rendering performance optimization, but not in depth. All of these are very important topics that may be necessary for you to learn (or for someone in your team), in addition to this book, to build complete, successful, and immersive VR applications.

Summary

In this chapter, we looked at virtual reality and realized that it can mean a lot of things to different people and can have different applications. There's no single definition, and it's a moving target. We are not alone, as everyone's still trying to figure it out. The fact is that virtual reality is a new medium that will take years, if not decades, to reach its potential.

VR is not just for games; it can be a game changer for many different applications. We identified over a dozen. There are different kinds of VR experiences, which we'll explore in the projects in this book.

VR headsets can be divided into those that require a separate processing unit (such as a desktop PC or a console) that runs with a powerful GPU and the ones that use your mobile phone for processing. In this book, we will use an Oculus Rift as an example of *desktop VR* and Google Cardboard as the example of *mobile VR*, although there are many alternative and new devices available.

We're all pioneers living at an exciting time. Because you're reading this book, you're one, too. Whatever happens next is literally up to you. As the personal computing pioneer Alan Kay said, "The best way to predict the future is to invent it."

So, let's get to it!

In the next chapter, we'll jump right into Unity and create our first 3D scene and learn about world coordinates and scaling. Then in *Chapter 3, VR Build and Run*, we'll build and run it on a VR headset, and we'll discuss how virtual reality really works.

2
Objects and Scale

You may remember building a diorama project for school from a shoebox as a child. We're going to make one today using Unity. Let's assemble our first scene, which is composed of simple geometric objects. Along the way, we'll talk a lot about **world scale**. In this chapter, we will discuss the following topics:

- A short introduction to the Unity 5 3D game engine
- Creating a simple diorama in Unity
- Making some measuring tools, including a unit cube and a Grid Projector
- Using **Blender** to create a cube with texture maps and import it into Unity

Getting started with Unity

If you don't have the Unity 3D game engine application installed on your PC yet, do that now! The fully-featured **Personal Edition** is free and runs on both Windows and Mac. To get Unity, go to `https://unity3d.com/get-unity/`, select the version that you want, click on **Download Installer**, and continue following the instructions. This book assumes version 5.1 of Unity.

For you beginners out there, we're going to take this first section nice and slow, with more hand-holding than what you'll get later on in the book. Furthermore, even if you already know Unity and have developed your own games, it may be worthwhile revisiting the fundamental concepts, since the rules sometimes are different when designing for virtual reality.

Starting a new Unity project

Create a new Unity project named VR_is_Awesome, or whatever you'd like.

To create a new Unity project, launch Unity from your operating system, and the **Open** dialog box will appear. From this dialog box, select **New Project**, which opens a **New project** dialog box, as shown in the following screenshot:

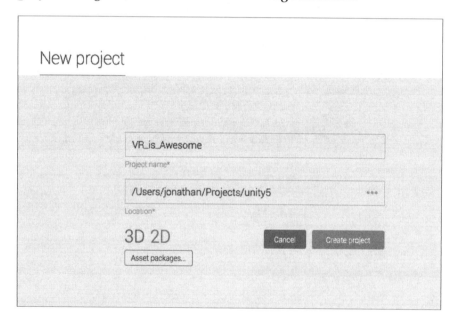

Fill in the name of your project and verify that the folder location is what you want. Ensure that **3D** is selected (on the lower left). There is no need to select any extra asset packages at this time, as we'll bring them in later if we need them. Click on **Create project**.

The Unity editor

Your new project opens in the Unity editor, as shown in the following screenshot (where I arranged the window panels in a custom layout to facilitate this discussion and highlighted a couple of panels):

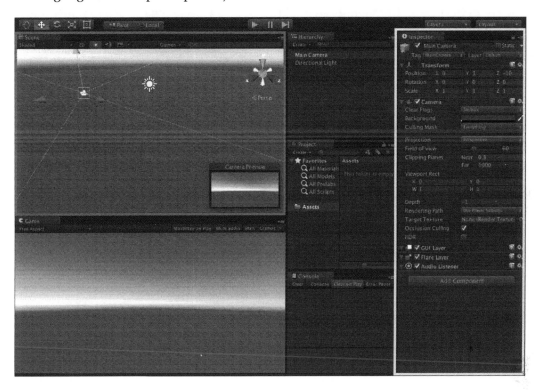

The Unity editor consists of a number of non-overlapping windows, or *panels*, which may be subdivided into *panes*. Here's a brief explanation of each panel that is shown in the preceding layout image (your layout may be different):

- The **Scene** panel on the upper left-hand side (highlighted) is where you can visually compose the 3D space of the current scene, including the placement of objects.

- Below the **Scene** panel (lower left-hand side) is the **Game** view, which shows the actual game camera view (presently, it is empty with an ambient sky). When in **Play Mode**, your game runs in this panel.

- In the center are the **Hierarchy**, **Project**, and **Console** panels (from the top to the bottom) respectively. The **Hierarchy** panel provides a tree view of all the objects in the current scene.

- The **Project** panel contains all the reusable resources for the project, including the ones imported as well as those that you'll create along the way.

- The **Console** panel shows messages from Unity, including warnings and errors from code scripts.

- On the right-hand side is the **Inspector** panel (highlighted), which contains the properties of the currently selected object. (Objects are selected by clicking on them in the **Scene**, **Hierarchy**, or the **Project** panel). The **Inspector** panel has separate panes for each component of the object.

- At the top is the main menu bar (on a Mac, this will be at the top of your screen, not at the top of the Unity window). There's a toolbar area with various controls that we'll use later on, including the *play* (triangle icon) button that starts Play Mode.

From the main menu bar **Window** menu, you can open additional panels, as needed. The editor's user interface is configurable. Each panel can be rearranged, resized, and tabbed by grabbing one of the panel tabs and dragging it. Go ahead, try it! On the upper right-hand side is a **Layout** selector that lets you either choose between various default layouts, or save your own preferences.

The default world space

A default empty Unity scene consists of a **Main Camera** component and a single **Directional Light** component, as listed in the **Hierarchy** panel and depicted in the **Scene** panel. The **Scene** panel also shows a perspective of an infinite reference ground plane grid, like a piece of graph paper with nothing on it yet. The grid spans across the x (red) and z (blue) axes. The y-axis (green) is up.

An easy way to remember the gizmo axis colors is by keeping in mind that R-G-B corresponds to X-Y-Z.

The **Inspector** panel shows the details of the currently selected item: Select the **Directional Light** with your mouse, either from the **Hierarchy** list or within the scene itself, and look at the **Inspector** panel for each of the properties and components associated with the object, including its transform. An object's transform specifies its position, rotation, and scale in the 3D world space. For example, a (0, 3, 0) position is 3 units above (Y direction) the center of the ground plane (**X** = 0, **Z** = 0). A rotation of (50, 330, 0) means that it's rotated 50 degrees around the *x*-axis and 330 degrees around the *y*-axis. As you'll see, you can change an object's transforms numerically here or directly with the mouse in the **Scene** panel.

Similarly, if you click on the **Main Camera**, it may be located at the (0, 1, -10) position with no rotation. That is, it's pointed straight ahead, towards the positive Z direction.

When you select the **Main Camera**, as shown in the preceding editor screenshot, a **Camera Preview** inset is added to the **Scene** panel, which shows the view that the camera presently sees. (If the **Game** tab is open, you'll see the same view there too). Presently, the view is empty and the reference grid does not get rendered, but a foggy horizon is discernible, with the grey ground plane below and the blue default ambient **Skybox** above.

Creating a simple diorama

Now, we will add a few objects to the scene to set up the environment, including a unit cube, a flat plane, a red ball, and a photographic backdrop.

Adding a cube

Let's add the first object to the scene—a unit-sized cube.

Within the **Hierarchy** panel, use the **Create** menu and choose **3D Object | Cube**. The same selection can also be found in the main menu bar's **GameObject** dropdown.

A default white cube is added to the scene, centered on the ground plane at the (0, 0, 0) position with no rotation and a scale of one, as you can see in the **Inspector** panel. This is the **Reset** setting, which can be found in the object's **Transform** component of the **Inspector** panel

The **Reset** values of the **Transform** component are **Position** (0, 0, 0), **Rotation** (0, 0, 0), and **Scale** (1, 1, 1).

If for some reason, your cube has other **Transform** values, set these in the **Inspector** panel or locate the small *gear* icon on the upper right-hand side of the **Inspector** panel's **Transform** component, click on it, and select **Reset**.

This cube has the dimensions of one unit on each side. As we'll see later, one unit in Unity corresponds to one meter in world coordinates. Its local center is the center of the cube.

Adding a plane

Now, let's add a ground plane object into the scene.

In the **Hierarchy** panel, click on the **Create** menu (or main **GameObject** menu) and choose **3D Object | Plane**.

A default white plane is added to the scene, centered on the ground plane at position (0, 0, 0). (If necessary, select **Reset** from the **Inspector** panel's **Transform** component's *gear* icon). Rename it to GroundPlane.

Note that at a scale of (1, 1, 1), Unity's plane object actually measures 10 by 10 units in **X** and **Z**. In other words, the size of GroundPlane is 10x10 units and its **Transform** component's **Scale** is 1.

The cube is centered at **Position** (0, 0, 0), just like the ground plane. However, maybe it doesn't look like it to you. The **Scene** panel may show a **Perspective** projection that renders 3D scenes onto a 2D image. The **Perspective** distortion makes the cube not seem centered on the ground plane but it is. Count the grid lines on the either sides of the cube! As you'll see, when it is viewed in VR and you're actually standing in the scene, it won't look distorted at all. This is shown in the following screenshot:

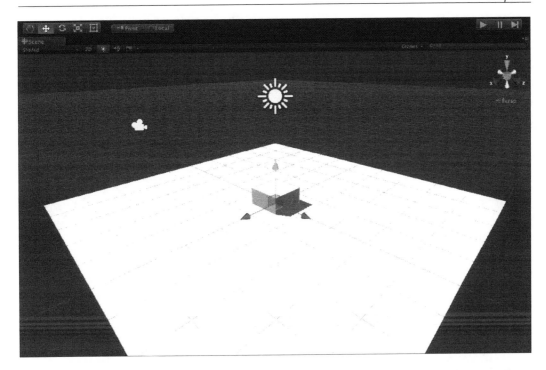

The cube is submerged in the ground plane because its local origin is at its geometric center—it measures 1 by 1 by 1 and its middle point is (0.5, 0.5, 0.5). This might sound obvious, but it is possible for the origin of a model to not be its geometric center (such as one of its corners). The **Transform** component's position is the world space location of the object's local origin. Let's move the cube as follows:

1. Move the cube onto the surface of the ground plane—in the **Inspector** panel, set its Y position to 0.5: **Position** (0, 0.5, 0).

2. Let's rotate the cube a bit around the y-axis. Enter 20 into its Y-rotation: **Rotation** (0, 0.5, 0).

Note the direction in which it rotates. That's 20 degrees clockwise. Using your left hand, give a thumbs-up gesture. See the direction your fingers are pointing? Unity uses a left-handed coordinate system. (There is no standard for the coordinate system *handedness*. Some software use left-handedness, others use right-handedness).

 Unity uses a left-handed coordinate system. The y-axis is up.

Adding a sphere and some material

Next, let's add a sphere.

Select **GameObject | 3D Object | Sphere** from the menu.

Like the cube, the sphere has a radius of 1.0, with its origin at the center.
(If necessary, select **Reset** from the **Inspector** panel's **Transform** component's *gear* icon). It's hard to see the sphere as it is embedded in the cube. We need to move the sphere's position.

This time, let's use the **Scene** panel's **Gizmos** component to move the object. In the **Scene** view, you can select graphical controls or gizmos to manipulate the objects' transforms, as illustrated in the following image, from the Unity documentations (`http://docs.unity3d.com/Manual/PositioningGameObjects.html`):

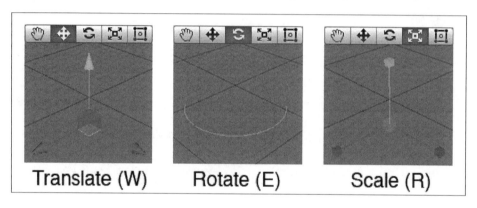

| Translate (W) | Rotate (E) | Scale (R) |

In the **Scene** panel, with the sphere selected, make sure that the **Translate** tool is active (second icon on the top left icon toolbar) and use the arrows of the x, y, and z axes to position it. I left mine at **Position** (1.6, 0.75, -1.75).

> A **gizmo** is a graphical control that lets you manipulate parameters of an object or a view. Gizmos have grab points or handles that you can click and drag with the mouse.

Before we go much further, let's save our work, as follows:

1. From the main menu bar, select **File | Save Scene** and name it `Diorama`.

2. Also, navigate to **File | Save Project** for good measure. Note that in the **Project** panel, the new scene object was saved in the top level **Assets** folder.

Let's add some color to the scene by making a couple of colored materials and applying them to our objects. Follow these steps:

1. In the **Project** panel, select the top-level **Assets** folder and select **Create | Folder**. Rename the folder to Materials.

2. With the Materials folder selected, select **Create | Material** and rename it to Red.

3. In the **Inspector** panel, click the white rectangle to the right of **Albedo**, which opens the **Color** panel. Choose a nice red.

4. Repeat the preceding steps to make a blue material too.

5. Select **Sphere** from the **Hierarchy** (or **Scene**) panel.

6. Drag the Red material from the **Project** panel into the **Inspector** panel for the sphere. The sphere should now look red.

7. Select **Cube** from the **Scene** (or **Hierarchy**) panel.

8. This time, drag the Blue material from the Project panel into the scene and drop it onto the cube. It should now look blue.

Save your scene and save the project. Here's what my scene looks like now (yours might be a little different, but that's OK):

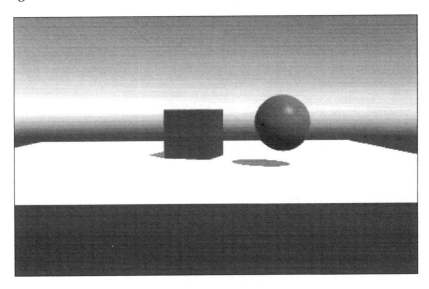

 Note that we're using the folders in Project/Assets/ directory to organize our stuff.

Changing the scene view

You can change the scene view any time in a number of ways, and this varies depending on whether you have a 3-button or a 2-button track pad, or Mac with only one button. Read up on it in the Unity manual, which can be found at `http://docs.unity3d.com/Manual/SceneViewNavigation.html`, to find out what works for you.

In general, combinations of left/right mouse clicks with *Shift/Ctrl/Alt* keys will let you perform the following actions:

- Drag the camera around.
- Orbit the camera around the current pivot point.
- Zoom in and out.
- *Alt* + right-click of the mouse swings the current eye orbit up, down, left, and right.
- When the **Hand** tool is selected (in the upper left icon bar), the right mouse button moves the eye. The middle-click of the mouse does a similar move.

In the upper right-hand side of the **Scene** panel, you have the **Scene View** gizmo, which depicts the current scene view orientation as shown in the following screenshot. It may indicate, for example, a **Perspective** view, with **X** extending back to the left and **Z** extending back to the right.

You can change the view to look directly along any of the three axes by clicking on the corresponding colored cone. Clicking on the small cube in the center changes the **Perspective** view to the **Orthographic** (nondistorted) view as shown in the following screenshot:

Before moving on, let's first align the scene view with the **Main Camera** direction. You may recall me saying that the default camera orientation, (0, 0, 0), is looking down the positive Z direction (back to front). Follow the following steps:

1. Click on the red **X** cone on the **Scene** view gizmo to adjust the view from the **Back** (back direction), looking forward.

2. Also, use the Hand tool (or the middle mouse-button) to slide the view up a tad.

Now, when you select the **Main Camera** component (from the **Hierarchy** panel), you will see that the **Scene** view is roughly similar to the **Camera Preview**, looking in the same direction. (See the screen capture image shown in the following section for what the scene and preview looks like with this view direction after we add the photo).

Adding a photo

Now, let's add a photo for the backdrop of our diorama.

In computer graphics, an image that is mapped onto an object is called a **texture**. While objects are represented in the X, Y, and Z world coordinates, textures are said to be in the U, V coordinates (such as pixels). We'll see that textures and UV maps can have their own scaling issues. Follow the following steps:

1. Create a plane by navigating to **GameObject | 3D Object | Plane** and rename it `PhotoPlane`.

2. Reset the plane's transform. In the **Inspector** panel, find the *gear* icon in the upper right-hand side of the **Transform** pane. Click on this icon and select **Reset**.

3. Rotate it by 90 degrees around the z-axis (set its **Transform** component's **Rotation** value of **Z** to `-90`). That's *minus 90*. So, it's standing up, perpendicular to the ground.

4. Rotate it by 90 degrees around the y-axis so that its front is facing us.

5. Move it to the end of the ground plane at **Position** value of **Z** = `5` and above, at **Position** value of **Y** = `5` (you may recall that the ground plane is 10x10 units).

6. Choose any photo from your computer to paste on this photo plane using Windows Explorer or Mac Finder. (Alternatively, you can use the `Grand Canyon.png` image that comes with this book).

7. In the **Project** panel, select the top-level **Assets** folder and navigate to **Create | Folder**. Rename the folder to Textures.

8. Drag the photo file into the Assets/Materials folder. It should automatically import as a texture object. Alternatively, you can right-click on the **Assets** folder, select **Import New Asset...**, and import the picture.

Select the new image **Texture** in the **Project** panel and review its settings in the **Inspector** panel. For whatever reason, even if the original photo was rectangular, the texture is square now (for example, 2048x2048) and looks squished. When you map it onto a square-shaped face, it will be squished there too. Let's see using the following steps:

1. Drag the photo texture from the **Project** panel onto the photo plane (in the **Scene** panel).

   Oops! In my case, the picture is rotated sideways (yours too?)

2. Select PhotoPlane (the photo plane) and set **Transform** component's **Rotation** value of **X** to 90 degrees.

   OK, it's upright, but still squished. Let's fix this. Check the original resolution of your photo and determine its aspect ratio. My Grand Canyon image was 2576x1932. When you divide its width by its height, you get the 0.75 ratio.

3. In Unity, set the PhotoPlane plane's **Transform** component's **Scale** value of **Z** to 0.75.

   Because its scale origin is the center, we also have to move it back down a bit.

4. Set **Position** value of **Y** to 3.75.

Why 3.75? The height started at 10. So, we scaled it to 7.5. The scaling of objects is relative to their origin. So now, half of the height is 3.75. We want to position the center of the photo plane 3.75 units above the ground plane.

We have the size and position set up, but the photo looks washed out. That's because the ambient lighting in the scene is affecting it. You might want to keep it that way, especially as you build more sophisticated lighting models and materials in your scenes. But for now, we'll un-light it.

With PhotoPlane selected, note that the photo's **Texture** component in the **Inspector** panel has its default **Shader** component as **Standard**. Change it to **Unlit | Texture**.

Here's what mine looks like; yours should be similar:

There! That looks pretty good. Save your scene and project.

Coloring the ground plane

If you want to change the ground plane color, create a new material (in the **Project** panel), name it Ground and drag it onto the ground plane. Then, change its **Albedo** color. I suggest using the dropper (icon) to pick an earth tone from the image in your photo plane.

Measurement tools

We've created a Unity scene, added a few primitive 3D objects and created a couple of basic textures, including a photograph. Along the way, we learned about positioning and transforming objects in Unity's 3D world space. The problem is that the actual size of stuff in your scene is not always obvious. You could be zoomed up or you may be using either a **Perspective** versus **Orthographic** view, or other features that affect the apparent size. Let's look at ways to deal with the scale.

Keeping a unit cube handy

I suggest keeping a unit cube handy in your **Hierarchy** panel. When it's not needed, just disable it (uncheck the checkbox in the top left-hand side of the **Inspector** panel). It can be used like a measuring stick or rather a measuring block, when needed. I use one to estimate actual world sizes of objects, distances between objects, heights and elevations, and so forth. Let's do it now.

Create a unit cube, name it `Unit Cube`, place it somewhere out of the way for now, such as **Position** (-2, 0.5, -2).

You can also add a tick-marked tape measure texture to its edges.

Leave it enabled for the time being.

Using a Grid Projector

I want to tell you about the **Grid Projector**, a handy tool that is used to visualize a scale in any Unity scene. It's one of the **Standard Assets** in the **Effects** package. So, you may need to import it into your project. To import, perform the following steps:

1. Select **Assets** in the main menu bar and then navigate to **Import Package | Effects**.

2. The **Import** dialog box pops up, containing the list of all the things that can get imported. If you want, just click on **All** and then select **Import**. However, we only really need the **Projectors** folder so that you can choose and import just that folder.

Now, we'll add a Projector to the scene, as follows:

1. Find the Grid Projector prefab located in the **Project** panel, navigating to the `Assets/Standard Assets/Effects/Projectors/Prefabs` folder.

2. Drag a copy of Grid Projector into your scene. Set its **Y** value of **Position** to 5 so that it's above the ground plane.

The default Grid Projector is facing downward (**Rotation** value of **X** = 90), which is usually what we want. In the **Scene** view, you can see the Orthographic projection rays. A Unity doc (`http://docs.unity3d.com/Manual/class-Projector.html`) explains a Projector as follows:

> *A Projector allows you to project a Material onto all objects that intersect its frustum.*

This means that the objects intersected by the projection rays will receive the projected material.

In this case, as you'd expect, the Projector material (also named `GridProjector`) has a "Grid" texture, which simply looks like a crosshair (see for yourself, in the `Assets/.../Projectors/Textures/Grid` object).

By default, the Projector shines the grid pattern as a light on the surface that it illuminates. In our scene, the `GroundPlane` plane is light. So the grid may not show up. Now follow the following steps:

With Grid Projector selected in the **Hierarchy** panel, locate the `GridProjector` Material component in the **Inspector** panel and change its **Shader** from **Hidden/ Projector Light** to **Hidden/Projector Multiply**.

It now paints white gridlines on black. To get a better feel of what's going on, change the scene view to a **Top** view orientation, as follows:

1. Click the green **Y** cone on the Scene view gizmo in the upper right-hand side of the **View** panel.

2. Also, click the little cube at the center of the gizmo to change from the **Perspective** to the **Orthographic** (non-distortion) view.

You should now be looking straight down onto the ground plane. With the Grid Projector selected (make sure that the Translate tool is active, which is the second icon in the top left icon toolbar), you can grab the Translate gizmo attached to the Projector and move it from side-to-side. The grid line will move accordingly. You might leave it at **Position** (-2.5, 5, -0.5) and avoid the projector blocking the directional light.

At this point, the built-in view reference grid might be confusing. So, turn it off in the following way:

1. In the **Scene** view panel, click on **Gizmos** (the menu with this name, which has options to control your gizmos) and uncheck **Show Grid**.

   OK, so what does this get us? We can see that the default grid size measures half the edge of the unit cube. In **Inspector**, the Projector component's **Orthographic** size value is 0.25.

2. Change the Projector's **Orthographic** Size value from 0.25 to 0.5.

3. Save the scene and the project.

Now, we have a 1-unit grid that can be turned on and projected onto the scene any time it is needed.

Let's leave it on for now because it looks kind of cool, as you can see in the following screenshot:

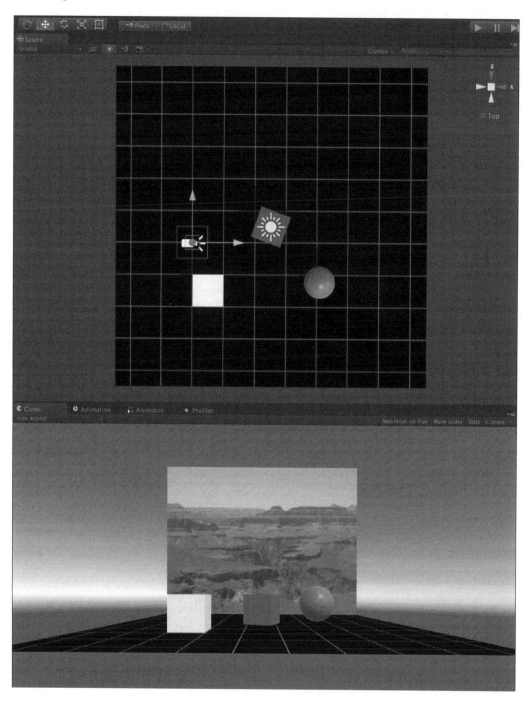

Measuring the Ethan character

How big is an avatar? Unity comes with a third-person character named Ethan. Let's add him to our scene. He's one of the **Standard Assets** in the **Characters** package. So, you may need to import that into your project.

To import, perform the following steps:

1. Select **Assets** in the main menu bar and then navigate to **Import Package | Characters**.

2. The **Import** dialog box pops up, containing the list of all the things that can get imported. Click **All** and then **Import**. The **ThirdPersonController** is a prefab (pre-built asset) located in the **Project** panel. This can be found by navigating to the Assets/Standard Assets/Characters/ThirdPersonCharacter/Prefabs folder.

3. Drag a copy of **ThirdPersonController** into your scene. The exact X and Z positions don't matter, but set the Y to 0 so that the character named Ethan is standing on GroundPlane. I left mine at (2.2, 0, 0.75).

Let's try it out:

1. Click on the *Play* icon at the top of the Unity window in the center, to start your game. Use the *W, A, S,* and *D* keys to move him around. *Run, Ethan! Run!*

2. Click on the *Play* icon again to stop the game and return to the edit mode.

So, how big is Ethan? According to Google search, the average height of a human male is 5' 6" or 1.68 meters (in USA, the average adult male is more like 5' 10" or 1.77 meters tall). Let's see how tall Ethan is when compared to these:

- Slide the unit cube next to Ethan using the Translate gizmo

  Alright, he's about 1.6 times its height

- Scale the unit cube's height (**Y**) to 1.6 and adjust its Y position to 0.8

Look again. As illustrated in the following screenshot, he's not quite 1.6. So Ethan is a little shorter than the average male (unless you include his pointy hairdo). Swinging my view around, I'm looking at Ethan right in the face, and by further adjusting the cube the eye level is about 1.4 meters. Make a note of this:

1. Restore the unit cube's **Scale** (1,1,1) and **Position** (-2, 0.5, -2).

2. Save the scene and the project.

The following screenshot shows the comparison of a cube 1.6 units tall and Ethan:

Importing from the Blender experiment

Unity offers some basic geometric shapes but when it comes to more complex models, you'll need to go beyond Unity. The Unity **Asset Store** has tons of amazing models (plus many other kinds of assets), and there are lots of other websites with large communities that share 3D models for fun and profit. Where do these models come from? Will you run into problems while importing them into Unity?

I know that this book is about Unity, but we're going on a short side adventure right now. We're going to use Blender (version 2.7x), a free and open source 3D animation suite (http://www.blender.org/), to make a model and then import it into Unity. Grab a coffee and strap yourself in!

The plan is not to build anything very fancy right now. We'll just build a cube and a simple texture map. The purpose of this exercise is to find out how well a one-unit cube in Blender imports with the same scale and orientation into Unity.

Feel free to skip this section or try a similar experiment using your favorite modeling software. If you prefer not to follow along or run into problems, a copy of the completed files created in this topic is available in the download package for this book.

An introduction to Blender

Open the Blender application. Dismiss the opening splash screen. You will be in the Blender editor, which is similar to what's shown in the following screenshot:

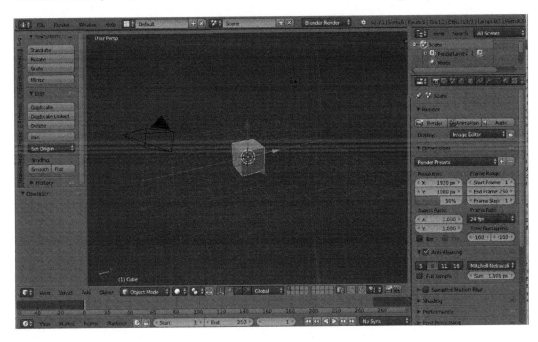

Like Unity, Blender consists of a number of non-overlapping windows, and their layout can be customized to suit your needs. However, the Blender interface can be more daunting, in part because it integrates a number of different editors that can be opened at the same time, in their own panels.

It's helpful to realize that the default view, as shown in the preceding screenshot, contains five different editors!

The most obvious editor is the large **3D View**, which I highlighted with a (red) rectangle. This is where you can view, move, and organize the objects in your Blender scene.

The following are the other editors that are opened:

- The **Info editor**, which can be seen along the top edge of the app, has global menus and information about the application
- The **Timeline editor**, which is present along the bottom edge of the app, is for animations
- The **Outliner editor**, in the upper right-hand side, has a hierarchical view of the objects in your scene
- The **Properties editor**, which can be seen to the right below the Outliner, is a powerful panel that lets you see and modify many properties of the objects in the scene

Each editor can have multiple panes. Let's consider the 3D View editor:

- The large area in the middle is the **3D Viewport**, where you can view, move, and organize the objects in your Blender scene.
- Just below the 3D Viewport is the editor **Header**, which is called so although it's at the bottom in this case. The Header is a row of menus and tools that provide great control over the editor, including view selectors, edit modes, transform manipulators, and layer management.
- On the left-hand side is the **Tool Shelf** containing various editing tools that can be applied to the currently selected object, which can be organized into tabbed groups. The **Tool Shelf** can be toggled open or closed by grabbing and sliding its edge or by pressing the key *T*.
- The 3D Viewport also has a **Properties** pane, which may be hidden by default and can be toggled open or closed by pressing the key *N*. It provides the property settings for the currently selected object.

In the upcoming instructions, we will ask you to change the **Interaction Mode** of the 3D View editor, say between the **Edit Mode** and **Texture Paint** mode. This is selected in the Header, as shown in the following screenshot:

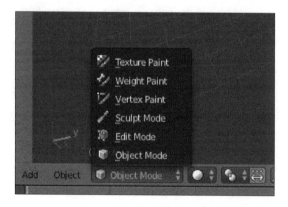

The other editors also have the Header panes. The Info editor (at the top of the app) is only a Header! The Outliner and Properties editors (on the right) have their Headers at the top of their panel rather than at the bottom.

Once you recognize this layout, it doesn't look so crowded and confusing.

The Properties editor Header has a wide set of icons, which act like tabs, to select the group of properties presented in the rest of the panel. Hovering your mouse over the icon (like any of the UI widgets here) will show a tooltip with a better hint as regards what it's for. It's pictured in the following images (in a couple of pages) when we get to using it.

The Blender layout is very flexible. You can even change a panel from one editor to another. At the far left of each Header is the **Editor Type** selector. When you click on it, you can see all the options.

In addition to the plethora of things that you can click on in the Blender interface, you can use just about any command using a keyboard shortcut. If you forget where to find a selection, press the *space bar* and type in your best guess of the command name that you're looking for. It just might pop up!

The following is the screenshot showing the **Editor Type** selector available in Blender:

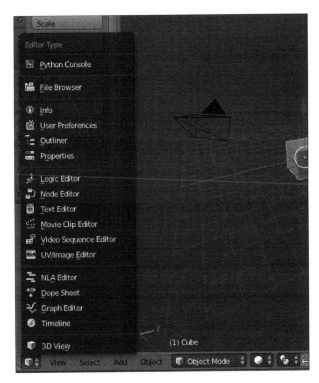

A unit cube

Now, let's build a unit cube in Blender.

The default scene may already have objects, including a cube, camera, and a light source, as shown earlier in the default Blender window. (Your start up settings may be different, since that can be configured).

If your startup scene does *not* contain a unit cube, create one, as follows:

1. Make sure that the scene is empty by deleting whatever is there in it (right-click to select, *X* key on the keyboard to delete).
2. Set the 3D cursor to the origin (0,0,0) using *Shift* + *S* (opens the **Snap** options list) | **Cursor To Center**.
3. In the left **Tool Shelf** panel, choose the **Create** tab and under **Mesh** select **Cube** to add a cube.

OK, now we're all on the same page.

Note that in Blender, the reference grid extends in the x and y axes, and z is up (unlike Unity, where the y-axis is up).

Furthermore, note that the default cube in Blender has the size of (2, 2, 2). We want a unit cube sitting on the ground plane at the origin. For this, follow the following steps:

1. Open the Properties pane with the keyboard *N* key.
2. Navigate to **Transform** | **Scale** and set **X, Y, Z** to (0.5, 0.5, 0.5).
3. Navigate to **Transform** | **Location** and set **Z** to 0.5.
4. Press the *N* key again to hide the pane.
5. You can zoom in using the scroll-wheel of the mouse.

For our purposes, also ensure that the current renderer is **Blender Render** (on the drop-down selector on the Info editor at the top of the app window in the center).

A UV Texture image

Next, we will create a **UV Texture image**, as follows:

1. Go into **Edit Mode** using the **Interaction Mode** selector in the bottom Header bar.

2. Select *all* (press the *A* key on keyboard twice) to make sure that all the faces are selected.

3. In the left **Tool Shelf** panel, select the **Shading/UVs** tab.

4. Under **UV Mapping** click on **Unwrap**, select **Smart UV Project** from the drop-down list, accept the default values, and click on **OK** (the result, shown in the following screenshot, also shows what the unwrapped cube looks like).

5. Now, go into the **Texture Paint** mode using the **Interaction Mode** selector in the bottom Header bar again.

6. We need to define a *paint slot* for our material. Click on **Add Paint Slot**, select **Diffuse Color**, name it CubeFaces, and press **OK**.

We can now start painting directly on the cube. Paint the front face first, as follows:

1. Make a smaller brush. In the left **Tool Shelf** panel, in the **Tools** tab, navigate to **Brush | Radius** and enter 8 px.

2. It may be easier to work in an orthographic view. From the menu bar at the bottom, navigate to **View | View Persp/Ortho**.

3. Then, navigate to **View | Front**.

4. You can zoom in or out using the mouse scroll-wheel, if needed.

5. With your best handwriting, write the word Front using the left-click of the mouse and draw.

6. Now, we'll do the same for the back face.

7. From the menu bar at the bottom, navigate to **View | Back** and select this face with a right-click.

8. With your best handwriting, write Back.

Repeat the above process for the left, right, top, and bottom faces. If at some point it's not painting, make sure that there's a current face selected. Try right-clicking on the face to reselect it. The result should look something like this (shown side-by-side both in the **3D View** editor with an orthographic perspective and the **UV/Image Editor**):

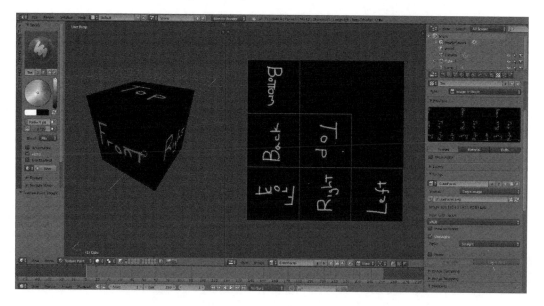

Now, we need to save the texture image and set up its properties, as follows:

1. Change the current **Editor Type** to **UV/Image Editor** using the selector on the far left of the Header at the bottom of the **3D View** editor.

2. Click on the **Browse Image to be linked** selector icon (just towards the left of **+** icon) and choose CubeFaces from the list.

3. The **Image** menu item on the menu bar at the bottom now has an asterisk (**Image***) indicating that there's an unsaved image. Click on it, select **Save As Image**, and save it as CubeFaces.png. Use a folder outside the Unity project.

4. On the right-hand side, in the Properties editor panel, find the long row of icons in its Header and select the **Texture** one (third from the last). It may be hidden if the panel isn't wide enough; you can scroll down with your mouse to show it, as shown in the following screenshot:

5. Within the **Texture** properties, change **Type** to **Image or Movie**.

6. Then, in the **Image** group of properties, click on the **Browse Image to be Linked** selector icon (as shown in the following screenshot) and choose CubeFaces:

7. You should see the labeled faces texture image in the **Preview** window.

Good! Let's save the Blender model, as follows:

1. Select **File** from the top main menu bar in the Info editor and click on **Save** (or press *Ctrl + S*).

2. Use the same folder as the one where you saved the texture image.

3. Name it UprightCube.blend and click on **Save Blender File**.

We should now have two files in a folder, UprightCube.blend and CubeFaces. png. I use a folder named Blender/ in the root of my Unity project. Note that alternatively, you can export to other standard formats, such as **FBX** (short for **Filmbox**).

Wow, that was a lot. Don't worry if you didn't get it all. Blender can be daunting. However, Unity needs models. You can always download someone else's models from the Unity **Asset Store** and other 3D model sharing sites. Don't be a wimp, learn to make your own. Ha ha! Seriously, it's a good thing to start to learn.

Importing into Unity

Back in Unity, we now want to import both the files, UprightCube.blend and CubeFaces.png, one at a time, as follows:

1. In the **Project** panel, select the top-level **Assets** folder, navigate to **Create | Folder**, and rename the folder to Models.

2. An easy way to import files into Unity is to just drag and drop the .blend file from the Windows Explorer (or Mac Finder) window into the **Project** panel **Assets/Models** folder and drag and drop the .png file into the **Assets/Textures** folder (or you can use the **Assets | Import New Asset...** from the main menu bar).

3. Add UprightCube to the scene by dragging it from the **Assets/Models** folder where it was just imported into the **Scene** view.

4. Set its position so that it's away from the other objects. I left mine at **Position** (2.6, 2.2, -3).

5. Drag the CubeFaces texture from the **Assets/Textures** folder into the **Scene** view, hovering over the just added UprightCube so that it receives the texture, and drop the texture onto the cube.

The scene should now look something like this:

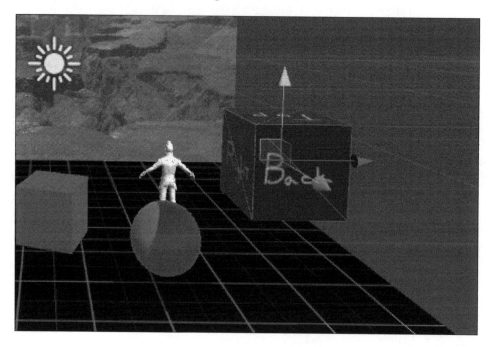

A few observations

The back of the cube is facing us. Is that a mistake? Actually, it makes sense since the current viewpoint is looking forward. So we should see the back of the cube. If you didn't notice already, the same goes for Ethan. It also seems like the cube has a one-unit dimension.

However, on closer examination, in the cube's **Inspector** panel, you'll see it imported with the scale that we gave it in Blender — (0.5, 0.5, 0.5). Also, it has an X-rotation of -90 (minus 90). Thus, if we reset the transform, that is, the scale to (1,1,1), it'll be 2 units in our world space and tipped over (so, don't reset it).

There's not much that we can do to compensate for the rotational adjustment without going back to Blender.

> Blender's default up direction is **Z**, while Unity's is **Y**. Importing with a -90 X-rotation adjusts for that. An imported scale can be adjusted in the object's **Inspector** panel's **Import Settings**.

The scaling issue can be fixed with further tweaking, as follows:

1. In the **Project** panel, select UprightCube that we imported. The **Inspector** panel shows its **Import Settings**.

2. Change **Scale Factor** from **1** to 0.5.

3. Click on **Apply**.

   The cube in the scene can now have **Scale** (1, 1, 1) and be a unit cube, like we'd expected.

4. With UprightCube selected in **Hierarchy**, change its **Transform** value of **Scale** to (1, 1, 1).

Before ending the preceding process, select UprightCube from the **Hierarchy** panel and drag it into the **Project** panel's **Assets** folder. (You may consider making an **Assets/Prefabs** subfolder and placing it into that). This makes it a reusable prefab, texture image and all.

There are some important lessons in this exercise (other than having learned a little bit of Blender) that apply to any 3D Unity project, including the VR ones. Normally, you will be importing models that are much more complex than a cube. You will likely run into issues related to data conversion, scale, orientation, and UV texture images that might be confusing at best. If this happens, try to break the problem into smaller, more isolated scenarios. Do little tests to gain insight on how applications exchange data and help you understand which parameter tweaks might be necessary.

Summary

In this chapter, we built a simple diorama, became more acquainted with the Unity editor, and learned about the importance of world scale in designing your scenes. We also set up several in-game tools to help us work with scaling and positioning in the future chapters. Lastly, we jumped into Blender, built a model with a UV texture, and learned some of the issues that can arise when importing these models into Unity.

In the next chapter, we'll set up a project with a virtual reality camera and build and run the project in your VR headset.

3
VR Build and Run

Yeah well, this is cool and everything, but where's my VR? I WANT MY VR!

Hold on kid, we're getting there.

In this chapter, we are going to set up a project that can be built and run with a virtual reality head-mounted display (HMD) and then talk more in depth about how the VR hardware technology really works. We will be discussing the following topics:

- The spectrum of the VR device integration software
- Installing and building a project for your VR device
- The details and defining terms for how the VR technology really works

 The projects in this book do not need to be implemented in sequence. You are free to skip around, as each chapter does not depend on its prior chapters. The exception is this chapter. Please implement the MeMyselfEye prefab, your target build device, and the Clicker class before moving on to the rest of the book.

VR device integration software

Before jumping in, let's understand the possible ways to integrate our Unity project with virtual reality devices. In general, your Unity project must include a camera object that can render stereographic views, one for each eye on the VR headset.

Software for the integration of applications with the VR hardware spans a spectrum, from built-in support and device-specific interfaces to the device-independent and platform-independent ones.

Unity's built-in VR support

Since Unity 5.1, support for the VR headsets is built right into Unity. At the time of writing this book, there is direct support for Oculus Rift and Samsung Gear VR (which is driven by the Oculus software). Support for other devices has been announced, including Sony PlayStation Morpheus. You can use a standard camera component, like the one attached to **Main Camera** and the standard character asset prefabs. When your project is built with **Virtual Reality Supported** enabled in **Player Settings**, it renders stereographic camera views and runs on an HMD.

The device-specific SDK

If a device is not directly supported in Unity, the device manufacturer will probably publish the Unity plugin package. An advantage of using the device-specific interface is that it can directly take advantage of the features of the underlying hardware.

For example, Steam Valve and Google have device-specific SDK and Unity packages for the Vive and Cardboard respectively. If you're using one of these devices, you'll probably want to use such SDK and Unity packages. (At the time of writing this book, these devices are not a part of Unity's built-in VR support.) Even Oculus, supported directly in Unity 5.1, provides SDK utilities to augment that interface (see, `https://developer.oculus.com/documentation/game-engines/latest/concepts/unity-intro/`).

Device-specific software locks each build into the specific device. If that's a problem, you'll either need to do some clever coding, or take one of the following approaches instead.

The OSVR project

In January 2015, **Razer Inc.** led a group of industry leaders to announce the **Open Source Virtual Reality** (**OSVR**) platform (for more information on this, visit `http://www.osvr.com/`) with plans to develop open source hardware and software, including an SDK that works with multiple devices from multiple vendors. The open source middleware project provides device-independent SDKs (and Unity packages) so that you can write your code to a single interface without having to know which devices your users are using.

With OSVR, you can build your Unity game for a specific operating system (such as Windows, Mac, and Linux) and then let the user configure the app (after they download it) for whatever hardware they're going to use. At the time of writing this book, the project is still in its early stage, is rapidly evolving, and is not ready for this book. However, I encourage you to follow its development.

WebVR

WebVR (for more information, visit `http://webvr.info/`) is a JavaScript API that is being built directly into major web browsers. It's like **WebGL** (2D and 3D graphics API for the web) with VR rendering and hardware support. Now that Unity 5 has introduced the WebGL builds, I expect WebVR to surely follow, if not in Unity then from a third-party developer.

As we know, browsers run on just about any platform. So, if you target your game to WebVR, you don't even need to know the user's operating system, let alone which VR hardware they're using! That's the idea anyway. New technologies, such as the upcoming **WebAssembly**, which is a new binary format for the Web, will help to squeeze the best performance out of your hardware and make web-based VR viable.

 For WebVR libraries, check out the following:
- **WebVR boilerplate**: `https://github.com/borismus/webvr-boilerplate`
- **GLAM**: `http://tparisi.github.io/glam/`
- **glTF**: `http://gltf.gl/`
- **MozVR** (the Mozilla **Firefox Nightly** builds with VR): `http://mozvr.com/downloads/`
- **WebAssembly**: `https://github.com/WebAssembly/design/blob/master/FAQ.md`

3D worlds

There are a number of third-party 3D world platforms that provide multiuser social experiences in shared virtual spaces. You can chat with other players, move between rooms through *portals*, and even build complex interactions and games without having to be an expert.

 For examples of 3D virtual worlds, check out the following:
- **VRChat**: `http://vrchat.net/`
- **JanusVR**: `http://janusvr.com/`
- **AltspaceVR**: `http://altvr.com/`
- **High Fidelity**: `https://highfidelity.com/`

For example, VRChat lets you develop 3D spaces and avatars in Unity, export them using their SDK, and load them into VRChat for you and others to share over the Internet in a real-time social VR experience. We will explore this in *Chapter 10, Social VR Metaverse*.

Creating the MeMyselfEye prefab

To begin, we will create an object that will be a proxy for the user in the virtual environment. This will be helpful later on, and it will simplify the conversations in this book, since different VR devices may use different camera assets. *Like an empty vessel for your VR soul...*

Let's create the object using the following steps:

1. Open Unity and the project from the last chapter. Then, open the `Diorama` scene by navigating to **File | Open Scene** (or double-click on the scene object in **Project** panel, under **Assets**).

2. From the main menu bar, navigate to **GameObject | Create Empty**.

3. Rename the object MeMyselfEye (hey, this is VR!).

4. Set its position up close into the scene, at **Position** (0, 1.4, -1.5).

5. In the **Hierarchy** panel, drag the **Main Camera** object into MeMyselfEye so that it's a child object.

6. With the **Main Camera** object selected, reset its transform values (in the **Transform** panel, in the upper right section, click on the *gear icon* and select **Reset**).

The **Game** view should show that we're inside the scene. If you recall the Ethan experiment that we did earlier, I picked a Y-position of 1.4 so that we'll be at about the eye level with Ethan.

Now, let's save this as a reusable prefabricated object, or *prefab*, in the **Project** panel, under **Assets** so that we can use it again in the other scenes in the other chapters of this book:

1. In **Project** panel, under **Assets**, select the top-level Assets folder, right-click and navigate to **Create | Folder**. Rename the folder Prefabs.

2. Drag the MeMyselfEye prefab into the **Project** panel, under Assets/Prefabs folder to create a prefab.

Now, let's configure the project for your specific VR headset.

 We will reuse this MeMyselfEye prefab in chapters throughout the book as a convenient generic VR camera asset in our projects.

Build for the Oculus Rift

If you have a Rift, you've probably already downloaded **Oculus Runtime**, demo apps, and tons of awesome games. To develop for the Rift, you'll want to be sure that the Rift runs fine on the same machine on which you're using Unity.

Unity has built-in support for the Oculus Rift. You just need to configure your **Build Settings...**, as follows:

1. From main menu bar, navigate to **File | Build Settings...**.

2. If the current scene is not listed under **Scenes In Build**, click on **Add Current**.

3. Choose **PC, Mac, & Linux Standalone** from the **Platform** list on the left and click on **Switch Platform**.

4. Choose your **Target Platform OS** from the **Select** list on the right (for example, **Windows**).

5. Then, click on **Player Settings...** and go to the **Inspector** panel.

6. Under **Other Settings**, check off the **Virtual Reality Supported** checkbox and click on **Apply** if the **Changing editor vr device** dialog box pops up.

To test it out, make sure that the Rift is properly connected and turned on. Click on the game *Play* button at the top of the application in the center. Put on the headset, and IT SHOULD BE AWESOME! Within the Rift, you can look all around—left, right, up, down, and behind you. You can lean over and lean in. Using the keyboard, you can make Ethan walk, run, and jump just like we did earlier.

Now, you can build your game as a separate executable app using the following steps. Most likely, you've done this before, at least for non-VR apps. It's pretty much the same:

1. From the main menu bar, navigate to **File | Build Settings....**

2. Click on **Build** and set its name.

3. I like to keep my builds in a subdirectory named `Builds`; create one if you want to.

4. Click on **Save**.

An executable will be created in your `Builds` folder. If you're on Windows, there may also be a `rift_Data` folder with built data. Run `Diorama` as you would do for any executable application—double-click on it. Choose the **Windowed** checkbox option so that when you're ready to quit, close the window with the standard *Close* icon in the upper right of your screen.

Build for Google Cardboard

Read this section if you are targeting Google Cardboard on Android and/or iOS.

A good starting point is the *Google Cardboard for Unity, Get Started* guide (for more information, visit `https://developers.google.com/cardboard/unity/get-started`).

The Android setup

If you've never built for Android, you'll first need to download and install the Android SDK. Take a look at Unity manual for *Android SDK Setup* (http://docs.unity3d.com/Manual/android-sdksetup.html). You'll need to install the **Android Developer Studio** (or at least, the smaller SDK Tools) and other related tools, such as Java (JVM) and the USB drivers.

It might be a good idea to first build, install, and run another Unity project without the Cardboard SDK to ensure that you have all the pieces in place. (A scene with just a cube would be fine.) Make sure that you know how to install and run it on your Android phone.

The iOS setup

A good starting point is Unity manual, *Getting Started with iOS Development* guide (http://docs.unity3d.com/Manual/iphone-GettingStarted.html). You can only perform iOS development from a Mac. You must have an Apple Developer Account approved (and paid for the standard annual membership fee) and set up. Also, you'll need to download and install a copy of the Xcode development tools (via the Apple Store).

It might be a good idea to first build, install, and run another Unity project *without* the Cardboard SDK to ensure that you have all the pieces in place. (A scene with just a cube would be fine). Make sure that you know how to install and run it on your iPhone.

Installing the Cardboard Unity package

To set up our project to run on Google Cardboard, download the SDK from https://developers.google.com/cardboard/unity/download.

Within your Unity project, import the CardboardSDKForUnity.unitypackage assets package, as follows:

1. From the **Assets** main menu bar, navigate to **Import Package | Custom Package...**
2. Find and select the CardboardSDKForUnity.unitypackage file.
3. Ensure that all the assets are checked, and click on **Import**.

Explore the imported assets. In the **Project** panel, the `Assets/Cardboard` folder includes a bunch of useful stuff, including the `CardboardMain` prefab (which, in turn, contains a copy of `CardboardHead`, which contains the camera). There is also a set of useful scripts in the `Cardboard/Scripts/` folder. Go check them out.

Adding the camera

Now, we'll put the Cardboard camera into `MeMyselfEye`, as follows:

1. In the **Project** panel, find `CardboardMain` in the `Assets/Cardboard/Prefabs` folder.
2. Drag it onto the `MeMyselfEye` object in the **Hierarchy** panel so that it's a child object.
3. With `CardboardMain` selected in **Hierarchy**, look at the **Inspector** panel and ensure the **Tap is Trigger** checkbox is checked.
4. Select the **Main Camera** in the **Hierarchy** panel (inside `MeMyselfEye`) and disable it by unchecking the **Enable** checkbox on the upper left of its **Inspector** panel.

Finally, apply theses changes back onto the prefab, as follows:

1. In the **Hierarchy** panel, select the `MeMyselfEye` object. Then, in its **Inspector** panel, next to **Prefab**, click on the **Apply** button.
2. Save the scene.

We now have replaced the default **Main Camera** with the VR one.

The build settings

If you know how to build and install from Unity to your mobile phone, doing it for Cardboard is pretty much the same:

1. From the main menu bar, navigate to **File | Build Settings...**.
2. If the current scene is not listed under **Scenes to Build**, click on **Add Current**.
3. Choose **Android** or **iOS** from the **Platform** list on the left and click on **Switch Platform**.
4. Then, click on **Player Settings...** in the **Inspector** panel.
5. For **Android**, ensure that **Other Settings | Virtual Reality Supported** is **unchecked**, as that would be for GearVR (via the Oculus drivers), not Cardboard Android!

6. Navigate to **Other Settings | PlayerSettings.bundleIdentifier** and enter a valid string, such as com.YourName.VRisAwesome.

7. Under **Resolution and Presentation | Default Orientation** set **Landscape Left**.

The Play Mode

To test it out, you *do not* need your phone connected. Just press the game's *Play* button at the top of the application in the center to enter **Play Mode**. You will see the split screen stereographic views in the **Game** view panel.

While in Play Mode, you can simulate the head movement if you were viewing it with the Cardboard headset. Use *Alt* + mouse-move to pan and tilt forward or backwards. Use *Ctrl* + mouse-move to tilt your head from side to side.

You can also simulate magnetic clicks (we'll talk more about user input in a later chapter) with mouse clicks.

Note that since this emulates running on a phone, without a keyboard, the keyboard keys that we used to move Ethan *do not* work now.

Building and running in Android

To build your game as a separate executable app, perform the following steps:

1. From the main menu bar, navigate to **File | Build & Run**.

2. Set the name of the build. I like to keep my builds in a subdirectory named Build; you can create one if you want.

3. Click on **Save**.

This will generate an Android executable .apk file, and then install the app onto your phone. The following screenshot shows the Diorama scene running on an Android phone with Cardboard (and Unity development monitor in the background).

Building and running in iOS

To build your game and run it on the iPhone, perform the following steps:

1. Plug your phone into the computer via a USB cable/port.
2. From the main menu bar, navigate to **File | Build & Run**.

This allows you to create an Xcode project, launch Xcode, build your app inside Xcode, and then install the app onto your phone.

Antique Stereograph (source https://www.pinterest.com/pin/493073859173951630/)

The device-independent clicker

There is one more thing I want to do, which will be very helpful in later chapters of this book. At the time of writing this book, VR input has not yet been settled across all platforms. Input devices may or may not fit under Unity's own **Input Manager** and APIs. In fact, input for VR is a huge topic and deserves its own book. So here, we will keep it simple.

As a tribute to the late Steve Jobs and a throwback to the origins of Apple Macintosh, I am going to limit these projects to mostly one-click inputs! Let's write a script for it, which checks for any click on the keyboard, mouse, or other managed device. (I have provided a detailed introduction to the Unity scripting in the next chapter, so please just follow along for now):

1. In the **Project** panel, select the top-level **Assets** folder.

2. Right-click and navigate to **Create | Folder**. Name it `Scripts`.

3. With the `Scripts` folder selected, right-click and navigate to `Create | C# Script`. Name it `Clicker`.

4. Double-click on the `Clicker.cs` file in the **Projects** panel to open it in the **MonoDevelop** editor.

5. Now, edit the `Script` file, as follows:

```
using UnityEngine;
using System.Collections;

public class Clicker {
  public bool clicked() {
    return Input.anyKeyDown;
  }
}
```

6. Save the file.

If you are developing for Google Cardboard, you can add a check for the Cardboard's integrated trigger when building for mobile devices, as follows:

```
using UnityEngine;
using System.Collections;

public class Clicker {
  public bool clicked() {
#if (UNITY_ANDROID || UNITY_IPHONE)
    return Cardboard.SDK.CardboardTriggered;
#else
    return Input.anyKeyDown;
#endif
  }
}
```

Any scripts that we write that require user clicks will use this `Clicker` file. The idea is that we've isolated the definition of a user click to a single script, and if we change or refine it, we only need to change this file.

How virtual reality really works

So, with your headset on, you experienced the diorama! It appeared 3D, it felt 3D, and maybe you even had a sense of actually being there inside the synthetic scene. I suspect that this isn't the first time you've experienced VR, but now that we've done it together, let's take a few minutes to talk about how it works.

The strikingly obvious thing is, VR looks and feels *really cool!* But why?

Immersion and *presence* are the two words used to describe the quality of a VR experience. The Holy Grail is to increase both to the point where it seems so real, you forget you're in a virtual world. *Immersion* is the result of emulating the sensory inputs that your body receives (visual, auditory, motor, and so on). This can be explained technically. *Presence* is the visceral feeling that you get being transported there—a deep emotional or intuitive feeling. You can say that immersion is the science of VR, and presence is the art. And that, my friend, is cool.

A number of different technologies and techniques come together to make the VR experience work, which can be separated into two basic areas:

* 3D viewing
* Head-pose tracking

In other words, displays and sensors, like those built into today's mobile devices, are a big reason why VR is possible and affordable today.

Suppose the VR system knows exactly where your head is positioned at any given moment in time. Suppose that it can immediately render and display the 3D scene for this precise viewpoint stereoscopically. Then, wherever and whenever you moved, you'd see the virtual scene exactly as you should. You would have a nearly perfect visual VR experience. That's basically it. *Ta-dah!*

Well, not so fast. Literally.

Stereoscopic 3D viewing

Split-screen stereography was discovered not long after the invention of photography, like the popular stereograph viewer from 1876 shown in the following picture (B.W. Kilborn & Co, Littleton, New Hampshire, see `http://en.wikipedia.org/wiki/Benjamin_W._Kilburn`). A stereo photograph has separate views for the left and right eyes, which are slightly offset to create parallax. This fools the brain into thinking that it's a truly three-dimensional view. The device contains separate lenses for each eye, which let you easily focus on the photo close up.

Similarly, rendering these side-by-side stereo views is the first job of the VR-enabled camera in Unity.

Let's say that you're wearing a VR headset and you're holding your head very still so that the image looks frozen. It still appears better than a simple stereograph. Why?

The old-fashioned stereograph has twin relatively small images rectangularly bound. When your eye is focused on the center of the view, the 3D effect is convincing, but you will see the boundaries of the view. Move your eyeballs around (even with the head still), and any remaining sense of immersion is totally lost. You're just an observer on the outside peering into a diorama.

Now, consider what an Oculus Rift screen looks like without the headset (see the following screenshot):

The first thing that you will notice is that each eye has a barrel shaped view. Why is that? The headset lens is a very wide-angle lens. So, when you look through it you have a nice wide field of view. In fact, it is so wide (and tall), it distorts the image (**pincushion effect**). The graphics software (SDK) does an inverse of that distortion (**barrel distortion**) so that it looks correct to us through the lenses. This is referred to as an **ocular distortion correction**. The result is an apparent **field of view (FOV)**, that is wide enough to include a lot more of your peripheral vision. For example, the Oculus Rift DK2 has a FOV of about 100 degrees. (We talk more about FOV in *Chapter 9, Using All 360 Degrees*).

Also of course, the view angle from each eye is slightly offset, comparable to the distance between your eyes, or the **Inter Pupillary Distance (IPD)**. IPD is used to calculate the parallax and can vary from one person to the next. (Oculus Configuration Utility comes with a utility to measure and configure your IPD. Alternatively, you can ask your eye doctor for an accurate measurement.)

It might be less obvious, but if you look closer at the VR screen, you see color separations, like you'd get from a color printer whose print head is not aligned properly. This is intentional. Light passing through a lens is refracted at different angles based on the wavelength of the light. Again, the rendering software does an inverse of the color separation so that it looks correct to us. This is referred to as a **chromatic aberration correction**. It helps make the image look really crisp.

Resolution of the screen is also important to get a convincing view. If it's too low-res, you'll see the pixels, or what some refer to as a **screen door effect**. The pixel width and height of the display is an oft-quoted specification when comparing the HMD's, but the **pixels per inch (ppi)** value may be more important. Other innovations in display technology such as **pixel smearing** and **foveated rendering** (showing a higher-resolution detail exactly where the eyeball is looking) will also help reduce the screen door effect.

When experiencing a 3D scene in VR, you must also consider the **frames per second (FPS)**. If FPS is too slow, the animation will look choppy. Things that affect FPS include the graphics processor (GPU) performance and complexity of the Unity scene (number of polygons and lighting calculations), among other factors. *This is compounded in VR because you need to draw the scene twice, once for each eye.* Technology innovations, such as GPUs optimized for VR, frame interpolation and other techniques, will improve the frame rates. For us developers, performance-tuning techniques in Unity, such as those used by mobile game developers, can be applied in VR. (We will talk more about performance optimization in *Chapter 8, Walk-throughs and Rendering*.) These techniques and optics help make the 3D scene appear realistic.

Sound is also very important—more important than many people realize. VR should be experienced while wearing stereo headphones. In fact, when the audio is done well but the graphics are pretty crappy, you can still have a great experience. We see this a lot in TV and cinema. The same holds true in VR. Binaural audio gives each ear its own stereo *view* of a sound source in such a way that your brain imagines its location in 3D space. No special listening devices are needed. Regular headphones will work (speakers will not). For example, put on your headphones and visit the *Virtual Barber Shop* at `https://www.youtube.com/watch?v=IUDTlvagjJA`. True 3D audio, such as **VisiSonics** (licensed by Oculus), provides an even more realistic spatial audio rendering, where sounds bounce off nearby walls and can be occluded by obstacles in the scene to enhance the first-person experience and realism.

Lastly, the VR headset should fit your head and face comfortably so that it's easy to forget that you're wearing it and should block out light from the real environment around you.

Head tracking

So, we have a nice 3D picture that is viewable in a comfortable VR headset with a wide field of view. If this was it and you moved your head, it'd feel like you have a diorama box stuck to your face. Move your head and the box moves along with it, and this is much like holding the antique stereograph device or the childhood **View Master**. Fortunately, VR is so much better.

The VR headset has a motion sensor (IMU) inside that detects spatial acceleration and rotation rate on all three axes, providing what's called the **six degrees of freedom**. This is the same technology that is commonly found in mobile phones and some console game controllers. Mounted on your headset, when you move your head, the current viewpoint is calculated and used when the next frame's image is drawn. This is referred to as **motion detection**.

Current motion sensors may be good if you wish to play mobile games on a phone, but for VR, it's not accurate enough. These inaccuracies (rounding errors) accumulate over time, as the sensor is sampled thousands of times per second, one may eventually lose track of where you are in the real world. This *drift* is a major shortfall of phone-based VR headsets such as Google Cardboard. It can sense your head motion, but it loses track of your head position.

High-end HMDs account for drift with a separate *positional tracking* mechanism. The Oculus Rift does this with an *inside-out positional tracking*, where an array of (invisible) infrared LEDs on the HMD are read by an external optical sensor (infrared camera) to determine your position. You need to remain within the *view* of the camera for the head tracking to work.

Alternatively, the Steam VR Vive Lighthouse technology does an outside-in positional tracking, where two or more dumb laser emitters are placed in the room (much like the lasers in a barcode reader at the grocery checkout), and an optical sensor on the headset reads the rays to determine your position.

Either way, the primary purpose is to accurately find the position of your head (and other similarly equipped devices, such as handheld controllers).

Together, the position, tilt, and the forward direction of your head — or the *head pose* — is used by the graphics software to redraw the 3D scene from this vantage point. Graphics engines such as Unity are really good at this.

Now, let's say that the screen is getting updated at 90 FPS, and you're moving your head. The software determines the head pose, renders the 3D view, and draws it on the HMD screen. However, you're still moving your head. So, by the time it's displayed, the image is a little out of date with respect to your then current position. This is called **latency**, and it can make you feel nauseous.

Motion sickness caused by latency in VR occurs when you're moving your head and your brain expects the world around you to change exactly in sync. Any perceptible delay can make you uncomfortable, to say the least.

Latency can be measured as the time from reading a motion sensor to rendering the corresponding image, or the *sensor-to-pixel* delay. According to Oculus' John Carmack:

> *"A total latency of 50 milliseconds will feel responsive, but still noticeable laggy. 20 milliseconds or less will provide the minimum level of latency deemed acceptable."*

There are a number of very clever strategies that can be used to *implement latency compensation*. The details are outside the scope of this book and inevitably will change as device manufacturers improve on the technology. One of these strategies is what Oculus calls the **timewarp**, which tries to guess where your head will be by the time the rendering is done, and uses that future head pose instead of the actual, detected one. All of this is handled in the SDK, so as a Unity developer, you do not have to deal with it directly.

Meanwhile, as VR developers, we need to be aware of latency as well as the other causes of motion sickness. Latency can be reduced by faster rendering of each frame (keeping the recommended FPS). This can be achieved by discouraging the moving of your head too quickly and using other techniques to make the user feel grounded and comfortable. Motion sickness in VR is discussed further in *Chapter 6, First-person Character*.

Another thing that the Rift does to improve head tracking and realism is that it uses a skeletal representation of the neck so that all the rotations that it receives are mapped more accurately to the head rotation. An example of this is looking down at your lap makes a small forward translation since it knows it's impossible to rotate one's head downwards on the spot.

Other than head tracking, stereography and 3D audio, virtual reality experiences can be enhanced with body tracking, hand tracking (and gesture recognition), locomotion tracking (for example, VR treadmills), and controllers with haptic feedback. The goal of all of this is to increase your sense of immersion and presence in the virtual world.

Summary

In this chapter, we discussed the different levels of device integration software and then installed the software that is appropriate for your target VR device. Setting up is not necessarily the smoothest process, but there are plenty of us early adopters doing it, so you can get help on the Internet if you get stuck. We also discussed what happens inside the hardware and software SDK that makes virtual reality work and how it matters to us VR developers.

In the next chapter, we'll work more on the `Diorama` scene and explore techniques to control objects in virtual reality. From a third-person perspective, we'll interact with objects in the scene (Ethan, the zombie) and implement look-based control.

4
Gaze-based Control

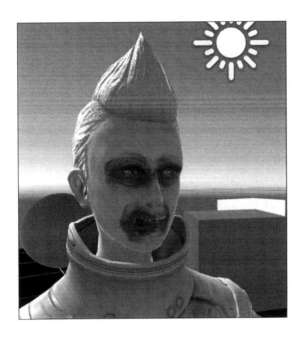

Up to this point, our diorama is a *third-person virtual reality experience*. When you go into it, you're like an observer or a third-person camera. Sure, you can look around and add controls that let you move the camera's viewpoint. However, any action in the scene is from a third-person perspective.

In this chapter, we'll pretty much stay in the third-person mode, but we'll get a little more personally involved. We will explore the techniques that can be used to control objects in your virtual world by looking and staring. Our character, Ethan, will be under your control, responding to where you look. Furthermore, we'll start programming the Unity scripts. Along the way, we will discuss the following topics:

- Adding **AI** (short for **artificial intelligence**) and **NavMesh** to our third-person character, Ethan
- Unity programming in C#
- Using our gaze to move a 3D cursor
- Shooting and killing Ethan, the zombie, to good effect

Ethan, the walker

A starting point for much of VR is gaming. So, we might as well start out from there, too! We are going to give our character, Ethan, a life of his own. Well, sort of (or not), because he's going to become a *zombie!*

We left off at the diorama, with Ethan hanging out. You can make him run around the scene if you have a keyboard or gamepad, but in today's VR having that is not guaranteed. In fact, if you're viewing the scene with a Google Cardboard, it's pretty unlikely that you'll have a handheld controller (notwithstanding the Bluetooth game controllers). Let's be honest. Even with the Oculus Rift, requiring a keyboard or a gamepad controller is not very user-friendly, since you can't see your hands. Perhaps, there's another way to make him move around. One technique is to use the direction of your gaze while wearing your VR headset.

Before we attempt this, we'll first transform Ethan into a zombie and have him walk around aimlessly without any user control. We'll do this by giving him some AI and write a script that sends him to random target locations.

Artificially intelligent Ethan

To start, we want to replace the `ThirdPersonController` prefab that we used initially with Unity's AI character, `AIThirdPersonController` using the following steps. Unity uses the word *artificial intelligence* loosely to mean *script-driven*. Perform the following steps:

1. Open the Unity project from the previous chapters with the `Diorama` scene, and have the **Characters** package imported from **Standard Assets**.

2. In the **Project** panel, open the `Standard Assets/Characters/ ThirdPersonCharacter/Prefabs` folder and drag `AIThirdPersonController` into the scene. Name it `Ethan`.

3. In the **Hierarchy** panel (or in **Scene**), select the previous `ThirdPersonController`, (the old Ethan). Then, in the **Inspector** panel's **Transform** pane, choose the *gear* icon on the upper right of the **Transform** pane and select **Copy Component**.

4. Select the new `Ethan` object (from the **Hierarchy** panel or **Scene**). Then, in the **Inspector** panel's **Transform** pane, choose the *gear* icon and select **Paste Component Values**.

5. Now you can delete the old `Ethan` object by selecting it from the **Hierarchy** panel, right-clicking to open options, and clicking on **Delete**.

Note that this controller has a **NavMesh Agent** component and an `AICharacterControl` script. The NavMesh Agent has parameters for how Ethan will move around the scene. The `AICharacterControl` script takes a target object where Ethan will walk to. Let's populate that, as follows:

1. Add an empty game object to the **Hierarchy** panel.

2. Reset its **Transform** values.

3. Name the game object as `WalkTarget`.

4. Select Ethan and drag `WalkTarget` into the **Target** property in the **Inspector** panel's **AI Character Control** pane.

At this point, we have an AI character in the scene (`Ethan`), an empty game object that will be used as a navigation target (`WalkTarget`), and we told the AI Character Controller to use this target object. When we run the game, wherever `WalkTarget` is, Ethan will go there. But not yet.

The Navmesh bakery

Ethan cannot just go walking around without being told where he's allowed to roam! We need to define a "NavMesh"—a simplified geometrical plane that enables a character to plot its path around obstacles.

Create a NavMesh by first identifying the static objects in the scene and then *baking* it:

1. Select each of the objects—the ground plane, the three cubes, and the sphere and in its **Inspector** panel, check off the **Static** checkbox (you can do each object separately or *Ctrl* + click to select multiple items at once).

2. Select the **Navigation** panel. If it's not already a tab in your editor, open the "Navigation" window from the main menu by navigating to **Window | Navigation**.

3. Click on the **Bake** button at the bottom of the panel.

The **Scene** view should now show a blue overlay where the NavMesh is defined, as shown in the following screenshot:

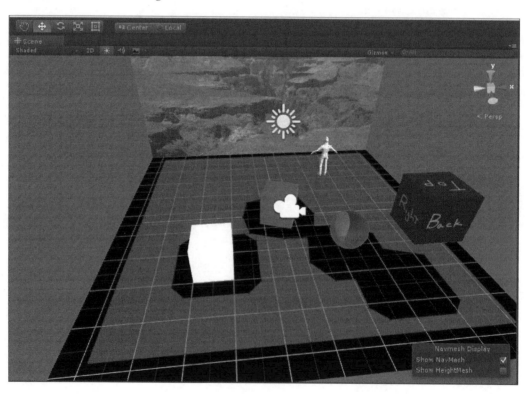

Let's test this out. Ensure that the **Game** panel's **Maximize on Play** is deselected. Click on the *Play* mode button (triangle at the top of editor). In the **Hierarchy** panel, select the `WalkTarget` object and ensure that the Translate gizmo is active in the **Scene** panel (press the *W* key on keyboard). Now, drag the red (X) and/or the blue (Z) arrow handles on the `WalkTarget` object to move it around the floor plane. As you do, Ethan should follow! Click on *Play* again to stop Play Mode.

A random walker in the town

Now, we'll write a script that moves the `WalkTarget` object to random places.

If you've done anything more that tinker with Unity, you've probably already written at least some scripts. We're going to use C# for the programming language. For this first script, we'll take it slow. We will attach the script to the `WalkTarget` object, as follows:

1. Select the `WalkTarget` object in the **Hierarchy** panel or the **Scene** view.
2. In its **Inspector** panel, click on the **Add Component** button.
3. Select **New Script**.
4. Name it `RandomPosition`.
5. Ensure that the **C Sharp** language is selected.
6. Click on **Create** and **Add**.
7. This should create a script component on the `WalkTarget` object. Double-click on the `RandomPosition` script in the slot to the right of **Script** in the **Inspector** pane to open it in the **MonoDevelop** code editor.

Interlude – a quick introduction to Unity programming

Unity does a lot of things—it manages objects, renders them, animates them, calculates the physics of those objects, and so on. Unity itself is a program. It's made of code—probably a lot of good code written by some very smart people. This internal Unity code can be accessed by you, the game developer, through the Unity point-and-click editor interface that we've already been using. Within the Unity editor, scripts are manifested as configurable components. However, it's also made more directly accessible to you through the Unity scripting API.

API (short for **application programming interface**), simply refers to published software functions that you can access from your own scripts. Unity's API is very rich and nicely designed. That's one reason why people have written amazing plugin add-ons for Unity.

There are many programming languages in the world. Unity has chosen to support the C# language from Microsoft (as well as a flavor of JavaScript, which has its limitations). Computer languages have a specific syntax that must be obeyed. Otherwise, the computer will not understand your script. In Unity, script errors (and warnings) appear in the **Console** panel of the editor as well as in the bottom footer of the app window.

The default script editor for Unity is an integrated development environment, or an IDE, called **MonoDevelop**. You can configure a different editor or an IDE if you want, like Microsoft's Visual Studio. MonoDevelop has some nice features such as auto-completion and pop-up help that understand the Unity documentation. C# scripts are text files that are named with a `.cs` extension.

In a Unity C# script, some of the words and symbols are a part of the C# language itself, some come from the Microsoft .NET Framework, and others are provided by the Unity API. And then there's the code that you write.

An empty default Unity C# script looks like this:

```
using UnityEngine;
using System.Collections;

public class RandomPosition : MonoBehaviour {

    // Use this for initialization
    void Start () {

    }

    // Update is called once per frame
    void Update () {

    }
}
```

Let's dissect it.

The first two lines indicate that this script needs some other stuff to run. The `using` keyword belongs to the C# language. The line using `UnityEngine`; says that we'll be using the `UnityEngine` API. The line using `System.Collections`; says that we also might use a library of functions named `Collections` to access lists of objects.

In C#, each line of code ends with a semicolon. Double slashes (`//`) indicate comments in the code, and anything from there to the end of that line will be ignored.

This Unity script defines a class named `RandomPosition`. **Classes** are like code templates with their own properties (variables) and behavior (functions). Classes derived from the `MonoBehaviour` base class are recognized by Unity and used when your game runs. The line public class `RandomPosition` : `MonoBehaviour` basically says, *we are defining a new public class named "RandomPosition", which inherits all the abilities of the "MonoBehaviour" Unity base class*, including the capability of the `Start()` and `Update()` functions. The body of the class is enclosed in a pair of curly braces (`{ }`).

When something is `public`, it can be seen by other code outside this specific script file. When it's `private`, it can only be referenced within this file. We want Unity to see the `RandomPosition` class.

Classes define variables and functions. A **variable** holds data values of a specific type, such as `float`, `int`, `boolean`, `GameObject`, `Vector3`, and so on. **Functions** implement logic (step-by-step instructions). Functions can receive *arguments*— variables enclosed in a parenthesis used by its code—and can return new values when it's done.

Numeric `float` constants, such as `5.0f`, require an `f` at the end in C# to ensure that the data type is a *simple* floating point value and not a *double-precision* floating point value.

Unity will automatically call some special `message` functions if you've defined them. `Start()` and `Update()` are two examples. Empty versions of these are provided in the default C# script. The datatype in front of a function indicates the type of value returned. `Start()` and `Update()` do not return values. So, they're `void`.

Each `Start()` function from all `MonoBehaviour` scripts in your game are called before the gameplay begins. It's a good place for data initialization. All the `Update()` functions are called during each time slice, or frame, while the game is running. This is where most of the action lies.

Once you've written or modified a script in the MonoDevelop mode, save it. Then, switch to the Unity editor window. Unity will automatically recognize that the script has changed and will reimport it. If errors are found, it will report them right away in the **Console** panel.

This is just some cursory introduction to Unity programming. As we work through the projects in this book, I will explain additional bits as they're introduced.

The RandomPosition script

Now, we want to move the WalkTarget object to a random location so that Ethan will head in that direction, wait a few seconds, and move the WalkTarget object again. That way, he'll appear to be wandering around aimlessly. We can do this with a script. Rather than developing the script incrementally, I'm presenting the finished version first, and we'll go through it line by line. The RandomPosition.cs script looks like this:

```
using UnityEngine;
using System.Collections;

public class RandomPosition : MonoBehaviour {

    void Start () {
        StartCoroutine (RePositionWithDelay());
    }

    IEnumerator RePositionWithDelay() {
        while (true) {
            SetRandomPosition();
            yield return new WaitForSeconds (5);
        }
    }

    void SetRandomPosition() {
        float x = Random.Range (-5.0f, 5.0f);
        float z = Random.Range (-5.0f, 5.0f);
        Debug.Log ("X,Z: " + x.ToString("F2") + ", " +
            z.ToString("F2"));
        transform.position = new Vector3 (x, 0.0f, z);
    }
}
```

This script defines a MonoBehaviour class named RandomPosition. The first thing we do when defining the class is declare any variables that we'll be using. A variable is a placeholder for a value. The value can be initialized here or assigned elsewhere, just as long as it has a value before the script needs to use it.

The meat of the script is further down—the function named SetRandomPosition(). Let's see what that does.

If you recall, the GroundPlane plane is 10 units square, with the origin in the middle. So, any (**X, Z**) location on the plane will be within the range from -5 to 5 along each axis. The line float x = Random.Range (-5.0f, 5.0f); picks a random value within the given range and assigns it to a new float x variable. We do the same thing to get a random z value. (Usually, I discourage *hardcoding* constant values like this instead of using variables, but I'm keeping things simple for illustration purposes).

The line Debug.Log ("X,Z: " + x.ToString("F2") + ", " + z.ToString("F2")); prints the x and z values in the **Console** panel when the game is running. It'll output something like X, Z: 2.33, -4.02 because ToString("F2") says round up to two decimal places. Note that we're using plus signs to combine the parts of the output string together.

We actually move the target to the given location with the line transform.position = new Vector3 (x, 0.0f, z);. We're setting the transform position of the object that this script is attached to. In Unity, values that have an X, Y, and Z are represented by the Vector3 objects. So, we create a new one with the x and z values that we generated. We give y=0 so that it sits on GroundPlane.

Each MonoBehaviour class has a built-in variable called this, which refers to the object that the script is attached to. That is, when the script is a component of an object and appears in its **Inspector** panel, the script can refer to its object as this. In fact, this is so obvious, if you want to call functions on the this object, you don't even need to say it. We could have said this.transform.position = ..., but the this object is implied and is normally omitted. On the other hand, if you had a variable for some other object (for example, GameObject that;), then you'd need to say that when you set its position, like that.transform.position = ...

The last mysterious bit is how we handle time delays in Unity. In our case, the transform position should get changed once every 5 seconds. It's solved in several parts:

1. In the `Start()` function, there's the line `StartCoroutine (RePositionWithDelay())`;. A **co-routine** is a piece of code that runs separately from the function from which it was called. So, this line kicks off the `RePositionWithDelay()` function in a co-routine.

2. Inside that, there's a `while (true)` loop, which as you might guess, runs forever (as long as the game is running).

3. It calls the `SetRandomPosition()` function, which actually repositions the object.

4. Then, at the bottom of this loop, we do a `yield return new WaitForSeconds (5)`; sentence, which basically says to Unity, *hey, go do what you want for 5 seconds and then come back here so that I can go through my loop again.*

5. For all of this to work, the `RePositionWithDelay` co-routine must be declared as the `IEnumerator` type (because the documentation says so).

This *co-routine / yield* mechanism, although an advanced programming topic, is a common pattern in time-sliced programs such as Unity.

Our script should be saved to a file named `RandomPosition.cs`.

We are now good to go. In the Unity editor, click on *Play*. Ethan is running from one place to another like a madman!

"Zombie-ize" Ethan!

Ok, that's pretty random. Let's adjust the NavMesh steering parameters to slow him down to a nice zombie-like pace. For that, perform the following steps:

1. Select `Ethan` in the **Hierarchy** panel.

2. Navigate to **Inspector | Nav Mesh Agent | Steering**, set the following:

   ◦ **Speed:** `0.3`
   ◦ **Angular Speed:** `60`
   ◦ **Acceleration:** `2`

Play again. He has slowed down. That's better.

One more finishing touch—let's turn him into a zombie. I have a texture image named `EthanZombie.png` that will help (included with this book). Perform the following steps:

1. From the **Assets** tab on the main menu, select **Import New Asset...**. Navigate to the files folder with the assets that came with this book.

2. Select the `EthanZombie.png` file.

3. Click on **Import**. For tidiness, ensure that it resides in the `Assets/Textures` folder. (Alternatively, you can just drag and drop the file from Windows Explorer into the **Project** panel folder.)

4. In the **Hierarchy** panel, unfold the `Ethan` object (click on the triangle) and select `EthanBody`.

5. In the **Inspector** panel, unfold the `EthanWhite` shader by clicking on the triangle-icon to the left of **Shader**.

6. Select the `EthanZombie` texture from the `Project Assets/Textures` folder.

7. Drag it onto the **Albedo** texture map. It's a small square just to the left of the **Albedo** label under **Main Maps**.

8. In the **Hierarchy** panel, select `EthanGlasses` and uncheck it to disable glasses in the **Inspector** panel. After all, zombies don't need glasses!

His portrait is featured at the top of this chapter! *What'd you say? That's a lame looking zombie??* Well, maybe he's just recently turned. Go ahead and make a better one yourself. Use Blender, Gimp, or Photoshop and paint your own (or even import a whole different zombie humanoid model to replace `EthanBody` itself).

Now, build the project and try it in VR.

We're looking from a third-person perspective. You can look around and watch what's going on. It's kind of fun, and it's pretty interesting. And it's passive. Let's get more active.

Go where I'm looking

In this next script, instead of being random, we'll send Ethan to wherever we look. In Unity, this is accomplished by using **ray casting**—like shooting a ray from the camera and seeing what it hits (for more information, visit `http://docs.unity3d.com/Manual/CameraRays.html`).

We're going to create a new script, which will be attached to WalkTarget like before, as follows:

1. Select the WalkTarget object in the **Hierarchy** panel or the **Scene** view.
2. In its **Inspector** panel, click on the **Add Component** button.
3. Select **New Script**.
4. Name it LookMoveTo.
5. Ensure that the **C Sharp** language is selected.
6. Click on **Create** and **Add**.

This should create a script component on the WalkTarget object. Double-click on it to open it in the MonoDevelop code editor.

The LookMoveTo script

In our script, each time Update() is called, we'll read where the camera is pointing (by using its transform position and rotation), cast a ray in that direction, and ask Unity to tell us where it hits the ground plane. Then, we'll use this location to set the WalkTarget object's position.

Here's the full LookMoveTo.cs script:

```csharp
using UnityEngine;
using System.Collections;

public class LookMoveTo : MonoBehaviour {
  public GameObject ground;

  void Update () {
    Transform camera = Camera.main.transform;
    Ray ray;
    RaycastHit hit;
    GameObject hitObject;

    Debug.DrawRay (camera.position,
      camera.rotation * Vector3.forward * 100.0f);

    ray = new Ray (camera.position,
      camera.rotation * Vector3.forward);
    if (Physics.Raycast (ray, out hit)) {
      hitObject = hit.collider.gameObject;
      if (hitObject == ground) {
        Debug.Log ("Hit (x,y,z): " + hit.point.ToString("F2"));
        transform.position = hit.point;
      }
```

```
        }
      }

    }
```

Let's go through the script a bit at a time.

```
    public GameObject ground;
```

The first thing the script does is declare a variable for the `GroundPlane` object. Since it's `public`, we can use the Unity editor to assign the actual object:

```
    void Update () {
        Transform camera = Camera.main.transform;
        Ray ray;
        RaycastHit hit;
        GameObject hitObject;
```

Inside `Update()`, we define a few local variables — camera, ray, hit, and hitObject, which have datatypes that are required by the Unity functions that we're going to use.

`Camera.main` is the current active camera object (that is, tagged as "MainCamera"). We get its current transform, which will be assigned to the camera variable:

```
        ray = new Ray (camera.position,
            camera.rotation * Vector3.forward);
```

Ignoring the handy `Debug` statements for a moment, we first determine the ray from the camera using `new Ray()`.

A **ray** can be defined by a starting position in the **X**, **Y**, and **Z** space and a direction vector. A **direction vector** can be defined as the relative offsets from a 3D starting point to some other point in space. The forward direction, where Z is positive, is (0, 0, 1). Unity will do the math for us. So, if we take a unit vector (`Vector3.forward`), multiply it by a 3-axis rotation (`camera.rotation`), and scale it by a length (`100.0f`), we'll get a ray pointing in the same direction as the camera measuring 100 units long.

```
    if (Physics.Raycast (ray, out hit)) {
```

Then, we cast the ray and see if it hit anything. If so, the `hit` variable will now contain more details about what was hit, including the specific object in `hit.collider.gameObject`. (The out keyword means that the `hit` variable value is filled in by the `Physics.Raycast()` function.)

```
        if (hitObject == ground) {
          transform.position = hit.point;
        }
```

We check whether the ray hit the GroundPlane object, and if so, we'll assign that as the position to move the WalkTarget object to the hit location.

 The == *compare* operator should not to be confused with =, which is the *assignment* operator.

This script contains two Debug statements, which are a useful way to monitor what's going on while a script is running in Play Mode. Debug.DrawRay() will draw the given ray in the **Scene** view so that you can actually see it, and Debug.Log() will dump the current hit position to the console if and when there's a hit.

Save the script, switch into the Unity editor, and perform the following steps:

1. With WalkTarget selected, in the **Inspector** panel, the LookMoveTo script component now has a field for the GroundPlane object.

2. From the **Hierarchy** panel, select and drag the GroundPlane game object onto the **Ground** field.

Save the scene. The script pane looks like this:

Then, click on *Play* button. Ethan should follow our gaze (at his own pace).

Adding a feedback cursor

Given it's not always obvious where your gaze is hitting the ground plane, we'll now add a cursor to the scene. It's really easy because what we've been doing is moving around an invisible, empty WalkTarget object. If we give it a mesh by using the following steps, it'll be visible:

1. In the **Hierarchy** panel, select the WalkTarget object.

2. Right-click on the mouse and navigate to **3D Object | Cylinder**. This will create a cylindrical object parented by WalkTarget. (Alternatively, you can use the **GameObject** tab on the main menu bar, and then drag and drop the object onto WalkTarget.)

3. Ensure that we're starting with the reset values of transform by clicking on **Reset** from the *gear* icon menu in the **Transform** pane.

4. Select the new cylinder and in its **Inspector** panel, change the **Scale** to (0.4, 0.05, 0.4). This will create a flat disk with a diameter of 0.4.

5. Disable its **Capsule Collider** by unchecking that checkbox.

6. In **Mesh Render**, you can also disable **Cast Shadows**, **Receive Shadows**, **Use Light Probes**, and **Reflection Probes**.

Now, try to play again. The cursor disk follows our gaze.

If you want, decorate the disk better with a colored material. Better yet, find an appropriate texture. For example, we used a grid texture in *Chapter 2*, *Objects and Scale*, for the GridProjector file (Standard Assets/Effects/Projectors/ Textures/Grid.psd). The file CircleCrossHair.png is provided with the files for this book. Drop the texture onto the cylinder cursor. When you do, set its **Shader** to **Standard**.

Observations

In this project, we got Ethan to follow where we're looking by moving the WalkTarget object to a position on the ground plane determined by ray casting from the camera and seeing where it intersected that plane.

You may have noticed that the cursor seems to get *stuck* when we slide our gaze over the cube and sphere. That's because the **physics engine** has determined which object is hit first, never getting to the ground plane. In our script, we have the conditional statement if (hitObject == ground) before moving WalkTarget. Without it, the cursor would float over any object in 3D-space where the cast ray hits something. Sometimes, that's interesting, but in our case, it is not. We want to keep the cursor on the ground. However now, if the ray hits something other than the ground, it doesn't get repositioned and seems *stuck*. Can you think of a way around it? Here's a hint—look up Physics.RaycastAll. Alright, I'll show you. Replace the body of Update() with the following code:

```
Transform camera = Camera.main.transform;
Ray ray;
RaycastHit[] hits;
GameObject hitObject;

Debug.DrawRay (camera.position, camera.rotation *
  Vector3.forward * 100.0f);

ray = new Ray (camera.position, camera.rotation *
  Vector3.forward);
hits = Physics.RaycastAll (ray);
```

```
for (int i = 0; i < hits.Length; i++) {
  RaycastHit hit = hits [i];
  hitObject = hit.collider.gameObject;
  if (hitObject == ground) {
    Debug.Log ("Hit (x,y,z): " +
      hit.point.ToString("F2"));
    transform.position = hit.point;
  }
}
```

On calling `RaycastAll`, we get back a list, or an array, of hits. Then we loop through each one looking for a ground hit anywhere along the path of the ray vector. Now our cursor will trace along the ground, whether or not there's another object in between.

Extra challenge: Another more efficient solution is to use the *layer system*. Create a new layer, assign it to the plane, and pass it as an argument to `Physics.raycast()`. Can you see why that's much more efficient?

If looks could kill

We got this far. We might as well try to kill Ethan (haha!). Here are the specifications for this new feature:

- Looking at Ethan hits him with our line-of-sight ray gun
- Sparks are emitted when the gun hits its target
- After 3 seconds of being hit, Ethan is killed
- When he's killed, Ethan explodes (we get a point) and then he respawns at a new location

The KillTarget script

This time, we'll attach the script to a new empty `GameController` object by performing the following steps:

1. Create an empty game object and name it `GameController`.
2. Attach a new C# script to it, using **Add Component**, named `KillTarget`.
3. Open the script in MonoDevelop.

Here's the completed `KillTarget.cs` script:

```
using UnityEngine;
using System.Collections;

public class KillTarget : MonoBehaviour {
  public GameObject target;
  public ParticleSystem hitEffect;
  public GameObject killEffect;
  public float timeToSelect = 3.0f;
  public int score;

  private float countDown;

  void Start () {
    score = 0;
    countDown = timeToSelect;
    hitEffect.enableEmission = false;
  }

  void Update () {
    Transform camera = Camera.main.transform;
    Ray ray = new Ray (camera.position, camera.rotation *
      Vector3.forward);
    RaycastHit hit;
    if (Physics.Raycast (ray, out hit) && (hit.collider.gameObject
      == target)) {
      if (countDown > 0.0f) {
        // on target
        countDown -= Time.deltaTime;
        // print (countDown);
        hitEffect.transform.position = hit.point;
        hitEffect.enableEmission = true;
      } else {
        // killed
        Instantiate( killEffect, target.transform.position,
          target.transform.rotation );
        score += 1;
        countDown = timeToSelect;
        SetRandomPosition();
      }
    } else {
      // reset
      countDown = timeToSelect;
```

```
        hitEffect.enableEmission = false;
    }
  }

  void SetRandomPosition() {
    float x = Random.Range (-5.0f, 5.0f);
    float z = Random.Range (-5.0f, 5.0f);
    target.transform.position = new Vector3 (x, 0.0f, z);
  }
}
```

Let's go through this. First, we declare a number of public variables, as follows:

```
public GameObject target;
public ParticleSystem hitEffect;
public GameObject killEffect;
public float timeToSelect = 3.0f;
public int score;
```

Like we did in the previous `LookMoveTo` script, our target will be Ethan. We're also adding a `hitEffect` particle emitter, a `killEffect` explosion, and a start value for the countdown timer, `timeToSelect`. Lastly, we'll keep track of our kills in the `score` variable.

The `Start()` method, which is called at the start of game play, initializes the score to zero, sets the `countDown` timer to its starting value, and turns off `hitEffect`.

Then, in the `Update()` method, like in the `LookMoveTo` script, we cast a ray from the camera and check whether it hits our target, Ethan. When it does, we check the `countDown` timer.

If the timer is still counting, we decrement its value by the amount of time that's gone by since the last time `Update()` was called, using `Time.deltaTime`, and make sure that `pickEffect` is emitting at the hit point.

If the ray is still on its target and the timer is done counting down, Ethan is killed. We explode, bump up the score by one, reset the timer to its starting value, and move (respawn) Ethan to a random new location.

For an explosion, we'll use one of Unity's standard assets found in the `ParticleSystems` package. To activate it, `killEffect` should be set to the prefab named `Explosion`. Then, the script *instantiates* it. In other words, it makes it an object in the scene (at a specified transform), which kicks off its awesome scripts and effects.

Lastly, if the ray did not hit Ethan, we reset the counter and turn off the particles.

Save the script and go into the Unity editor.

 Extra challenge: Refactor the script to use co-routines to manage the delay timing, like we did in the `RandomPosition` script at the start of this chapter.

Adding particle effects

Now, to populate the `public` variables, we will perform the following steps:

1. First, we need the `ParticleSystems` package that comes with Unity standard assets. If you do not have them, navigate to **Assets | Import Package | ParticleSystems**, choose **All**, and then click on **Import**.

2. Select `GameController` from the **Hierarchy** panel and go to the **Kill Target (Script)** pane in the **Inspector** panel.

3. Drag the `Ethan` object from the **Hierarchy** panel onto the **Target** field.

4. From the main menu bar, navigate to **GameObject | Particle System** and name it `SparkEmitter`.

5. Reselect `GameController` and drag `SparkEmitter` onto the **Hit Effect** field.

6. In the **Project** panel, find the `Explosion` prefab in `Assets/Standard Assets/ParticleSystems/Prefabs`, drag the `Explosion` prefab onto the **Kill Effect** field.

The script pane looks like the following screenshot:

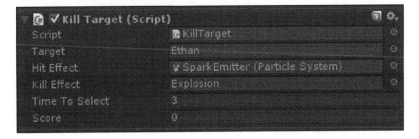

We created a default particle system that will be used as the sparks emitter. We need to set that up to our liking. I'll get you started, and you can play with it as you desire, as follows:

1. Select SparkEmitter from the **Hierarchy** panel.

2. And in its **Inspector** panel, under **Particle System**, set the following values:

   ° **Start Size**: 0.15,

   ° **Start Color**: pick a red/orange color

   ° **Start Lifetime**: 0.3,

   ° **Max Particles**: 50.

3. Under **Emission**, set **Rate**: 100.

4. Under **Shape**, set **Shape**: **Sphere** and **Radius**: 0.01.

5. For performance, under **Renderer**, set **Cast Shadows**: **Off**, **Receive Shadows**: un-check, and **Reflection Probes**: **Off**.

Here's what my **Scene** view looks like as I run Play Mode and zap Ethan in the chest:

When Ethan is shot, the hitEffect particle system is activated. After 3 seconds (or whatever value you set in the TimeToSelect variable), his *health* is depleted, the explosion effect is instantiated, the score is incremented, and he respawns at a new location. In the next chapter, we'll see how we can show the current score to the player.

Cleaning up

One last thing before we're done — let's clean up the **Assets** folder a bit and move all the scripts into a `Assets/Scripts/` subfolder. Select the **Project Assets** folder in **Project**, create a folder, name it `Scripts`, and drag all your scripts into it.

Summary

In this chapter, we explored the relationship between the VR camera and objects in the scene. We first made Ethan (the zombie) walk randomly around the scene and enabled to move by using a NavMesh, but then, we directed his wanderings using a 3D cursor on the X, Z ground plane. This cursor follows our gaze as we look around the scene in virtual reality. Lastly, we also used our gaze to shoot a ray at Ethan, causing him to lose health and eventually explode.

These look-based techniques can be used in non-VR games, but in VR, it's very common and almost essential. We'll be using them more in the later chapters of this book too.

In the next chapter, we will look at the various ways to present the user with information and input widgets in VR. **User interface (UI)** conventions found in desktop applications and video games may not work well in VR, because they operate in *Screen Space*. However, as we'll see, there are numerous other effective ways that you can use to approach UI that do make sense in virtual worlds.

World Space UI

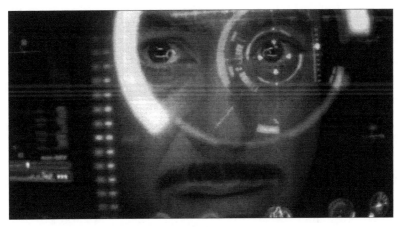

"Iron Man 3" Marvel Studios, Paramount Pictures, 2013 (source http://www.geek.com/mobile/
wearable-computing-is-back-google-reportedly-making-hud-glasses-1465399/)

Graphical user interface (GUI) or just UI, usually refers to on-screen
two-dimensional graphics, which overlay the main gameplay and present
information to the user with status messages, gauges, and input controls
such as menus, buttons, sliders, and so on.

In Unity 5, UI elements always reside on a **canvas**. The Unity manual quotes the
canvas component as the following:

> *The Canvas component represents the abstract space in which the UI is laid out
> and rendered. All UI elements must be children of a GameObject that has a Canvas
> component attached.*

In conventional video games, UI objects are usually rendered in a **screen space**
canvas as an overlay. Screen space UI is analogous to a piece of cardboard pasted
on your TV or monitor, overlaying the game action behind it.

However, that doesn't work in VR. If you attempt to use screen space for UI in virtual reality, you'll run into issues. Since there are two stereographic cameras, you need separate views for each eye. While conventional games may co-opt the edges of the screen for UI, *virtual reality has no screen edges!*

Instead in VR, we use various approaches that place the user interface elements in **World Space** rather than screen space. In this chapter, I characterized a number of these types. We'll define these types in detail and give examples of the same throughout this chapter:

- **Visor heads-up display**: In visor **heads-up display (HUD)** the user interface canvas appears at the same spot in front of your eyes regardless of the head movement

- **Reticle cursors**: Similar to visor HUD, a crosshair or a pointer cursor is used to choose things in the scene

- **Windshield HUD**: This is a pop-up panel floating in 3D space like a windshield in a cockpit

- **Game element UI**: The canvas is in the scene as a part of the gameplay, like a scoreboard in a stadium

- **Info bubble**: This is a UI message that is attached to objects in the scene, like a thought bubble hovering over a character's head

- **In-game dashboard**: This is a control panel that is a part of the gameplay, usually at the waist or desk height

- **Responsive object UI**: UI information need not necessarily be present in the field of view at all times, but it is invoked in a relevant context

The differences in these UI techniques basically come down to where and when you show the canvas and how the user interacts with it. In this chapter, we're going to try each of these in turn. Along the way, we'll also continue to explore user input with head movement and gestures as well as button clicks.

Note that some of the projects in this chapter use the scene completed in the previous chapter, *Chapter 4, Gaze-based Control,* but are separate and not directly required by the other chapters in this book. If you decide to skip any of it or not save your work, that's OK.

A reusable default canvas

Unity's UI canvas provides lots of options and parameters to accommodate the kinds of graphical layout flexibility that we have come to expect not only in games, but also from the web and mobile apps. With this flexibility comes additional complexity. To make our examples in this chapter easier, we'll first build a reusable prefab canvas that has our preferred default settings.

Create a new canvas and change its **Render Mode** to **world space** as follows:

1. Navigate to **GameObject | UI | Canvas**.

2. Rename the canvas as DefaultCanvas.

3. Set **Render Mode** to **world space**.

The **Rect Transform** component defines the grid system on the canvas itself, like the lines on a piece of graph paper. It is used for the placement of UI elements on the canvas. Set it to a convenient 640 x 480, with a 0.75 aspect ratio. The **Rect Transform** component's width and height are different from the world space size of the canvas in our scene. Let's configure the **Rect Transform** component using the following steps:

1. In **Rect Transform**, set **Width** = 640 and **Height** = 480.

2. In **Scale**, set **X, Y, Z** to (0.00135, 0.00135, 0.00135). This is the size for one of our pixels in world space units.

3. Now, position the canvas centered on the ground plane one unit above (0.325 is half of 0.75).

   In **Rect Transform**, set **Pos X, Pos Y, Pos Z** to (0, 1.325, 0).

Next, we will add an empty **Image** element (with a white background) to help us visualize the otherwise transparent canvas and provide an opaque background for the canvas when we need one (we can also use a **Panel** UI element):

1. With DefaultCanvas selected, navigate to **GameObject | UI | Image** (ensure that it's created as a child of DefaultCanvas; if not, move it under DefaultCanvas).

2. With the **Image** selected, on the upper left of its **Rect Transform** pane, there is an **anchor presets** button (shown in the following screenshot). Selecting it opens the **anchor presets** dialog box. Press and hold the *Alt* key to see the **stretch** and **position** options and choose the one on the bottom-right corner (**stretch-stretch**). Now, the (blank) image is stretched to fill the canvas:

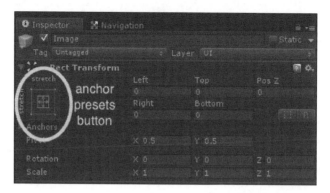

3. Double-check your **Image** settings based on the default properties for the Image child of the DefaultCanvas as shown in the following screenshot:

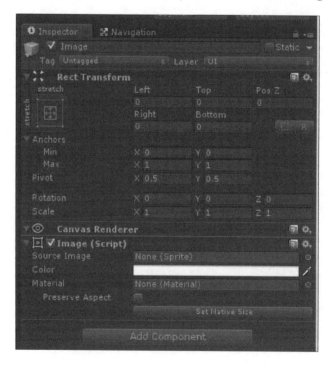

Add a **Text** element with useful default settings, as follows:

1. With `DefaultCanvas` selected, navigate to **GameObject | UI | Text** (ensure that it's created as a child of `DefaultCanvas`, if not, move it under `DefaultCanvas`). The words **New Text** should appear on the canvas.

2. With the **Text** selected, set **Alignment** to **Center Align** and **Middle Align** and set **Vertical Overflow** to **Overflow**. Set the **Scale** to (4, 4, 4).

3. With the **Image** selected, set its **anchor presets** button to (**stretch - stretch**) using the widget on the upper left of its **Rect Transform** pane.

4. Double-check your **Text** settings based on the default properties for the `Text` child of the `DefaultCanvas` as shown in the following screenshot:

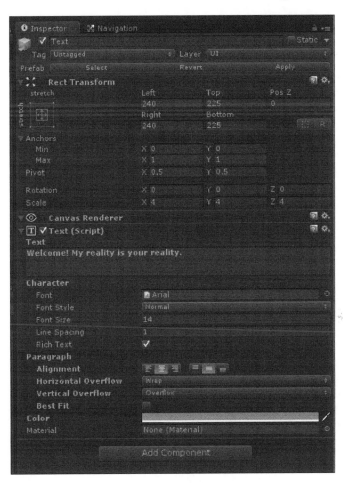

Increase the pixel resolution to give cleaner text fonts by keeping DefaultCanvas selected and setting the **Canvas Scaler | Dynamic Pixels Per Unit** to 10.

Finally, save your work as a prefab asset that you can reuse throughout the chapter in the following manner:

1. If necessary, in **Project Assets**, create a new folder named Prefabs.

2. Drag the DefaultCanvas object into the Project Assets/Prefabs folder to create a prefab.

3. Delete the DefaultCanvas instance in the **Hierarchy** panel now.

4. Double-check the DefaultCanvas setting against the properties shown in the following screenshot:

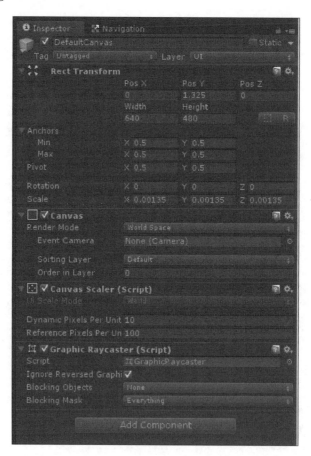

OK, glad we got that out of the way! Now, we can use the DefaultCanvas prefab with different VR user interfaces.

A canvas has a **Rect Transform** component, which defines the grid system on the canvas itself, like the lines on a piece of graph paper. It is used for the placement of UI elements on the canvas. This is different from the size and position of a canvas object in world space.

The visor HUD

A heads-up display, or HUD, is a floating canvas in your field of view that overlays the gameplay scene. In VR vernacular, there are two variations of HUDs. I'll call these variations the *visor HUD* and the *windshield HUD*. This section looks at the first one.

In visor HUD, the UI canvas is attached to the camera. It doesn't appear to respond to your head movement. When you move your head, it appears to be *stuck to your face*. Let's look at a nicer way of visualizing it. Let's suppose that you're wearing a helmet with a visor and the UI appears projected onto the surface of the visor. There may be contexts where this is OK in virtual reality, but it is likely to break the sense of immersion. So, it should generally only be used either when the visor is a part of the gameplay, or if the intent is to take you out of the scene, such as the utility menus for the hardware or the system.

Let's make a visor HUD with a welcome message as follows, and see for ourselves how it feels:

1. In the **Hierarchy** panel, unfold the `MeMyselfEye` object and then drill down to the **Main Camera** object (for Oculus, we placed it as an immediate child of `MeMyselfEye`; for Cardboard, you need to go deeper to `CardboardMain/Head/`).

2. From the **Project** panel, drag the `DefaultCanvas` prefab onto the `Camera` object so that it becomes a child of `Camera`.

3. In the **Hierarchy** panel, with the canvas selected, rename the canvas to `VisorCanvas`.

4. In the **Inspector** panel for the canvas, change the **Rect Transform** component's **Pos X, Pos Y, Pos Z** to (`0, 0, 1`).

5. Unfold `VisorCanvas` and select the child **Text** object.

6. In the **Inspector** panel, change the text from **Default Text** to **Welcome! Mi reality es su reality**. (You can enter line breaks in the input text area.)

7. Change the text color to something bright, such as green.

8. Disable the `Image` object so that only the text shows, by unchecking its **Enable** checkbox in **Inspector**.

9. Save the scene, and try it in VR.

Here's a capture of the Rift screen with the `VisorCanvas`:

In VR, when you move your head around, the text follows along as if it's attached to a visor in front of your face.

 A visor HUD canvas and reticle cursor canvas are set as a child object of the camera.

Now, go ahead and either disable `VisorCanvas`, or just delete it (in the **Hierarchy** panel, right-click on it and click on **Delete**) because we're going to show the welcome message in a different way in a later topic. Next, we'll look at a different application of this technique.

The reticle cursor

A variant of the visor HUD that is essential in first-person shooter games is a *reticle* or crosshair cursor. The analogy here is that you're looking through a gun-sight or an eyepiece (rather than a visor), and your head movement is moving in unison with the gun or turret itself. You can do this with a regular game object (for example, Quad + texture image), but this chapter is about UI. So, let's use our canvas, as follows:

1. Find your **Main Camera** object in the **Hierarchy** panel.

2. From the **Project** panel, drag the `DefaultCanvas` prefab onto the camera object so that it becomes a child of the camera. Name it `ReticleCursor`.

3. Set the **Rect Transform** component's **Pos X, Pos Y, Pos Z** to (0, 0, 1).

4. Delete its child objects—**Image** and **Text**.

5. Add a raw image child by selecting from the main menu bar navigating through **GameObject | UI | Raw Image** and making sure that it's a child of `ReticleCursor`.

6. In the **Raw Image** panel's **Rect Transform**, set **Pos X, Pos Y, Pos Z** to (0, 0, 0) and **Width, Height** to (22, 22). Then, choose a noticeable **Color** such as red in the **Raw Image (Script)** properties.

7. Save the scene and try it in VR.

If you'd like a nicer looking reticle, in the **Raw Image (Script)** properties, populate the **Texture** field with a cursor image. For example, click on the tiny *circle* icon on the far right of the **Texture** field. This opens the **Select Texture** dialog. Find and select a suitable one, such as the `Crosshair` image. (A copy of `Crosshair.gif` is included with this book.) Just be sure to change the **Width** and **Height** to the size of your image (`Crosshair.gif` is 22 x 22 in size) and ensure that the **Anchor** is set to **middle-center**.

We set its **Pos Z** to `1.0` so that the reticle floats in front of you at a one meter distance. A fixed distance cursor is fine in most UI situations. For example, this cursor in fine when you're picking something from a flat canvas that is also at a fixed distance from you.

However, this is world space. If another object is between you and the reticle, the reticle will be obfuscated.

Also, if you look at something much farther away, you'll refocus your eyes and have trouble viewing the cursor at the same time. (To emphasize this problem, try moving the cursor closer. For example, if you change the **Pos Z** of the ReticleCursor to 0.5 or less, you might have to go cross-eyed to see it!) To compensate for these issues, we can ray cast and move the cursor to the actual distance of the object that you're looking at, resizing the cursor accordingly so that it appears to stay the same size. Here's a cheap version of this idea:

1. With ReticleCursor selected, click on **Add Component | New Script**, name it CursorPositioner, and click on **Create** and **Add**.

2. Open the script in MonoDevelop by double-clicking on the name.

Here's the CursorPositioner.cs script:

```
using UnityEngine;
using UnityEngine.EventSystems;
using System.Collections;

public class CursorPositioner : MonoBehaviour {
  private float defaultPosZ;

  void Start () {
    defaultPosZ = transform.localPosition.z;
  }

  void Update () {
    Transform camera = Camera.main.transform;
    Ray ray = new Ray (camera.position, camera.rotation *
      Vector3.forward);
    RaycastHit hit;
    if (Physics.Raycast (ray, out hit)) {
      if (hit.distance <= defaultPosZ) {
        transform.localPosition = new Vector3 (0, 0, hit.distance);
      } else {
        transform.localPosition = new Vector3 (0, 0, defaultPosZ);
      }
    }
  }
}
```

The **Rect Transform** component's **Pos Z** is found in the script in transform. localPosition. This script changes it to hit.distance if it's less than the given **Pos Z**. Now, you can also move the reticle to a more comfortable distance, such as **Pos Z** = 2.

An excellent tutorial by @eVRydayVR shows how to implement both, distance and size compensated world space reticles. You can visit `https://www.youtube.com/watch?v=LLKYbwNnKDg`, which is a video titled *Oculus Rift DK2 – Unity Tutorial: Reticle*.

We just implemented our own cursor reticle, but many VR SDKs now also provide cursors (for Oculus Rift, see `OVRCrosshair.cs`, and in Cardboard, it is a part of the `GazeInputModule.cs` utility), although they may or may not include distance and size compensation.

The windshield HUD

The term *heads-up display*, or HUD, originates from its use in aircraft, where a pilot is able to view information with the head positioned in such a way that they are looking forward rather down at their instrument panels. Owing to this usage, I'll refer it as *windshield HUD*. Like visor HUD, the information panel overlays the gameplay, but it isn't attached to your head. Instead, you can think of it as attached to your seat while in a cockpit or at the dentist.

A visor HUD is like the UI canvas—it is attached to your head.
A windshield HUD is like it's attached to your seat.

Let's create a simple windshield HUD by performing the following steps:

1. From the **Project** panel, drag the `DefaultCanvas` prefab onto the `MeMyselfEye` object in the **Hierarchy** panel so that it becomes a child of `MeMyselfEye`.

2. Rename it to `HUDCanvas`.

3. With `HUDCanvas` selected, set the **Rect Transform** component's **Pos X**, **Pos Y**, **Pos Z** to (`0,0.4,0.8`).

4. Now, we'll set the **Text** component. With **Text** under `HUDCanvas` selected, change the text to **Welcome! Mi reality es su reality**. Also, change the color to something bright, such as green.

5. This time, we'll make the panel translucent. Select the image from **Image** under `HUDCanvas` and select its color swatch. Then in the **Color** dialog, modify the **Alpha ("A")** channel from `255` to about `115`.

That's pretty straightforward. When you view it in VR, the canvas starts out just in front of you, but as you look around, its position seems to remain stationary and relative to the other objects in the scene as shown in the following screenshot:

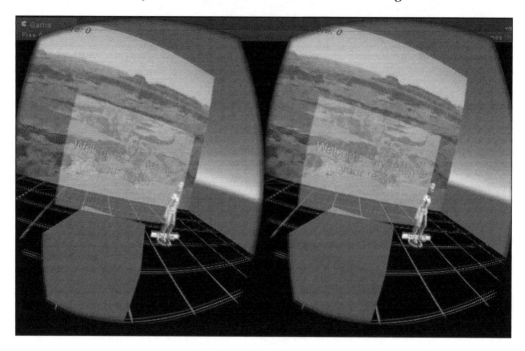

As we'll see in the next chapter, *Chapter 6, First-person Character*, when a first-person character moves through the scene, the HUD canvas will stay in front of you, at the same relative position to your body object, MeMyselfEye.

You might have realized that it's possible for objects in the scene to obfuscate the HUD panel since they're all occupying the same world space. If you need to prevent this, you have to ensure that the canvas is always rendered last so that it appears in front of any other objects regardless of its position in 3D-space. In a conventional monoscopic game, you can do this by adding a second camera for the UI and changing its render priority. In stereoscopic VR, you have to accomplish this differently, possibly requiring that you write a custom shader for your UI object (an advanced topic).

A variant of this HUD is to turn the canvas so that it's always facing you, while its position in 3D-space is fixed. See the section named *The info bubble* of this chapter to learn how to code this.

For kicks, let's write a script that removes the welcome message canvas after 15 seconds, as follows:

1. With HUDCanvas selected, click on **Add Component | New Script**, name the script as DestroyTimeout, and click on **Create** and **Add**.

2. Open the script in MonoDevelop.

Here's the DestroyTimeout.cs script:

```
using UnityEngine;
using System.Collections;

public class DestroyTimeout : MonoBehaviour {
  public float timer = 15.0f;

  void Start () {
    Destroy (gameObject, timer);
  }
}
```

The HUDCanvas will disappear after the timer runs out when the game starts up.

 A windshield HUD canvas is set as a child object of the first-person avatar, a sibling object of the camera.

In this example, we start to move further towards a first-person experience. Imagine sitting in a car or the cockpit of an aircraft. The HUD is projected on the windshield in front of you, but you're free to move your head to look around. In the scene's **Hierarchy** panel, there's a first-person object (MeMyselfEye) that contains the camera rig, and possibly your avatar body and the other furnishings surrounding you. When the vehicle moves in the game, the entire cockpit moves in unison, including the camera rig and the windshield. We'll work with this more later in this chapter and *Chapter 6, First-person Character*.

The game element UI

When Ethan gets killed, the score value in the GameController object's KillTarget script is updated, but we don't show the current score to the player (set up in the previous chapter). We'll do that now—adding a scoreboard into the scene at the top left corner of the backdrop PhotoPlane image:

1. From the **Project** panel, drag the DefaultCanvas prefab directly into the **Scene** view.

2. Rename it ScoreBoard.

3. With ScoreBoard selected, set the **Rect Transform** component's **Pos X**, **Pos Y**, **Pos Z** to (-2.8, 7, 4.9) and **Width**, **Height** to (3000, 480).

4. With **Text** under ScoreBoard selected, set **Font Size** to 100 and a noticeable color such as red for the **Text**.

5. Enter the **Score: 0** sample string for **Text**.

6. Disable **Image** under ScoreBoard by unchecking the **Enable** checkbox, or deleting it.

We added another canvas to the scene, sized and placed it where we want, and formatted the text for display. It should look like this:

Now, we need to update the KillTarget.cs script, as follows:

```
using UnityEngine;
using UnityEngine.UI;
using System.Collections;

public class KillTarget : MonoBehaviour {
  public GameObject target;
  public ParticleSystem hitEffect;
  public GameObject killEffect;
  public float timeToSelect = 3.0f;
  public int score;
```

```
public Text scoreText;

private float countDown;

void Start () {
  score = 0;
  countDown = timeToSelect;
  hitEffect.enableEmission = false;
  scoreText.text = "Score: 0";
}

void Update () {
  Transform camera = Camera.main.transform;
  Ray ray = new Ray (camera.position, camera.rotation *
    Vector3.forward);
  RaycastHit hit;
  if (Physics.Raycast (ray, out hit) && (hit.collider.gameObject
    == target)) {
    if (countDown > 0.0f) {
      // on target
      countDown -= Time.deltaTime;
      // print (countDown);
      hitEffect.transform.position = hit.point;
      hitEffect.enableEmission = true;
    } else {
      // killed
      Instantiate( killEffect, target.transform.position,
        target.transform.rotation );
      score += 1;
      scoreText.text = "Score: " + score;
      countDown = timeToSelect;
      SetRandomPosition();
    }
  } else {
    // reset
    countDown = timeToSelect;
    hitEffect.enableEmission = false;
  }
}

void SetRandomPosition() {
  float x = Random.Range (-5.0f, 5.0f);
  float z = Random.Range (-5.0f, 5.0f);
  target.transform.position = new Vector3 (x, 0.0f, z);
}
}
```

After saving the script file, go back into Unity editor, select GameController in the **Hierarchy** panel, and then drag and drop the **Text** object under ScoreBoard from **Hierarchy** onto the **Score Text** field in **Kill Target (Script)**.

Run the scene in VR. Each time you kill Ethan (by staring at him), your score will be updated on ScoreBoard on the upper left of PhotoPlane.

A game element UI canvas is a part of the scene like any other game object.

This was an example of using an object that's a part of the scene for information display. Our example is pretty simplistic. You might want to make a nicer modeled scoreboard, like the one you'd see in a stadium or something. The point is, it's a part of the scene and to see the message you might have to actually turn your head and, well, look at it.

The info bubble

In a comic book, when a character says something, it's shown in a *speech bubble*. In many online social worlds, participants are represented by avatars and if you hover above someone's avatar, their name is displayed. I'll call this type of user interface an *info bubble*.

Info bubbles are located in world space at a specific 3D position, but the canvas should always be facing the camera. We can ensure this with a script.

In this example, we'll display the **X, Z** location of the WalkTarget object (set up in the previous chapter), controlled by the LookMoveTo.cs script. To add the info bubble, perform the following steps:

1. From the **Project** panel, drag the DefaultCanvas prefab directly into the **Scene** view on top of WalkTarget under GameController so that its a child of WalkTarget.
2. Rename it to InfoBubble.
3. With InfoBubble selected, set the **Rect Transform** component's **Pos X, Pos Y, Pos Z** to (0, 0.2, 0).
4. With **Text** under InfoBubble selected, set the **Rect Transform** component's **Pos X, Pos Y, Pos Z** to (0, 0, 0) and **Right, Bottom** to 0, 0.
5. With **Image** under InfoBubble selected, set **Scale** to (0.7, 0.2, 1).
6. Enter the **X:00.00, Z:00.00** sample string for **Text**.

Verify that the canvas and text look roughly the right size and position and adjust the text as you please.

Now, we will modify the LookMoveTo.cs script to show the current WalkTarget **X**, **Z** position. Open the script in the MonoDevelop editor, and add the following code:

```
using UnityEngine;
using UnityEngine.UI;
using System.Collections;

public class LookMoveTo : MonoBehaviour {
  public GameObject ground;
  public Transform infoBubble;

  private Text infoText;

  void Start () {
    if (infoBubble != null) {
      infoText = infoBubble.Find ("Text").GetComponent<Text> ();
    }
  }

  void Update () {
    Transform camera = Camera.main.transform;
    Ray ray;
    RaycastHit[] hits;
    GameObject hitObject;

    ray = new Ray (camera.position, camera.rotation *
      Vector3.forward);
    hits = Physics.RaycastAll (ray);
    for (int i=0; i < hits.Length; i++) {
      RaycastHit hit = hits [i];
      hitObject = hit.collider.gameObject;
      if (hitObject == ground) {
        if (infoBubble != null) {
          infoText.text = "X:" + hit.point.x.ToString("F2") + ",
            Z:" + hit.point.z.ToString("F2");

          infoBubble.LookAt(camera.position);
          infoBubble.Rotate ( 0.0f, 180.0f, 0.0f );
        }
```

```
            transform.position = hit.point;
        }
    }
}


}
```

The line `using UnityEngine.UI;` states that this script will need access to the Unity UI API. We defined a `public Transform infoBubble` variable, which will be set to the `WalkTarget/InfoBubble` object. We also defined a private **Text** the `infoText` variable, which gets set to the `InfoBubble` object's **Text** object. The script assumes that the given `InfoBubble` has a child **Text** UI object.

So, the `infoText text` object has a text component, which has a text string property! You can see what I mean in Unity editor. If you examine the **Inspector** panel while `InfoBubble/Text` is selected, you'll see that it contains a **Text (Script)** component, which has a **Text** field. This **Text** field is where we write our messages. So in `Setup()`, we find the `WalkTarget/InfoBubble/Text` object assigning the **Text** object to `infoText`, and then in `Update()`, we set the string value of `infoText.text` so that the score is shown on the bubble canvas.

Also, in `Update()`, we transformed the `infoBubble` canvas so that it's always facing us using `infoBubble.LookAt()` and passing it the camera position. The result of `LookAt()` has the canvas facing away from us. So, we also need to rotate it around the *y*-axis by 180 degrees.

Save the script and drag the `InfoBubble` object from **Hierarchy** onto the **Info Bubble** slot in the **Look Move To (Script)** component. If you don't assign the `InfoBubble` canvas, the script will still run because we test for `null` objects before we reference them.

 An info bubble UI canvas is attached to other game objects, moving when they move and always facing the camera (like a billboard).

Run the scene in VR, and you'll see that `WalkTarget` has a little info bubble telling us about its **X, Z** position.

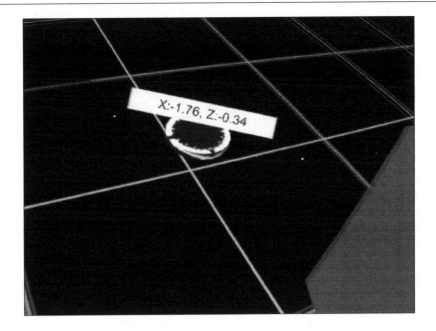

 Extra challenge: Want to try something else? Implement a health meter bar for Ethan. Use the `countDown` variable in the `KillTarget` script to determine his percent health, and show a health meter (horizontal bar) above his head when it's not 100 percent.

Info bubbles are useful when you need to display UI messages that belong to specific objects in the scene and may move in concert with the objects.

An in-game dashboard with input events

An in-game dashboard is a UI display that is integrated into the game itself. A typical scenario is an automobile or a space ship, where you are seated in a cockpit. At waist level (desk level) is a panel with a set of controls, gauges, information displays, and so on. Dashboards generally feel more natural in a seated VR experience.

A few pages back, we discussed windshield HUDs. Dashboards are pretty much the same thing. One difference is that the dashboard may be more obviously a part of the level environment and not simply an auxiliary information display or a menu.

In fact, dashboards can be a very effective mechanism to control VR motion sickness. Researchers have found that when a VR user has a better sense of being grounded and has a consistent *horizon line* in view, he's much less likely to experience nausea while moving around a virtual space. The opposite being a floating one-dimensional eyeball with no sense of self or grounding, which is asking for trouble. (See the *Oculus Best Practices* for this and other great tips by visiting `https://developer.oculus.com/documentation/intro-vr/latest/concepts/bp_intro/`).

In this example, we'll make a simple dashboard with a Start/Stop button. For now, the buttons will operate a water hose in the scene to help fend off the zombies. (*Why not?*). This project uses the scene created in the previous chapter.

This project is a bit more complicated than you might expect. However, if you've ever had to build anything in Minecraft, you know that even the simple things may require assembling multiple parts. Here's what we will do:

- Create a dashboard canvas with two functional buttons—Start and Stop
- Add a water hose to the scene and wire it to the buttons
- Write a simple version of the script that activates the buttons
- Highlight a button by looking at it
- Improve the script to activate the button only if it's highlighted
- Modify the reticle cursor (created earlier) so that its enabled only when looking at the dashboard
- Consider mechanisms to *click* with different VR hardware

So let's get to it.

Creating a dashboard with buttons

First, let's create a dashboard with a Start and a Stop button, as follows:

1. From the **Project** panel, drag the `DefaultCanvas` prefab onto the `MeMyselfEye` object in the **Hierarchy** panel so that it becomes a child.
2. Rename it to `Dashboard`.
3. With `Dashboard` selected, set the **Rect Transform** component's **Pos X, Pos Y, Pos Z** to (`0`, `-1`, `0.2`) and its **Rotation** to (`60`, `0`, `0`).
4. Disable or delete the **Text** child object of `Dashboard`.

This places the dashboard one meter below our eyes and a little out in front.

For a *work-in-progress* look, if you'd like, I've included an image sketch of a vehicle dashboard that you can use, as follows:

1. Import the `DashboardSketch.png` file into your **Project** (such as the `Assets/Textures` folder).

2. Add a new **GameObject | UI | Raw Image** as a child of `Dashboard`.

3. Drag the `DashboardSketch` texture from the **Project** panel onto the **Texture** field of the **Raw Image** component.

4. Set its **Rect Transform** component's **Pos X, Pos Y, Pos Z** to (0,0,0), **Width** to `140`, and **Height** to `105`.

5. It should be **Anchored** at **middle-center** (0.5,0.5) in **X, Y**, and **Pivot**, with **Rotation** (0,0,0).

6. Set **Scale** to (4.5,4.5,4.5).

Next we will add the Start and Stop buttons. They can go anywhere you'd like on the canvas, but the sketch has two nice spaces predefined for them:

1. Add a new **GameObject | UI | Button** as a new child of `Dashboard`. Name it `StartButton`.

2. Set its **Rect Transform** component's **X, Y, Z** to (-48, 117, 0), ser **Width, Height** to (60, 60), and **Anchored** to **center-middle** (0.5). No **Rotation** and **Scale** of 1.

3. In the button's **Image (Script)** component pane, for **Source Image**, click on the tiny circle on the far right to open the **Select Sprite** picker and choose **ButtonAcceleratorUpSprite** (which you may have imported into the `Assets/Standard Assets/CrossPlatformInput/Sprites` folder).

4. In the button's **Button (Script)** component pane, for **Normal Color**, I liked RGB (89,154,43) and set **Highlighted Color** to (105, 255, 0).

5. Similarly, create another button named `StopButton` with the **Rect Transform** component's **X, Y, Z** (52, 118, 0), set **Width, Height** to (60, 60), for **Source Image** select **ButtonBrakeOverSprite**, choose **Normal Color** (236, 141, 141) and **Highlighted Color** (235, 45, 0).

The result should look like this:

2001 Audi A6 (source (http://www.justanswer.com/audi/6sskf-audi-a6-audi-a6-51-reg-centre-dashboard.html#re.v/174/)

One last thing. If you're using the ReticleCursor that was created earlier in this chapter with the CursorPositioner.cs script, we want the dashboard itself to have a collider for the script. We can achieve this by performing the following steps:

1. With Dashboard selected, right-click for options, and navigate to **3D Object | Plane**.
2. Set its **Position** to (0,0,0), **Rotation** to (270,0,0) and **Scale** to (64,1,48).
3. Disable its **Mesh Renderer** (but leave its **Mesh Collider** enabled).

Now the dashboard has a plane child that isn't rendered, but its collider will be detected when CursorPositioner does its ray cast.

Having a single toggle button with pressed and released states might be better than separate Start and Stop buttons. When we're done with this chapter, go ahead and figure out how to do it!

We just created a world space canvas that should appear in VR at waist or desk level. We decorated it with a dashboard sketch and added two UI buttons. Now, we'll wire up the buttons to specific events.

Linking the water hose to the buttons

Let's first give the buttons something to do, such as the action of turning on a fire hose. If we aim it strategically, it might even fend off rogue zombies. Coincidentally, the Unity **Particle Systems** under **Standard Assets** that we imported earlier has a water hose that we can use. Add it to the scene, as follows:

1. If you haven't done so already, import the **Particle Systems** standard asset from the main menu bar and navigating to **Assets | Import Package | ParticleSystems**.

2. In the **Project** panel, find the Assets/Standard Assets/Particle Systems/Prefabs/Hose prefab and drag it into the **Scene** view.

3. Set its **Transform** component's **X, Y, Z** to (-3, 0, 1.5) and **Rotation** to (340, 87, 0).

4. Ensure that **Hose** is enabled (check its **Enable** checkbox).

5. Unfold the **Hose** in **Hierarchy** so that you can see its child **WaterShower** particle system. Select it.

6. In **Inspector**, in the **Particle System** properties pane, look for **Play On Awake** and uncheck it.

Note that the **Hose** object in **Hierarchy** has a **WaterShower** child object. This is the actual particle system that we will control with the buttons. It should start *off*.

The **Hose** prefab itself comes with mouse-driven script that we don't want to use, so disable it, as follows:

1. With **Hose** selected, disable (uncheck) its **Hose (Script)**.

2. Also disable (uncheck) the **Simple Mouse Rotator (Script)** component.

Now we will wire up StartButton to the **WaterShower** particle system, by telling the buttons to listen for the OnClick() events, as follows:

1. Unfold the **Hose** in **Hierarchy** so that you can see its child **WaterShower** particle system.

2. In **Hierarchy**, select StartButton (under MeMyselfEye/Dashboard).

3. Note that the **On Click()** pane in the **Inspector** is empty. Click on the *Plus* (+) icon on the lower right of that pane to reveal a new field labeled **None (Object)**.

4. Drag the **WaterShower** particle system from **Hierarchy** onto the **None (Object)** field.

5. Its function selector the default value is **No Function**. Change it to **ParticleSystem | Play()**.

OK. The steps are similar for the StopButton, as follows:

1. In **Hierarchy**, select StopButton.

2. Click on the *Plus* (**+**) icon on the lower right of its **On Click()** pane.

3. Drag the **WaterShower** from **Hierarchy** onto the **None (Object)** field.

4. Its function selector the default value is **No Function**. Change it to **ParticleSystem | Stop()**.

The Start and Stop buttons *listen for OnClick() events,* and when one comes, it will call the **WaterShower** particle system's Play() and Stop() functions respectively. To make it work, we need to press the buttons.

Activating buttons from the script

Before we give the user a way to press the buttons, let's see how we can do this from a script. Create a new script on GameController, as follows:

1. With GameController selected, press **Add Component | New Script** to create a script named ButtonExecuteTest.

2. Open the script in MonoDevelop.

In the following script, we turn the hose on and off in five second intervals, as follows:

```
using UnityEngine;
using UnityEngine.EventSystems;
using System.Collections;

public class ButtonExecuteTest : MonoBehaviour {
  private GameObject startButton, stopButton;
  private bool on = false;
  private float timer = 5.0f;

  void Start () {
    startButton = GameObject.Find ("StartButton");
    stopButton = GameObject.Find ("StopButton");
  }

  void Update () {
```

```
      timer -= Time.deltaTime;
      if (timer < 0.0f) {
        on = !on;
        timer = 5.0f;

        PointerEventData data = new PointerEventData
          (EventSystem.current);
        if (on) {
          ExecuteEvents.Execute<IPointerClickHandler> (startButton,
            data, ExecuteEvents.pointerClickHandler);
        } else {
          ExecuteEvents.Execute<IPointerClickHandler> (stopButton,
            data, ExecuteEvents.pointerClickHandler);
        }
      }
    }
  }
}
```

The script manages a Boolean on value, which says that if the hose is on or off. And it has a timer which counts down from five seconds on each update. We use the private keyword for variables that are only used within this script, whereas the public ones can be viewed and modified via the Unity editor and other scripts. For startButton and stopButton, I decided to use GameObject.Find() to get them rather than having you drag and drop them in the Unity editor.

In this script, we introduced the UnityEngine.EventSystems. *Events* are a way for different components to talk to one another. When an event occurs, such as a button press, a function in another script may get called. In our case, we're going to trigger an event corresponding to the start button press, and another corresponding to the stop button press.

The meat of our script is in the ExecuteEvents.Execute functions. Since we set up the button to respond to the OnClick() events, we just need to send such an event to the button that we want to execute. When we want to turn the hose on, we call ExecuteEvents.Execute<IPointerClickHandler> (startButton, data, ExecuteEvents.pointerClickHandler). When we want to turn it off, we call the same for stopButton. The API requires a PointerEventData object to be included with the arguments. So, we also provide that. (For more information on scripting Unity events, visit http://docs.unity3d.com/Manual/EventSystem.html.)

Save the script and click on **Play**. The hose should turn on and off every five seconds (as if a cat were walking on the dashboard).

Now that we tested the event system connection between the button clicks and the hose, we can disable this script before moving on to the next one.

Breaking down a complex feature into bite-sized pieces and testing them separately is an excellent implementation strategy.

Look to highlight a button

Meanwhile, let's detect when the user is looking at a button and highlight it. Although **Button** is a Unity UI object, it needs to be detected with a ray cast. There may be other ways to accomplish this, but here we will add a game object sphere to each button, tag it as `Button` and cast a ray to detect it. First, add the spheres by performing the following steps:

1. In the **Hierarchy** panel, select `StartButton` (under `MeMyselfEye/ Dashboard`), right-click for options, and navigate to **3D Object | Sphere**.

2. Set its **Transform** component's **Scale** to (52, 52, 52) so that it fits the button size.

3. To add a tag named `Button`, near the top of the **Inspector** panel, click on the **Tag** selector, click on **Add Tag**, and then select the *Plus* (**+**) icon to add a row to the tag list. Enter the name `Button` in place of **New Tag**.

4. We're tagging the sphere child of `StartButton`. So, click on the sphere in **Hierarchy** again so that its **Inspector** panel is visible again. Then, click on the **Tag** selector. This time, `Button` should be included in the list. Select it.

The following screenshot shows the sphere on the button in **Scene** and tagged `Button` in **Inspector** before we disable its **Mesh Renderer**:

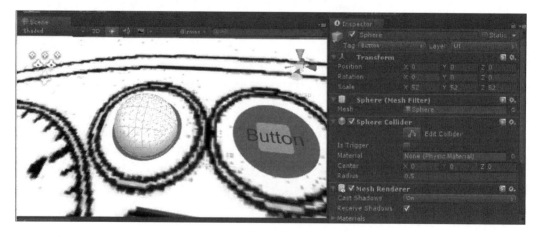

Disable the sphere's **Mesh Renderer** by unchecking the **Mesh Renderer** checkbox.

Also, repeat these steps for `StopButton`.

Now, create a new script on `GameController`, as follows:

1. With `GameController` selected, if you haven't already, disable the previous `ButtonExecuteTest` script now by unchecking its **Enable** checkbox.

2. With `GameController` selected, navigate to **Add Component | New Script** to create a script named `ButtonExecute`.

3. Open the script in MonoDevelop.

In the following `ButtonExecute.cs` script, we tell the button to become highlighted when you look at it:

```
using UnityEngine;
using UnityEngine.EventSystems;
using System.Collections;

public class ButtonExecute : MonoBehaviour {
  private GameObject currentButton;

  void Update () {
    Transform camera = Camera.main.transform;
    Ray ray = new Ray(camera.position, camera.rotation *
      Vector3.forward );
    RaycastHit hit;
    GameObject hitButton = null;
    PointerEventData data = new PointerEventData
      (EventSystem.current);
    if (Physics.Raycast (ray, out hit)) {
      if (hit.transform.gameObject.tag == "Button") {
        hitButton = hit.transform.parent.gameObject;
      }
    }
    if (currentButton != hitButton) {
      if (currentButton != null) { // unhighlight
        ExecuteEvents.Execute<IPointerExitHandler> (currentButton,
          data, ExecuteEvents.pointerExitHandler);
      }
      currentButton = hitButton;
      if (currentButton != null) { // highlight
        ExecuteEvents.Execute<IPointerEnterHandler>
          (currentButton, data,
          ExecuteEvents.pointerEnterHandler);
      }
    }
  }
}
```

Much of this script should look familiar to you by now. On each frame's `Update()` function, we cast a ray from the camera, looking for a hit of an object tagged `Button` (the button's sphere). So, we take its parent (the UI button itself) as `hitButton`. We remember `currentButton` that's highlighted between the calls to `Update()`. So, we can detect whether the new hit is the same or different (or nothing at all, null).

This script executes two new events on the `Button` object. In the previous `ButtonExecuteTest.cs` script, we executed a *click* event (`pointerClickHandler`). This time, we will execute *enter* and *exit* events to highlight and remove the highlight respectively (with `pointerEnterHandler` and `pointerExitHandler`).

Save the script and *Play*. When you gaze at a button, it should highlight, and when you gaze away from it, it should remove the highlight.

Looking and then clicking to select

To be a functional dashboard, the buttons should operate when they're clicked. Let's use the generic `Clicker` class that we wrote in *Chapter 3, VR Build and Run*, which checks for user clicks on the keyboard, mouse, or the Cardboard trigger.

At the top of the `ButtonExecute.cs` script's class definition, add the following:

```
public class ButtonExecute : MonoBehaviour {
    private GameObject currentButton;
    private clicker = new Clicker ();
```

Then the changes made to the `ButtonExecute.cs` script are pretty simple. At the bottom of `Update()`, make the following changes:

```
    ...
    if (currentButton != hitButton) {
      if (currentButton != null) { // unhighlight
        ExecuteEvents.Execute<IPointerExitHandler> (currentButton,
          data, ExecuteEvents.pointerExitHandler);
      }
      currentButton = hitButton;
      if (currentButton != null) { // highlight
        ExecuteEvents.Execute<IPointerEnterHandler>
          (currentButton, data,
          ExecuteEvents.pointerEnterHandler);
      }
    }
    if (currentButton != null) {
      if (clicker.clicked()) {
        ExecuteEvents.Execute<IPointerClickHandler>
          (currentButton, data,
```

```
            ExecuteEvents.pointerClickHandler);
      }
   }
```

After the setting of highlighting, if there's still one highlighted and any key is pressed (keyboard or mouse), we'll take that as a select and click on the UI button.

We now have an in-game dashboard with buttons that respond to user input, which controls the behavior of an object (water hose) in the scene.

Looking and staring to select

Instead of using a clicker, we can use a time-based selection to click on the button. To make this work, we'll keep a countdown timer while staring at a button, much like the one that we used to kill Ethan in the previous chapter. The `ButtonExecute.cs` script now looks like this:

```
using UnityEngine;
using UnityEngine.EventSystems;
using System.Collections;

public class ButtonExecute : MonoBehaviour {
  public float timeToSelect = 2.0f;
  private float countDown;
  private GameObject currentButton;
  private clicker = new Clicker ();

  void Update () {
    Transform camera = Camera.main.transform;
    Ray ray = new Ray(camera.position, camera.rotation *
      Vector3.forward );
    RaycastHit hit;
    GameObject hitButton = null;
    PointerEventData data = new PointerEventData
      (EventSystem.current);
    if (Physics.Raycast (ray, out hit)) {
      if (hit.transform.gameObject.tag == "Button") {
        hitButton = hit.transform.parent.gameObject;
      }
    }
    if (currentButton != hitButton) {
      if (currentButton != null) { // unhighlight
        ExecuteEvents.Execute<IPointerExitHandler> (currentButton,
          data, ExecuteEvents.pointerExitHandler);
```

```
    }
    currentButton = hitButton;
    if (currentButton != null) { // highlight
      ExecuteEvents.Execute<IPointerEnterHandler>
        (currentButton, data,
        ExecuteEvents.pointerEnterHandler);
      countDown = timeToSelect;
    }
  }
  if (currentButton != null) {
    countDown -= Time.deltaTime;
    if (clicker.clicked() || countDown < 0.0f) {
      ExecuteEvents.Execute<IPointerClickHandler>
        (currentButton, data,
        ExecuteEvents.pointerClickHandler);
      countDown = timeToSelect;
    }
  }
}
}
```

When a button is highlighted, the countDown timer starts. When it reaches zero, we consider that to be a click. *Does it work for you? Wooohooo!!!*

So this was a relatively complex project. The goal was to create a dashboard with buttons that turn a hose on and off. We broke it down into discrete steps, added the objects and components a step at a time, and tested each step to make sure that it works as expected before moving on. If you tried to implement this all at once or blew through it without testing, things can (and will) go wrong, and it'll be much harder to figure out where the problem cropped up.

Extra challenge: This feature can be further enhanced for different purposes. For example, it can be used to give the user a feedback that the countdown is running, perhaps by animating a selection cursor (such as concentric circles). Also, further feedback can be given when the click event is executed. For example, the **Button** UI object has a **Transition** option called **Animation** that might be helpful. Also, consider audio cues.

A responsive object UI with head gestures

The last UI technique that I'll discuss is where the UI elements are not necessarily visible at all times. Rather, they may be invoked in context as a part of the gameplay. I call this a *responsive object UI*.

For example, in conventional video games, you might have an ammunition gauge that's always visible. In VR, you can wait for the user to look down at the weapon in his hands, and then an ammo meter on the weapon lights up, showing its status.

In this example, we are going to make the dashboard that we just built appear only when we can infer that it is the user's intent to access it. The mechanism should feel quite natural—you look down towards you feet quickly and the dashboard slides out, and when you look away after a few seconds it tucks itself in again.

Using the head position

Let's try just using the camera angle to tell if you're looking down, say within 60 degrees of looking straight down. Create a new script on the `GameController` named `HeadGesture.cs`, which checks whether you're facing down, as follows:

```
using UnityEngine;
using System.Collections;

public class HeadGesture : MonoBehaviour {
  public bool isFacingDown = false;

  void Update () {
    isFacingDown = DetectFacingDown ();
  }

  private bool DetectFacingDown () {
    return (CameraAngleFromGround () < 60.0f);
  }

  private float CameraAngleFromGround () {
    return Vector3.Angle (Vector3.down, Camera.main.transform.rotation
* Vector3.forward);
  }
}
```

This script defines a HeadGesture class with a handy public variable, isFacingDown, which is updated during each Update(). I put it into its own class so that it is reusable and we can call it from other scripts. The details are broken out into smaller single-purpose functions.

The DetectFacingDown() function checks whether the camera angle is within 60 degrees of straight down.

In CameraAngleFromGround(), we get the angle of the current camera relative to straight down, returning a value between 0 and 180 degrees.

Internally, Unity uses a **Quaternion** data structure to represent orientations and rotations in three dimensions, which is optimal for calculations and accuracy. The Unity editor lets us specify angles as Euler rotations (pronounced *oiler*) as degree rotations around the *x*, *y*, and *z* axes. See http://docs.unity3d.com/ScriptReference/Quaternion.html.

Now, create another new script also on the GameController and name it FlippinDashboard.cs, which flips opens the dashboard when you're looking down, as follows:

```
using UnityEngine;
using System.Collections;

public class FlippinDashboard : MonoBehaviour {
  private HeadGesture gesture;
  private GameObject dashboard;
  private bool isOpen = true;
  private Vector3 startRotation;

  void Start () {
    gesture = GetComponent<HeadGesture> ();
    dashboard = GameObject.Find ("Dashboard");
    startRotation = dashboard.transform.eulerAngles;
    CloseDashboard ();
  }

  void Update () {
    if (gesture.isFacingDown) {
      OpenDashboard ();
    } else {
      CloseDashboard ();
    }
```

```
      }

      private void CloseDashboard() {
        if (isOpen) {
          dashboard.transform.eulerAngles = new Vector3 (180.0f,
            startRotation.y, startRotation.z);
          isOpen = false;
        }
      }

      private void OpenDashboard() {
        if (!isOpen) {
          dashboard.transform.eulerAngles = startRotation;
          isOpen = true;
        }
      }
    }
```

This script references the other `HeadGesture` component. In fact, it finds the component instance from the same `GameController` and *asks it* during each update whether the user is looking down (`gesture.isFacingDown`). In this case, we're using the `public` variable of the `HeadGesture` class from another script rather than in the Unity editor's **Inspector** panel.

In `Start()`, we initialize `startRotation` of the dashboard in its opened position, like it's set in the Unity editor. Then, we close the dashboard initially.

The `Update()` function checks whether the user is in `isFacingDown` gesture, and opens the dashboard. Otherwise, it closes the dashboard. The `CloseDashboard()` function closes it by setting its **X** rotation to 180 degrees, but only if it's already open. The `OpenDashboard()` function restores the rotation to the open settings, but only if it's presently closed.

When you *Play* the scene, the dashboard starts folded up. When you look down, it unfolds. When you look away, it folds up again. That's a responsive object UI!

Using head gestures

There are many ways to improve this behavior. One idea is that instead of opening the dashboard by simply looking down, the user must look down quickly, as though there's intent in the gesture of looking down. In other words, if you casually look down, the dashboard doesn't open. If you look down quickly, it does. This is a simple example of a head *gesture* input.

Separating functional units in your program into their own class, like we did with `HeadGesture`, makes your code more modular, reusable, testable, and maintainable.

Let's change the `HeadGesture` script to do it that way, as follows:

```
using UnityEngine;
using System.Collections;

public class HeadGesture : MonoBehaviour {
  public bool isFacingDown = false;
  public bool isMovingDown = false;

  private float sweepRate = 100.0f;
  private float previousCameraAngle;

  void Start () {
    previousCameraAngle = CameraAngleFromGround ();
  }

  void Update () {
    isFacingDown = DetectFacingDown ();
    isMovingDown = DetectMovingDown ();
  }

  private float CameraAngleFromGround () {
    return Vector3.Angle (Vector3.down, camera.transform.rotation
      * Vector3.forward);
  }

  private bool DetectFacingDown () {
    return (CameraAngleFromGround () < 60.0f);
  }

  private bool DetectMovingDown () {
    float angle = CameraAngleFromGround ();
    float deltaAngle = previousCameraAngle - angle;
    float rate = deltaAngle / Time.deltaTime;
    previousCameraAngle = angle;
    return (rate >= sweepRate);
  }
}
```

We now detect a downward movement and set a public `isMovingDown` function.

The `DetectMovDown()` function gets the camera **X** rotation (angle) each time `Update()` is called and compares it with `previousCameraAngle` from the previous frame. Then, we calculate the rotational rate in seconds (rate), and check whether the rate exceeds a threshold (`sweepRate`). Then, it counts as a gesture. I've found out that a sweep rate of `100.0` works pretty well, but you can experiment.

Add the `isMovingDown` detection to the `FlippingDashboard` script and replace `Update()`, as follows:

```
void Update() {
  if (gesture.isMovingDown) {
    OpenDashboard ();
  } else if (!gesture.isFacingDown) {
    CloseDashboard ();
  }
}
```

I also discovered that it's a little too sensitive, and adding a two second delay before closing the dashboard once you look up again helps. Add a timer, as follows:

```
private Vector3 startRotation;
private float timer = 0.0f;
private float timerReset = 2.0f;

. . .

void Update() {
  if (gesture.isMovingDown) {
    OpenDashboard ();
  } else if (!gesture.isFacingDown) {
    timer -= Time.deltaTime;
    if (timer <= 0.0f) {
      CloseDashboard ();
    }
  } else {
    timer = timerReset;
  }
}
. . .
```

To summarize, we have a dashboard that starts in a folded-up position and opens when you look down at it. At first, we simply used the angle of your gaze to decide to open it. Then, we enhanced it so that it opens only when you look down in a gesture (as if indicating intent) and it doesn't open if you casually look down.

Extra challenge: Can you figure out how to add a side-to-side head gesture—nod up and down for *On* and shake left to right for *Off*? How about tapping on the side of your headset? Does that count as a click? This idea has gotten a lot of love and hate from commenters (http://www.reddit.com/r/oculus/comments/2cl3wp/tap_the_side_of_the_rift_to_select/).

When implementing the head-gesture input, it's important to distinguish between casually looking around from an intended gesture and maintaining the user's sense of immersion in the VR experience.

Our current implementation is a kind of a cheap trick. For one, we only look back by one frame (for example, 1/60th of a second), whereas gestures would better be measured over multiple frames. Also, gestures certainly can be more complex. Even head nods can have acceleration, deceleration, and bounce. Also, it can vary from one person to the next. There are emerging third-party solutions that promise to provide more complete and robust solutions, including all kinds of head gestures as well as gesture detection from hand and body sensors.

When implementing a head-gesture input, it is important that the code is able to distinguish between casually looking around versus an intended gesture and maintain a sense of immersion in the VR experience.

Lots of experimentation is needed by all of us to gain a better understanding of how gestures play in VR. I encourage you to further explore this new user interface vocabulary.

Summary

In Unity, user interfaces that are based on a canvas object and the event system include buttons, text, images, sliders, and input fields, which can be assembled and wired to objects in the scene.

In this chapter, we took a close look at various world space UI techniques and how they can be used in virtual reality projects. We considered ways in which UI for VR differs from UI for conventional video games and desktop applications. Also, we implemented over a half of a dozen of them, demonstrating how each can be constructed, coded, and used in your own projects. Our C# scripting got a little more advanced, probing deeper into the Unity engine API and modular coding techniques.

You now have a broader vocabulary to approach UI in your VR projects. Some of the examples in this chapter can be directly applicable in your own work. However, not all need to be home-grown. VR UI tools are increasingly being provided in VR headset SDKs, open source VR middleware projects, and third-party Unity Assets Store packages.

In the next chapter, we will add a first-person character controller to our scene. We'll learn about avatars and methods to control navigation in VR so that we can comfortably move around inside the virtual world. Also, we'll learn about managing one of the negative aspects of virtual reality experiences—VR motion sickness.

6
First-person Character

Ninja on Segway illustration by Alaric Holloway, used with permission

Surprisingly, we have gotten this far in a book about VR and are still only using a fixed position third-person camera! This was intentional.

The typical approach when one starts to build a VR application is to immediately place the user directly into the scene as a first-person character. After all, wearing a VR headset is inherently a first-person point of view. However, virtual reality does not always need to be from a first-person perspective. Watching and controlling the action from a third-person point of view, such as a diorama with live actors, is a legitimate approach. In fact, some research indicates that fast-paced action games, which can unavoidably cause motion sickness when played in VR from a first-person point of view, may benefit from a third-person perspective instead.

That said, in this chapter, we will now move ourselves into a controllable first-person character and explore techniques to move around the virtual world.

In this chapter, we will discuss the following topics:

- Unity's character objects and components
- Controlling navigation with buttons and/or head movement
- Calibrating your avatar
- Separating your head from your body
- Exploring techniques to maintain a sense of self in VR
- The issues around VR motion sickness

 Note that the projects in this chapter are separate and not directly required by the other chapters in this book. If you decide to skip any of it or not save your work, that's OK.

Understanding the Unity characters

A first-person character is such a key asset in a VR project that we really should understand its components inside out. So, before we go about building one for our project, it would be a good idea to take a close look at the built-in components and standard assets that Unity provides.

Unity components

As you probably know, each Unity game object contains a set of associated **components**. Unity includes many types of built-in components, which you can see by browsing the **Component** menu in the main menu bar. Each component adds properties and behaviors to the object that it belongs to. A component's properties are accessible via the Unity editor's **Inspector** panel and scripts. A script attached to a game object is also a type of component, and may have properties that you can set in the **Inspector** panel.

The component types used to implement first-person characters include the **Camera**, **Character Controller**, and/or **Rigidbody**, and various scripts. Let's review each of these standard components.

The Camera component

The Camera component specifies the viewing parameters that are used to render the scene on each frame update. Any object with a Camera component is considered a *camera object*. Naturally, we've been using a camera in our scenes since we started, and we've been accessing it in the scripts that we've written.

A stereographic VR camera object renders two views, one for each eye. In VR, the camera controller scripts read data from the headset's motion sensors to determine the current head pose (position, direction, and rotation) and set the cameras' transform appropriately.

The Rigidbody component

When you add a Rigidbody component to any Unity game object, it will benefit from the calculations that are performed by the **physics engine**. Rigidbodies have parameters for gravity, mass, and drag, among others. During game play, the physics engine calculates each rigid object's *momentum* (mass, speed, and direction).

Rigid objects interact with other rigid objects. For example, if they collide, they'll bounce off each other and the parameters of the interaction can be controlled using a **physic material** with properties, such as friction and bounce factor.

Rigidbodies can be flagged as *kinematic*, which is usually only used when the object is driven by animation or scripts. Collisions will not affect kinematic objects, but they will still affect the motion of other Rigidbodies. It's mostly used when objects are chained together with *joints*, like the ones connecting a humanoid's bones or a swinging pendulum.

Any rigid object, given a child camera object, becomes a rigid first-person character. Then, you can add scripts to handle user input to move, jump, look around, and so on.

The Character Controller component

Like a Rigidbody, the **Character Controller** (CC) component is used for collision detection and character movement. It needs scripts to handle the user input to move, jump, and look around, too. However, it doesn't automatically have the physics built in.

The CC component is specifically designed for character objects because characters in a game often are not really expected to behave the same as other physics-based objects. It can be used instead of, or in addition to, a Rigidbody.

The CC component has a built-in **Capsule Collider** behavior to detect collisions. However, it doesn't automatically use the physics engine to *respond* to the collision.

For example, if a CC object hits a rigid object, such as a wall, it will just stop. It won't bounce. If a rigid object, such as a flying brick hits a CC object, the brick will get deflected (bounce) based on its own properties, but the CC object will not be affected. Of course, if you want to include behavior like this on the CC object, you can program that in your own scripts.

The CC component does have an especially good support for one force in its scripting API—*gravity*. Built-in parameters are specifically related to keeping the object's feet on the ground. For example, the **Step Offset** parameter defines how high a step the character can hop onto rather than being an obstacle that blocks his way. Similarly, the **Slope Limit** parameter says how big an incline is too steep and whether it should be treated like a wall. In your scripts, you can use the Move() method and the IsGrounded variable to implement character behavior.

Unless you script it, a CC object has no momentum and can stop on a dime. It feels very precise, but this could also lead to a jerky movement. The opposite is so for Rigidbody objects, which feel more fluid because they have momentum, acceleration and deceleration, and obey the laws of physics. In VR, we'd ideally like some combination of the two.

Unity Standard Assets

The **Characters** package in Unity **Standard Assets** comes with a number of third- and first-person character prefab objects. These prefab objects are compared in the following tables:

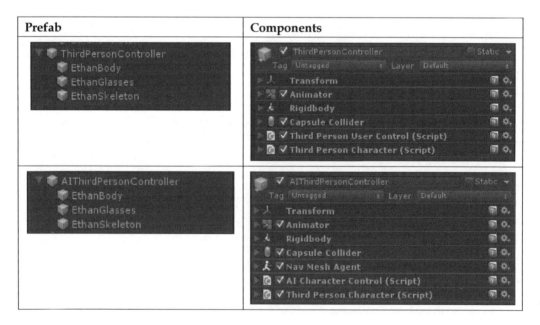

Prefab	Components
ThirdPersonController EthanBody EthanGlasses EthanSkeleton	ThirdPersonController — Static Tag Untagged Layer Default Transform Animator Rigidbody Capsule Collider Third Person User Control (Script) Third Person Character (Script)
AIThirdPersonController EthanBody EthanGlasses EthanSkeleton	AIThirdPersonController — Static Tag Untagged Layer Default Transform Animator Rigidbody Capsule Collider Nav Mesh Agent AI Character Control (Script) Third Person Character (Script)

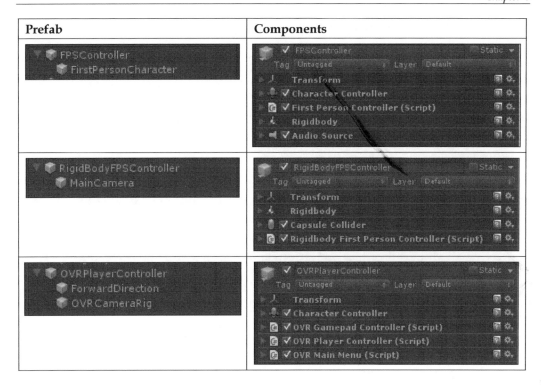

Prefab	Components

Let's discuss this in more detail.

ThirdPersonController

We've already used both of the third-person prefabs, ThirdPersonController and AIThirdPersonController, in *Chapter 2*, *Objects and Scale*, and *Chapter 4*, *Gaze-based Control*, respectively.

The ThirdPersonController prefab has child objects that define the character's body, namely, our friend Ethan. He is a rigged avatar (from the .fbx file), which means that humanoid animations can be applied to make him walk, run, jump, and so on.

The ThirdPersonController prefab uses a Rigidbody for physics and Capsule Collider for collision detection.

It has two scripts. A ThirdPersonUserControl script takes user input, such as keyboard presses, and tells the character to move, jump, and so on. A ThirdPersonCharacter script implements physics behind movements and calls the animations that are needed for running, crouching, and so on.

AIThirdPersonController

The AIThirdPersonController prefab is identical to the ThirdPersonController prefab, but the former adds a NavMeshAgent and an AICharacterControl script, which constrains where and how the character can move around the scene. If you recall, in *Chapter 4, Gaze-based Control*, we used the AICharacterController to make Ethan walk around the scene and avoid bumping into objects.

FirstPersonController

The FPSController prefab is a first-person controller that uses both a CC component and a Rigidbody. It has a child camera attached to it. When the character moves, the camera moves with it.

> The core distinction between third-person controller prefabs and first-person controller prefabs is the child object. Third-person controller prefabs have a rigged humanoid child object, while first-person controller prefabs have a camera child object.

Its body mass is set to a low value (1) and IsKinematic is enabled. This means that it will have limited momentum and does not react to other rigid objects, but it can be driven by animations.

Its FirstPersonController script offers a plethora of parameters for running, jumping, audible footsteps, and more. The script also includes parameters and animations for a *head bob*, which bounces the camera in a natural way when the character is moving. If you use the FPSController script in your VR project, *be sure to disable any head bob features* or you might need to clean the puke off your keyboard!

RigidBodyFPSController

The RigidBodyFPSController prefab is a first-person controller with a Rigidbody but no CC component. Like FPSController, it has a child camera object. When the character moves, the camera moves with it.

A RigidBodyFPSController prefab's body mass is more substantial, set to 10, and is not kinematic. That is, it *can* get bounced around when it collides with other objects. It has a separate Capsule Collider component with ZeroFriction physic material. The RigidBodyFirstPersonController script is different from the FPSController one, but the former has a lot of similar parameters.

Why am I going through all of this detail here?

If you've built any non-VR projects in Unity, then you've most likely used these prefabs. However, you might not have paid much attention to how they're assembled. Virtual reality is experienced from the first-person perspective. Our implementation toolbox is Unity. It is critical that you really understand Unity's tools to manage and control this first-person experience.

Making a first person

For making a first person feature, let's take an *agile* approach to development. This means (in part) that we'll start by defining our new feature, or story, with a set of requirements. Then, we'll incrementally build and test this feature, one requirement at a time, by iterating and refining our work as we go along. Experimentation is not only allowed, it's encouraged.

Agile software development is a broad term for methodologies that encourage small incremental and iterative developments in a fashion that's easy to respond to the changing and refined requirements.

Feature: *As a first-person character, when I start walking, I will move through the scene in the direction I am looking until I indicate to stop walking.*

Here are the requirements to achieve this feature:

- Move in the direction you're looking
- Keep your feet on the ground
- Don't pass through solid objects
- Don't fall off the edge of the world
- Step over small objects and handle uneven terrain
- Start and stop moving with a head gesture (look down) or by clicking an input device

This sounds reasonable.

Move in the direction you're looking

We already have a MeMyselfEye object containing the camera rig. We're going to turn it into a first-person controller. Our first requirement is to move about the scene in the direction you're looking. Add a script named HeadLookWalk. Keeping it simple, let's start by performing the following steps:

1. Select the MeMyselfEye object in the **Hierarchy** panel.

2. In the **Inspector** panel, select **Add Component | New Script** and name it HeadLookWalk.

Then, open the script and code it, as follows:

```
using UnityEngine;
using System.Collections;

public class HeadLookWalk : MonoBehaviour {
  public float velocity = 0.7f;

  void Update () {
    Vector3 moveDirection = Camera.main.transform.forward;
    moveDirection *= velocity * Time.deltaTime;
    transform.position += moveDirection;
  }
}
```

The normal walking speed for humans is about 1.4 meters per second. Let's be cool and travel half that velocity at 0.7 m/s. During Update(), we check the current direction in which the camera is facing (camera.transform.forward) and move the MeMyselfEye transform position in this direction at the current velocity.

Note the coding shortcuts for the self-modification of a variable. The last two lines of the preceding code could have been written out like this:

```
moveDirection = moveDirection * velocity * Time.deltaTime;
transform.position = transform.position  + moveDirection;
```

Here, I used the *= and += operators instead.

Save the script and the scene and try it in VR.

When you look forward, you move forward. Look left, move left. Look right, move right. It works!

Look up... *Whoa!! Did you expect that?! We're freakin' flying!* You can move up, down, and all around as if you're Superman or a pilot of a drone. Presently, `MeMyselfEye` has no mass and physics, and does not respond to gravity. Nonetheless, it meets our requirement—to move in the direction you're looking. So let's continue.

Keep your feet on the ground

The next requirement wants you to keep your feet on the ground. We know that `GroundPlane` is flat and positioned at **Y** = 0. So, let's just add this simple constraint to the `HeadLookWalk` script, as follows:

```
void Update () {
  Vector3 moveDirection = Camera.main.transform.forward;
  moveDirection *= velocity * Time.deltaTime;
  moveDirection.y = 0.0f;
  transform.position += moveDirection;
}
```

Save the script and try it in VR.

Not bad. Now, we can move around the **Y** = 0 plane.

On the other hand, you're like a ghost, readily passing through the cube, sphere, and the other objects.

Don't pass through solid objects

The third requirement states—*don't pass through solid objects*. Here's an idea. Give it a Rigidbody component and let the physics engine take care of it by performing the following steps:

1. Select the `MeMyselfEye` object in the **Hierarchy** panel.
2. In the **Inspector** panel, navigate to **Add Component | Physics | Rigidbody**.

Try it in VR.

Whoa!! What the...? It was going fine there for a second, but as soon as you knock into the cube, you go spinning out of control in wild directions, like a spacewalk gone wrong in the movie *Gravity*. Well, that's a Rigidbody for you. Forces are being applied in all directions and axes. Let's add some constraints, as follows:

In the **Inspector** panel's **Rigidbody** pane, check off the checkboxes for **Freeze Position: Y** and **Freeze Rotation: X** and **Z**.

Try it in VR.

Now that's pretty nice! You're able to move by looking in a direction, you're not flying (the Y position is constrained), and you don't pass through solid objects. Instead, you slide past them since only the Y rotation is allowed.

Assuming that your `KillTarget` script is still running (from *Chapter 4, Gaze-based Control*), you should be able to stare at Ethan until he explodes. Do it, make Ethan explode... *Whoa!* We just got blown out of here by the explosion, spinning out of control in wild directions again. Maybe we're just not ready for this powerful physics engine yet. We can probably address this in the scripting, but for the time being, let's abandon the Rigidbody idea. We'll come back to it in the next chapter.

You may recall that CC includes a Capsule Collider and supports movement that is constrained by collisions. We'll try that instead, as follows:

1. In the **Inspector** panel, click on the **Rigidbody** pane's *gear* icon and select **Remove Component**.

2. In the **Inspector** panel, navigate to **Add Component | Physics | Character Controller**.

Modify the `HeadLookWalk` script, as follows:

```
using UnityEngine;
using System.Collections;

public class HeadLookWalk : MonoBehaviour {
  public float velocity = 0.7f;

  private CharacterController controller;

  void Start () {
    controller = GetComponent<CharacterController>();
  }

  void Update () {
    Vector3 moveDirection = Camera.main.transform.forward;
    moveDirection *= velocity * Time.deltaTime;
    moveDirection.y = 0.0f;
    controller.Move(moveDirection);
  }
}
```

Instead of updating `transform.position` directly, we called the built-in `CharacterController.Move()` function and let it do it for us. It knows that the characters should behave with certain constraints.

Save the script and try it in VR.

This time, when we bump into objects (a cube or sphere), we kind of go over it and then remain in the air. The `Move()` function does not apply gravity to the scene for us. We need to add that to the script, which isn't so hard (see the Unity API docs at `http://docs.unity3d.com/ScriptReference/CharacterController.Move.html`).

However, there is a simpler way. The `CharacterController.SimpleMove()` function applies gravity to the movement for us. Just replace the whole `Update()` function with the following one-liner:

```
void Update () {
  controller.SimpleMove(Camera.main.transform.forward *
    velocity);
}
```

The `SimpleMove()` function takes care of gravity and also handles `Time.deltaTime`. So, all that we need to give it is the movement direction vector. Also, since it's introducing gravity, we don't need the **Y** = 0 constraint either. Much simpler.

Save the script and try it in VR.

Awesome! I think we've met all the requirements so far. *Just don't go walking off the edge...*

Don't fall off the edge of the world

Now that we have gravity, if we walk off the edge of the ground plane, you'll fall into oblivion. Fixing this isn't a first-person character thing. Just add some railings to the scene.

Use cubes, scale them to the desired thickness and length, then move them into position. Go ahead and do it. I won't give you the step-by-step instructions for it. For example, I used these transforms:

- **Scale**: 0.1, 0.1, 10.0
- Railing 1: **Position**: -5, 1, 0
- Railing 2: **Position**: 5, 1, 0
- Railing 3: **Position**: 0, 1, -5; **Rotation**: 0, 90, 0
- Railing 4: **Position**: 0, 1, 5; **Rotation**: 0, 90, 0

Try it in VR. Try to walk through the railings. Whew! This is safer.

Stepping over small objects and handling uneven terrain

While we're at it, add a few things to walk on and over, such as a ramp and other obstacles. The result will look something like this:

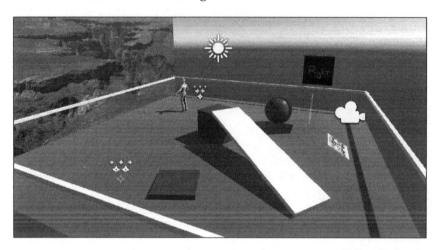

Try it in VR. Walk up the ramp and step off the cube. Hey, this is fun!

The CC component is taking care of the requirement to step over small objects and handle uneven terrain. You might want to tinker with its **Slope Limit** and **Step Offset** settings.

Start and stop moving

The next requirement is *to start and stop moving with a click or a head gesture*. First, we'll implement the click by using the `Clicker` class that we wrote in *Chapter 3, VR Build and Run*, which checks whether any keys are pressed on the keyboard, mouse, or the Cardboard trigger.

Modify the `HeadLookWalk` script, as follows:

```
using UnityEngine;
using System.Collections;

public class HeadLookWalk : MonoBehaviour {
  public float velocity = 0.7f;
  public bool isWalking = false;

  private CharacterController controller;
```

```
    private Clicker clicker = new Clicker();

  void Start() {
    controller = GetComponent<CharacterController> ();
  }

  void Update () {
    if (clicker.clicked()) {
      isWalking = !isWalking;
    }
    if (isWalking) {
      controller.SimpleMove (Camera.main.transform.forward *
        velocity);
    }
  }
}
```

By adding a Boolean `isWalking` flag, we can switch the forward movement on and off, which can be signaled by a key press.

Using head gestures to start/stop

To add a head gesture trigger for walking, we can use the `HeadGesture` class that we made in *Chapter 5, World Space UI* (assuming its still attached to a `GameController` object in your scene). We can modify the `HeadLookWalk` script, but let's keep this in a separate script that ties them together, as follows:

1. Select the `MeMyselfEye` object in the **Hierarchy** panel.

2. In the **Inspector** panel, select **Add Component | New Script** and name it `GestureWalk`.

Then, open the script and code it, as follows:

```
using UnityEngine;
using System.Collections;

public class GestureWalk : MonoBehaviour {
  private HeadLookWalk lookWalk;
  private HeadGesture gesture;

  void Start () {
    lookWalk = GetComponent<HeadLookWalk> ();
    gesture = GameObject.Find ("GameController").
GetComponent<HeadGesture> ();
```

```
      }

   void Update () {
     if (gesture.isMovingDown) {
        lookWalk.isWalking = !lookWalk.isWalking;
     }
   }
}
```

We've made the code more modular by separating the gesture input from the look-walk controller, modifying the HeadLookWalk Class's public variable, isWalking.

Now, we can also switch the forward movement on and off with a head-down gesture. *Look ma, no hands!* You can walk around, start, and stop in VR without a keyboard, mouse, or a game controller. (It should be noted that this example is for fun. I'm not necessarily advocating that this is a good mechanism to use in your applications.)

User calibrations

How tall are you? Are you presently sitting or standing? Am I referring to your real-life human self or your player inside the virtual world? Your first-person VR experience may not feel right if your virtual self isn't calibrated.

Mind you, I am not referring to your VR headset's physical configurations. For example, **Oculus Configuration Utility** lets you calibrate the settings for *eye relief* (how far the HMD lenses are from your eyes) and **Interpupillary Distance** (**IPD**) (distance between your eyes), which affect the low-level distortion rendering that is performed by the SDK drivers. Although those may be important to have a satisfactory experience, I'm referring to calibrating the in-game character in the scene with you—the player.

A character's height

I do not know whether you've been paying much attention to the first-person camera height, but it appears that we shrunk recently. Before this chapter, the eye-level of the camera was set to be eye-to-eye with Ethan. Now, we're looking at his chest. What happened?

If you've been following along, in *Chapter 3, VR Build and Run*, we created a
MeMyselfEye object located at 1.4 meters as shown in the following screenshot
(MeMyselfEye has **Position** component's **Y** = 1.4) to be at about eye-level with
Ethan. The camera child object has a relative position of (0,0,0) so that it's coincident:

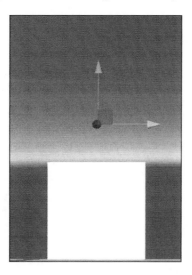

Then, earlier in this chapter, we added a Character Controller component to
MeMyselfEye, which includes a Capsule Collider with a default height of 2.0.
The Transform.position prefab now represents the center of the capsule as
shown in the following screenshot:

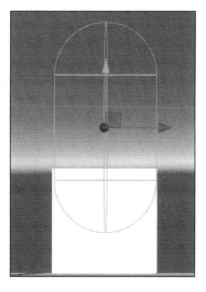

Then, when we play the scene (and call `SimpleMove`), gravity kicks in, dropping the object so that it makes contact with the ground, moving the center and the camera to **Y**= `1.0` as shown in the following screenshot. (You can see this happen immediately when you press the Play Mode):

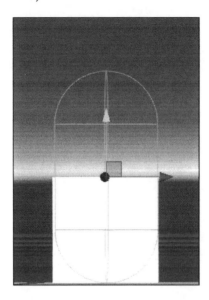

We need to clean this up.

Feature: *As a first-person character, my eye-level should be at 1.4 meters.*

Perform the following steps:

1. With `MeMyselfEye` selected in the **Hierarchy** panel, set its **Transform** component's **Position** value of **Y** to `1.08`.

2. With its child VR **Main Camera** selected, set its **Transform** component's **Position** value of **Y** to `0.4`.

3. If you still have the dashboard that we built in *Chapter 5, World Space UI,* in this scene, with the `Dashboard` child selected, set its **Rect Transform** component's **Pos Y** to `-0.6`.

The capsule's full height is 2.0. So, we set its position to **Y** = `1.08`. Why the extra 0.08? It has a default **Skin Width** of 0.08 (*skin* is a Unity fudge factor that lets characters fit through narrow passages). We want the camera height to be 0.4 above the center of the capsule. We will also adjust the dashboard as before to be one meter below the eye level. (These are my settings. For example, you can set the skin to `0.001` and the capsule height to `1.6` and make other adjustments accordingly.)

Real-life height of a player

If you're actually 1.6 meters tall (5 feet, 3 inches), then this eye level may feel normal when you play the character in VR. If you're actually taller (or shorter), it may feel weird.

At this point, you need to ask yourself, *what is the intent of the application or game?* Are you playing as a kid that's Ethan's size? Alternatively, do you want to create a VR experience that makes you feel that you are being transported into a virtual world? Is your character standing up or sitting down?

The first case is easier. Let's say that you're in a VR game. Let's say you're *Mario* or *Luigi*. Then, you're playing a short guy, and it's OK to see the world from that height. You're not going to be six feet tall, even if that's how tall you are in real life. Likewise, if you're *Bowser*, you'll need to be about ten feet tall. So whatever height you, the game designer, chooses will be fine.

The second case, where you're designing an experience to transport the actual user to a new virtual place, you will want the camera height close to the actual player's eye level. Depending on your project, it might be fine to pick the average human height worldwide (1.7 meters).

If you want to fine-tune it, your app can have a calibration menu that lets users enter their actual height or choose from a list, such as *Short / Average / Tall*. The Oculus Rift includes a **Configuration Utility** that lets you predefine one or more user profiles. This includes height and gender, which are accessible to all the Rift apps through their API.

If your character is sitting, the eye-level height may be less of an issue because we're accustomed to sitting at desks of a standard height (for example, 28 inches) and adjusting our chairs to meet that height.

When virtual reality equipment advances to the point where hand and body sensors are more common, we'll need calibration tools and user profiles to help players feel more at home in their virtual bodies.

 When you're impersonating a character in a game, you set the camera to the character's height. When you're virtually transporting the user into a new virtual place, you want to set the camera to their actual eye level.

Recentering

Sometimes in VR, the view presented in the headset is not quite in sync with your body's orientation. Device SDKs provide functions to reset the orientation of the headset with respect to the real-world space. This is often referred to as the **recentering** of the view.

For the Oculus Rift, you might add a script that listens for a specific key press, such as the *R* key to *recenter* the view or a utility HUD menu button, and calls `InputTracking.Recenter()`.

Google Cardboard has a similar function to reset the HMD orientation. It of course, doesn't have positional tracking. Only the orientation and motion sensors are reset by calling `Cardboard.SDK.Recenter()`.

Maintaining a sense of self

In VR, you could just be a floating one-dimensional eyeball in virtual space (like our initial `Diorama` camera), a normal human being, or maybe some full-bodied space creature. We have focused on walking around the scene and discussed how to set the camera height to the eye level. The implication was that someone experiencing VR has a sense of their own body. However, the camera height actually only makes sense when there's also a ground plane or some other stable reference point in your vicinity. When you're flying around like a bird, plane, or Superman, then the body height may not matter much.

Yet in the physical world, we all *really do* have bodies, and our brains kind of expect that. Issues surrounding the sense of self can get very psychological, philosophical, and even religious. Also, it's mind-bending what VR might eventually be able to do in this regard. For now, we should focus on what we need in order to help make our VR experiences comfortable for our visitors.

> *He who experiences the unity of life sees his own Self in all beings, and all beings in his own Self, and looks on everything with an impartial eye.*
>
> – Buddha

Head-body disconnect

When reading up on virtual reality headsets, much is said about positional tracking and head pose. This is very important for the provision of immersive VR experiences. Unfortunately, you're probably just a nobody.

Most of us don't have body-tracking features in our VR setup and have only the head-tracking features (unless you're reading this book well after its been written, you're a very special, early adopter of body-tracking equipment, or you've been tinkering with **Microsoft Kinect**). This means that when you look around (for example, from left to right), your software cannot know whether you moved just your head (from the neck up) or kept your head still but moved your whole body (for example, you just swiveled in your chair). Of course, real life bodies, like rigged avatars, can also twist the shoulders, hips, legs, and so on. Furthermore, eye tracking is another matter altogether—looking around without moving either your head or your body.

What does this mean? While wearing a VR headset, let's suppose that your first-person character has an avatar body. Suppose you're in a multiuser virtual world where other players can see you. If you turn your head, shouldn't only your avatar's head move? This makes sense. Until you start walking forward, your whole body probably should turn to face the direction in which you're going.

Consider another scenario. Suppose you're seated in the cockpit of a spaceship. You can move your head to look around where you're seated. However, your input controls direct where your ship is going.

You're getting the picture. Head-motion controls are not necessarily connected to your body (or spaceship) controls. However, I don't have body tracking. Also, while the Rift (and similar devices) has positional tracking, mobile VR headsets, such as GearVR and Google Cardboard, don't even have that.

Let's see what we can do about this.

Head and body...

Feature: *As a first-person character, when I am walking, then I can look down and see my feet facing the direction I'm going; When I'm not walking but looking around, my feet do not rotate.*

To build this, we're going to divide MeMyselfEye into separate head and body objects that can rotate independently and give the body some feet that point in the direction we're walking, as follows:

1. With MeMyselfEye selected in the **Hierarchy** panel, create an empty object by right-clicking and choosing **Create Empty**. Rename it to MeBody.

2. Find your **Main Camera** under MeMyselfEye, create an empty object by right-clicking and choosing **Create Empty**, and rename it to MeHead.

Now, our script can know the rotational look direction of the head, which is different from the facing direction of the body.

Whereas Unity wants you to think in terms of a *camera* in the scene, I prefer to think in terms of the *player*. Remember that the player is wearing an HMD. *Her head is inside the HMD*. The HMD, also known as the camera object, has positional tracking. You don't need to rename the camera, but if you did, the hierarchy will look like this:

Although we named the container of our body parts as `MeBody`, it can be more than virtual flesh and blood. If you're driving a car, it can include the car body. It can include anything that's attached to you or anything that you might be carrying, such as a weapon. If your app will support hand-held motion controllers and other tracking devices, these body parts and scripts will also be parented by `MeBody`.

...And feet

Let's add feet to the body. I have included an image file, `flip-flops.png`, with this book. (Otherwise, use anything that indicates a forward direction). Perform the following steps:

1. Import the `flip-flops.png` texture by navigating to **Import New Asset...** under **Assets**.

2. Create a new material in the **Project** panel and name it `FlipFlops`.

3. Drag the flip-flops texture onto the `FlipFlops` material's **Albedo** map and choose **Rendering Mode** as **Cutout**.

4. Create a **Quad** object (by navigating to **GameObject | 3D Object | Quad**) as a child of `MeMyselfEye/MeBody`, name it `Feet`, and set its **Transform** component's **Position** to (0, -1, 0) and it's **Rotation** to (90, 0, 0) so that it lies flat on the ground plane.

5. With `Feet` selected in **Hierarchy**, drag the `FlipFlops` material onto the **Inspector** panel.

If you try it now in VR, the feet are there, but they are not pointing in the direction in which we are walking. We need another script. For that, perform the following steps:

1. Select the `MeMyselfEye` object in the **Hierarchy** panel.

2. In the **Inspector** panel, select **Add Component | New Script** and name it `BodyWalk`.

Then, open the script and code it, as follows:

```
using UnityEngine;
using System.Collections;

public class BodyWalk : MonoBehaviour {
  private HeadLookWalk lookWalk;
  private Transform head;
  private Transform body;

  void Start () {
    lookWalk = GetComponent<HeadLookWalk> ();
    head = Camera.main.transform;
    body = transform.Find ("MeBody");
  }

  void Update () {
    if (lookWalk.isWalking) {
      body.transform.rotation = Quaternion.Euler (new Vector3
        (0.0f, head.transform.eulerAngles.y, 0.0f));
    }
  }
}
```

In the script, we are assuming a specific hierarchy — the script is a component of MeMyselfEye and it has a direct child named MeBody.

Now, when walking, we not only move MeMyselfEye in the direction we're looking, we rotate its body in the same direction. Since we're standing vertically, the body rotates about the *y*-axis only and the **X** and **Z** rotations are zeroed.

Save the script and try it in VR.

What big feet you have, my dear! OK, it's not a body and the feet are too big. Also, they aren't animated as you walk, but we have something to build on. Just showing flipflops attached to the first-person character goes a long way in giving you a sense of being grounded. It could be a skateboard or Segway instead. You're not just a floating one-dimensional point anymore.

If you still have the dashboard from *Chapter 5*, *World Space UI*, in your scene, you should now also move it as a MeBody child so that it follows the direction in which you're walking too.

The following screenshot shows the flipflops from the first-person character view:

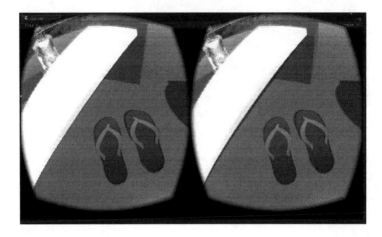

The body avatar

Let's try a full-body avatar. Unless you have a different humanoid that you prefer, we can use a clone of Ethan for our body, as follows:

1. In the **Project** panel, locate the Ethan prefab at Standard Assets/ ThirdPersonCharacter/Models/Ethan and drag it into the **Hierarchy** panel under MeMyselfEye/MeBody.

2. Set its **Transform** component's **Position** to (0, -1, -0.2).

The **Y** position = -1. So, his feet are on the ground. The camera is at **Z** = 0. So, **Z** = -0.2 puts the front of Ethan's face behind the camera.

Try it in VR.

It's a good start. We can walk around with a body. However, it has issues, and that's what we're here to discuss, but not necessarily fix today:

- **No animations**: Ethan is frozen in *T-pose*. You know that Ethan is a rigged humanoid who can do all sorts of walking and running. Setting this up in MeMyselfEye will take some work.

- **Positional tracking**: Unlike Cardboard, the awesome positional tracking features of Oculus Rift, and similar devices means that the given head pose not only changes the rotation, but also its position in world space. Our scripts don't account for this. If you keep your head in the same position and just look around, it seems OK. However, if you start leaning over, back, or any which way, you'll find yourself having a true out-of-body experience. (For example, lean back a distance and you'll see the back of Ethan's head in view.)

- **No head constraint**: Unless your character is Linda Blair (*The Exorcist*) or an owl, it might be weird to be able to turn your head all the way around. When you're not in the *walk* mode and just looking around, if you turn your gaze past your shoulder, the script should rotate the body accordingly to save your neck.

Another big issue—these flipflops are way too big for my feet! This can be seen in the following screenshot:

There are other considerations when planning a first-person avatar with respect to the actual player, such as gender and skin color.

The default Oculus Rift demo in **Configuration Utility** has the player sitting in a desk chair, but has no body. When you look down, all you see is a chair. Other games might provide a body without a head, which limits the need to sync the avatar with the VR head pose.

If you decide not to pursue this fullbody avatar idea for now, just delete it.

Virtual David le nose

One reason to have an avatar body is to help reduce motion sickness by giving the user a spatial context and a sense of being grounded. Virtual reality is very young, and people are exploring new, innovative ways. Maybe you don't need a whole body. Maybe you only need a nose!

According to David Whittinghill, a researcher at Purdue University, (`http://www.purdue.edu/newsroom/releases/2015/Q1/virtual-nose-may-reduce-simulator-sickness-in-video-games.html`), adding a virtual nose in your field of view may help reduce motion sickness. Since we're in a mood to experiment, let's try it.

Back in the *The visor HUD* section, and the *The reticle cursor* section, in *Chapter 5, World Space UI*, we parented objects under the VR camera object so that it appears to be *stuck to your face*. This sounds appropriate for a nose! Perform the following steps:

1. Import the `david-le-nose.png` texture that is provided with this book.

2. Create a new material, name it `Nose`, and drag the `.png` texture onto the material.

3. In the `Nose` material, set its **Shader** as **Unlit | Transparent Cutout**.

4. Also, adjust its **Mesh Renderer** to no shadows (unchecking the **Cast Shadows**, **Receive Shadows**, and **Use light Probes** options).

5. Locate the **Main Camera** object and create a new quad so that it becomes a child of the camera. Name it `Nose`.

6. Set the **Nose** quad's **Transform** component's **Position** to (`0, 0, 0.3`) so that it's in front of your face.

7. Drag the `Nose` material onto the `Nose` quad.

Try it out in VR. Keep it if you like. A first-person character wearing a nose is shown in the following screenshot:

Audio cues

Lest we forget, audio is an important dimension of virtual reality. As another quick demo, let's add audible footsteps to our first-person character, as follows:

1. With `MeMyselfEye` selected, navigate to **Add Component | Audio | Audio Source**.
2. In the **Audio Source** component, in the **Audio Clip** field, click on the *circle* icon (far right) to open the **Select AudioClip** dialog box and choose `Footstep01`.
3. Uncheck the **Play On Awake** checkbox.
4. Check off the **Loop** checkbox.

Now, we can modify the `BodyWalk` script, as follows:

```
using UnityEngine;
using System.Collections;

public class BodyWalk : MonoBehaviour {
  private HeadLookWalk lookWalk;
  private AudioSource footsteps;
  private Transform head;
  private Transform body;

  void Start () {
    lookWalk = GetComponent<HeadLookWalk> ();
    footsteps = GetComponent<AudioSource> ();
    head = Camera.main.transform;
    body = transform.Find ("MeBody");
  }

  void Update () {
    if (lookWalk.isWalking) {
      body.transform.rotation = Quaternion.Euler (new Vector3
        (0.0f, head.transform.eulerAngles.y, 0.0f));
      if (!footsteps.isPlaying) {
        footsteps.Play ();
      }
    } else { // not walking
      footsteps.Stop ();
    }
  }
}
```

Now, whenever you're walking, you'll hear footsteps.

Locomotion, teleportation, and sensors

We just implemented a simple look-based mechanism to move through a virtual reality scene. You could of course decide to stick with a keyboard, joystick, or a gamepad to control your character like a conventional video game. New techniques for locomotion and teleportation control are continuously being tried. Here are some ideas:

- **Look to walk**: Walk in the direction of your gaze. Your feet stay on the ground, animated. This is the mechanism that we previously implemented.

- **The hover disc**: Step onto a hover disc to begin moving. Step off it when you're done. This requires a way to indicate the action of stepping on and stepping off.

- **Segway**: Like the hover disc but you move forward and turn by leaning into it, and slow down or stop by leaning back.

- **The Superman fly**: Jump to take off, fly by looking, and crouch to land. With positional hand controllers, you can stretch your hands out to your sides to glide and in front to go up or down. Also, take off by leaping over tall buildings in a single bound.

- **The grappling "look"**: Stare at a location, eject a hook (or a *spidey* web) on a rope, which attaches and you swing through the space.

- **The third-person runner**: When you start moving quickly, the camera steps away from the first-person view to the third-person view while you're traveling. When you're done, it returns to the first-person view.

- **Pilot**: You're sitting in the cockpit of a vehicle, driving it with various controls.

- **Ride on rails**: A passive ride through the scene, such as a roller coaster or a tour bus. There are no user controls for where you're going, but you can look around.

- **Look-at targets**: The scene includes targets that you can stare at, press a button, and you get teleported to the location in the scene.

- **Walk-through portals**: Teleport by walking through a portal or a doorway. This is a common mechanism that is used to jump between scenes or levels.

How many more can you think of? We will implement a few of these in the coming chapters.

Hardware input devices will have a big impact on how we control our first-person character. At this time, we're limited by the available hardware. For this book, I had to take the lowest common denominator of Oculus and Cardboard. So, we cannot necessarily assume any input devices, not even the humble handheld gamepad, keyboard, or mouse.

However, in the near future, this will change. We already have **Microsoft Kinect**, **Leap Motion**, **Valve Lighthouse**, **Oculus Touch**, and other technologies to experiment with. As the hand- and body-tracking input becomes more common, developers will have more options for the implementation of locomotion and teleportation mechanics in virtual reality applications. Devices may include the following:

- **Gamepad**: Here today, a traditional gamepad controller or a keyboard (WASD) and/or a mouse input device can certainly be used in VR applications. The problem is that it's hard to see which button to press when your eyes are covered. An **Xbox One** controller will ship with the Oculus Rift consumer versions.

- **HMD touchpad**: Samsung Gear VR includes a small touchpad on the side for user input.

- **Positional game controller**: A handheld controller that includes positional tracking and motion sensors can be used to drive your character as well as use hand gestures. A few strategically placed buttons can also be effective. There's one for each hand. Examples of handheld controllers are Valve Lighthouse and Oculus Touch.

- **Wearable motion sensors**: In addition to your head and hands, if you're wearing motion sensors on your torso, legs, or feet, the game can sense all kinds of body movement.

- **Body-tracking cameras**: We can use infrared or other camera technology with body recognition and tracking software, such as Microsoft Kinect.

- **Treadmills**: VR treadmills and related devices detect when and where you're walking. Walk around using your feet and legs? How strange!

- **Voice commands**: Speak your mind rather than push buttons.

- **Gesture recognition**: With hand recognition, gesture input vocabularies will be established (for instance, everyone now knows about swipe and pinch on smartphones.)

- **Eye tracking**: This detects where your eyeballs are looking, and, perhaps, recognize glances and other eye gestures.

Facial Expression Recognition, Alpha Brain Waves... and the list can go on.

People have joked about tongue-based input controllers. A presentation that was made in 1991 makes fun of the *Nose Gesture Interface* (for more information, visit `http://www.powershow.com/view4/44dcae-ZjBjY/A_Nose_Gesture_Interface_Device_Extending_Virtual_Realities_powerpoint_ppt_presentation.`)

As new input devices and recognition software emerge for the consumer market, they will accelerate the expectations of VR users and force your implementation of first-person characters to provide the most immersive VR experiences.

Managing VR motion sickness

VR motion sickness, or simulator sickness, is a real symptom and a concern for virtual reality. Researchers, psychologists, and technologists with a wide array of specializations and PhDs are studying the problem to better understand the underlying causes and find solutions.

A cause of VR motion sickness is a lag in screen updates, or latency, when you're moving your head. Your brain expects the world around you to change exactly in sync. Any perceptible delay can make you feel uncomfortable, to say the least.

Latency can be reduced by faster rendering of each frame, keeping the recommended frames per second. Device manufacturers such as Oculus and others see this as their problem to solve, in both hardware and device-driver software. GPU and chip manufacturers see it as a processor performance and throughput problem. We will undoubtedly see leaps and bounds in improvements over the coming years.

At the same time, as VR developers, we need to be aware of latency and other causes of VR motion sickness. Developers need to look at it like it's our problem too, because ultimately, it comes down to performance and ergonomics. With an ongoing dichotomy of mobile VR versus desktop VR, there will always be upper bounds on the performance of the devices that our players will be using.

It's not just technology. I can get nauseous riding a real-world roller coaster. So, why wouldn't a VR one have a similar effect?

Things to consider that help improve your players' comfort and safety include the following:

- **Don't move fast**: When moving or animating a first-person character, don't move too fast. High-speed first-person shooter games that work on gaming consoles and desktop PCs may not work out so well in VR.

- **Look forward**: When moving through a scene, if you're looking to the side rather than straight ahead, you're more likely to feel nauseous.

- **Don't turn your head too fast**: Discourage users from turning their head quickly with the VR headset on. The latency in updating the HMD screen is aggravated by larger changes in the viewport in small time slices.

- **Offer comfort mode**: When a scene requires you to quickly turn yourself a lot of times, provide a ratcheted rotation mechanism, also known as comfort mode, which lets you change the direction in which you look in larger increments.

- **Use a third-person camera**: If you have high-speed action but you don't necessarily intend to give the user a thrill ride, use a third-person camera view.

- **Stay grounded**: Provide visual cues that help the user stay grounded, such as horizon lines, nearby objects in your field of view, and relative fixed-position objects, such as dashboards and body parts.

- **Provide an option to recenter the view**: Mobile VR devices, in particular, are subject to drift and the need to be recentered on occasion. With wired VR devices, it helps you avoid getting tangled in HMD wires. As a safety issue, recentering your view relative to the real world may help you avoid hitting furniture and walls in the physical space.

- **Don't use cut scenes**: In traditional games (and movies), a technique that can be used to transition between levels is to show a 2D cut scene movie. This does not work in VR if the head motion detection is disabled. It breaks the immersion and can cause nausea. An alternative is to simply fade to black and then open the new scene.

- **Optimize rendering performance**: It behooves all VR developers to understand the underlying causes of latency — specifically rendering performance — and what you can do to optimize it, such as lowering the poly count and choosing lighting models carefully. Learn to use performance monitoring tools in order to keep the frames per second within the expected and acceptable limits. More on this will be discussed in *Chapter 8, Walk-throughs and Rendering*.

- **Encourage users to take breaks**: Alternatively, you can maybe just provide a puke-bag with your game!

Summary

In this chapter, we took a deep dive into what it means to have a first-person character in Unity and virtual reality. We started by dissecting the **Characters** prefabs under Unity's **Standard Assets** and the components that they use, including Camera, Character Controller, and/or Rigidbody.

Then, we developed our own first-person character, starting with the static positioned VR camera rig that we used for our `Diorama` scene. We incrementally added features to move in the direction of your gaze, gravity, solid-object collisions, and use head gestures to start and stop walking. We made adjustments for camera height and explored the relationship between a first-person head versus a body in virtual reality. Lastly, we reviewed some of the factors that VR developers should think about to provide a comfortable VR experience and avoid motion sickness.

It is not my intent to say that you should always build your own first-person controllers instead of using the prefabs provided by Unity or VR integration packages. However, you certainly might need to take one of them apart and customize it. After this chapter, you should have a better idea of what this might entail.

In *Chapter 7*, *Physics and the Environment*, we'll explore uses of Rigidbody, the Unity physics engine, and physic materials, plus a bit of 3D modeling using Blender.

Physics and the Environment 7

Parkour jumper: THOR/Parkour Foundations/Flickr, Creative Commons (source `https://www.flickr.com/photos/geishaboy500/2911897958/in/album-72157607724308547/`)

In the previous chapters, the first-person character was mostly limited to the X-Z ground plane. This chapter will focus more on the *y*-axis, as we explore adding physics to the virtual experience. You will see how properties and materials based on physics can be added to objects, as well as how one can transfer physical forces between objects using the C# scripting.

In this chapter, you will learn the following topics:

- The Unity physics engine, the Unity Rigidbody component, and physic materials
- Transferring physical forces from one object to another with scripting
- Implementing velocity and gravity on first-person characters
- Interacting with the environment, including headshots and jump gestures
- Building models in Blender

Note that the projects in this chapter are separate and are not directly required by the other chapters in this book. If you decided to skip any of it or not save your work, that's OK.

Unity physics

In Unity, the behavior of an object that is based on physics is defined separately from its mesh (shape), materials (UV texture), and the renderer properties. The items that play into physics include the following:

- **The Rigidbody component**
- **The Collider component**
- **The Physic Material**
- **The project Physics Manager**

Basically, physics (in this context) is defined by the positional and rotational forces that affect the transform of an object, such as gravity, friction, momentum, and collisions with other objects. It is not necessarily a perfect simulation of physics in the real world because it's optimized for performance and separation of concerns to facilitate animation. Besides, virtual worlds might just need their own laws of physics that aren't found in our God-given universe!

Unity 5 integrates the **NVIDIA PhysX** engine, a real-time physics calculation middleware, which implements classical Newtonian mechanics for games and 3D applications. This multiplatform software is optimized to utilize fast hardware processors when present. It is accessible via the Unity scripting API.

A key to physics is the Rigidbody component that you add to objects. Rigidbodies have parameters for gravity, mass, and drag, among others. Rigidbodies can automatically react to gravity and collisions with other objects. No extra scripting is needed for this. During gameplay, the engine calculates each rigid object's momentum and updates its transform position and rotation.

 Details on Rigidbodies can be found at `http://docs.unity3d.com/ScriptReference/Rigidbody.html`.

Unity projects have a global gravity setting, found in the project's Physics Manager by navigating to **Edit | Project Settings | Physics**. As you might expect, the default gravity setting is a **Vector3** with values (0, -9.81, 0) that apply a downward force to all Rigidbodies. Gravity is in meters per second squared.

 Rigidbodies can automatically react to gravity and collisions with other objects. Extra scripting is not needed for this.

In order to detect a collision, both the colliding objects must have a Collider component. There are built-in colliders with basic geometric shapes such as a cube, sphere, cylinder, and a capsule. A mesh collider can assume an arbitrary shape. If you can, it's best to use one or more basic collider shapes that approximately fit the actual object rather than a mesh collider to reduce the expense of calculating the actual collisions during gameplay. (If you do, a mesh collider must be marked as convex and be limited to 255 triangles.)

When rigid objects collide, the forces pertinent to each object in the collision are applied to the others. The values of the resulting forces are calculated based on the objects' current velocity and body mass. Other factors are also taken into consideration, such as gravity and drag (that is, resistance). Furthermore, you have options to add constraints to freeze the position or rotation of a given object in any of its *x*, *y*, and *z* axes.

The calculations can be further affected when a Physic Material is assigned to the object's Collider, which adjusts the friction and the bounciness effects of the colliding objects. These properties will be applied only to the object that owns the Physic Material. (Note that it's really spelled *Physic Material* rather than *Physics Material* for historical reasons.)

So, let's say that Object A (Ball) hits Object B (Brick). If Object A has bounciness and Object B does not, Object A will have an impulse applied in the collision, but Object B will not. However, you have options to determine how their friction and bounciness combine, as we'll see next. It's not necessarily an accurate simulation of real-world physics. It's a game engine, not a computer-aided engineering modeler.

From a scripting point of view, Unity will trigger events (also known as *messages*) when objects collide (`OnTriggerEnter`), each frame while objects are collided (`OnTriggerStay`), and when they've stopped colliding (`OnTriggerExit`).

If this sounds daunting, read on. The rest of this chapter breaks it down into understandable bits and pieces.

Bouncy balls

Feature: *When a ball drops from mid-air and hits the ground, it bounces back up and down, and up again, diminished by gravity.*

We are going to start simply with a new scene that consists of a ground plane and a sphere. Then, we'll add physics to it, a bit at a time, as follows:

1. Create a new scene by navigating to **File | New Scene**.
2. Then, navigate to **File | Save Scene As...** and name it `BallsFromHeaven`.
3. Create a new plane by navigating to **GameObject | 3D Object | Plane** and reset its position using the **Transform** component's *gear* icon | **Reset**.
4. Create a new sphere by navigating to **GameObject | 3D Object | Sphere** and rename it `BouncyBall`.
5. Set its **Scale** to (0.5, 0.5, 0.5) and **Position** to (0, 5, 0) so that it's above the center of the plane.
6. Drag the **Red** material from **Project Assets** (created in *Chapter 2, Objects and Scale*) onto it so that it looks like a bouncy ball.

The new Unity scene defaults come with **Directional Light** and **Main Camera**. It's OK to use this **Main Camera** for the time being.

Click on *Play* button. Nothing happens. The ball just sits in mid-air and doesn't move.

Now, let's give it a Rigidbody, as follows:

1. With `BouncyBall` selected, in **Inspector**, navigate to
   Add Component | Physics | Rigidbody.

2. Click on *Play* button. It drops like a lead balloon.

Let's make it bounce, as follows:

1. In the **Project** panel, select the top-level **Assets** folder, navigate to
   Create | Folder, and rename it to `Physics`.

2. With the `Physics` folder selected, create a material by navigating to
   Assets | Create | Physic Material.

3. Name it `Bouncy`.

4. Set its **Bounciness** value to `1`.

5. With the `BouncyBall` sphere selected in **Hierarchy**, drag the `Bouncy` asset
   from **Project** onto the sphere's **Collider** material field in **Inspector**.

Click on *Play* button. It bounces, but it does not go very high. We used the maximum
value for **Bounciness** as `1.0`. What's slowing it down? It's not the **Friction** settings.
Rather, the **Bounce Combine** is set to **Average**, which determines how much of the
bounciness of the ball (1) is mixed with that of the plane (0). So, it diminishes rapidly
over time. We want the ball to retain all its bounciness. We will accomplish this,
as follows:

1. Change the `Bouncy` object's **Bounce Combine** to **Maximum**.

2. Click on *Play* button.

Much better. Actually, too much better. The ball keeps bouncing back up to its
original height, ignoring gravity. Now, change the **Bounciness** to `0.8`. The bounces
diminish, and the ball will eventually come to a stop.

Let's check it out in VR, as follows:

1. Delete the default **Main Camera** from the **Hierarchy** root.

2. Drag the `MeMyselfEye` prefab from **Project Assets** into the scene.
   Set its **Position** to (`0`, `1`, `-4`).

Run it in VR. Pretty neat! Even the simplest things look impressive in VR.

OK, let's have some fun. Make it rain bouncy balls! To do this, we'll make the ball a prefab and write a script that instantiates new balls, dropping them from random positions, as follows:

1. Drag the `BouncyBall` object from **Hierarchy** into `Project Assets/Prefabs` folder, making it a prefab.

2. Delete the `BouncyBall` object from the **Hierarchy**, since we'll be instantiating them with a script.

3. Create an empty game controller object to attach the script to by navigating to **GameObject | Create Empty**. Rename it `GameController`.

4. In **Inspector**, navigate to **Add Component | New Script**, name it `BallsFromHeaven`, and open the script in MonoDevelop.

Edit the script so that it looks like this:

```
using UnityEngine;
using System.Collections;

public class BallsFromHeaven : MonoBehaviour {
  public GameObject ball;
  public float startHeight = 10f;
  public float fireInterval = 0.5f;

  private float nextBallTime = 0.0f;

  void Update () {
    if (Time.time > nextBallTime) {
      nextBallTime = Time.time + fireInterval;
      Vector3 position = new Vector3( Random.Range (-4.0f, 4.0f),
        startHeight, Random.Range (-4.0f, 4.0f) );
      Instantiate( ball, position, Quaternion.identity );
    }
  }
}
```

The script drops a new ball from `startHeight` at the rate of every `fireInterval` seconds (an interval of 0.5 means that a new ball is dropped every half second). The new ball position is at a random **X-Z** coordinate between `-4` and `4`. The `Instantiate()` function adds a new ball into the scene **Hierarchy**.

Save the script. We now need to populate the **Ball** field with the BouncyBall prefab, as follows:

1. With GameController selected in **Hierarchy**, drag the BouncyBall prefab from Project Assets/Prefabs folder onto the **Ball** slot in the **Balls From Heaven (Script)** panel in **Inspector**.

2. Be sure to use the BouncyBall prefab from **Project Assets** so that can be instantiated.

3. Save the scene. Run it in VR. Fun!

This is what I get:

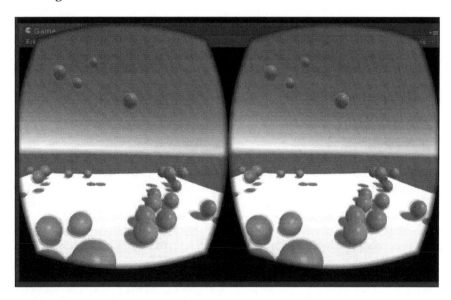

Watch the **Hierarchy** panel as new balls are instantiated. Note that some balls end up bouncing off the plane platform but remain in the **Hierarchy** panel. We need to clean this up by adding a script that destroys the balls that are out of play, as follows:

1. Select the BouncyBall prefab in Project Assets/Prefabs.

2. Navigate to **Add Component | New Script**, name it DestroySelf, and open it in MonoDevelop.

Here's a `DestroySelf.cs` script, which will destroy the object if its **Y** position is well below the ground plane (**Y** = 0):

```
using UnityEngine;
using System.Collections;

public class DestroySelf : MonoBehaviour {
  void Update () {
    if (transform.position.y < -5f) {
      Destroy (gameObject);
    }
  }
}
```

Whenever you have a script that instantiates objects, you must be aware of the lifecycle of the object and possibly arrange to destroy it when it is no longer needed.

In summary, we created a sphere with a Rigidbody and added a Physic Material with a **Bounciness** property of 0.8 and **Bounce Combine** to **Maximum**. Then, we waved the `BouncyBall` as a prefab and wrote a script to instantiate new balls that drop from above.

Headshots

Wouldn't it be fun to actually play with these bouncy balls? Let's make a game – try to aim the ball at a target using headshots. For this game, balls drop one at a time from above and bounce off your forehead (face), aiming for a target.

Feature: *When a ball drops from above your head, you bounce it off your face and aim for a target.*

To implement this, place a cube collider on the `MeMyselfEye` head, parented by the VR camera, so our head pose will move the face of the cube. I decided a cube shaped collider will be better for this game than a sphere or capsule, because it provides a flat face (like a paddle) that will make the bounce direction more predictable. Balls will drop out of the sky. For a target, we'll use a flattened cylinder. We'll add audio cues to indicate when a new ball has been released, and when a ball hits the target.

Create a new scene and implement the head as follows:

1. Navigate to **File | Save Scene As** and name it BallGame.

2. Delete the BallsFromHeaven script component attached to GameController using *gear* icon **Remove Component**. We won't need it.

3. In **Hierarchy**, unfold MeMyselfEye drilling down to the **Main Camera** object and select it.

4. In **Inspector**, navigate to **Add Component | Physics | Box Collider**.

5. With GameController selected, navigate to **Add Component | Audio | Audio Source**.

6. Click on the small *circle-shaped* icon on the far right of the **AudioClip** field of **Audio Source** to open the **Select AudioClip** dialog box and choose the clip named Jump.

7. With GameController selected, navigate to **Add Component | New Script**, name it BallGame, and open it in MonoDevelop.

Note the box collider in the **Scene** view; it encases the head/camera of your first-person character (as shown in following image). We'll play the Jump sound clip (provided with the **Characters** package of Unity's **Standard Assets**) to indicate when a new ball is dropped.

Here's the BallGame.cs script:

```
using UnityEngine;
using System.Collections;

public class BallGame : MonoBehaviour {
  public GameObject ball;
  public float startHeight = 10f;
  public float fireInterval = 5f;

  private float nextBallTime = 0.0f;
  private GameObject activeBall;
  private Transform head;
  private AudioSource audio;

  void Start () {
    head = Camera.main.transform;
    audio = GetComponent<AudioSource> ();
  }
```

```
   void Update () {
     if (Time.time > nextBallTime) {
       nextBallTime = Time.time + fireInterval;
       audio.Play ();
       Vector3 position = new Vector3( head.position.x,
         startHeight, head.position.z + 0.2f );
       activeBall = Instantiate( ball, position,
         Quaternion.identity ) as GameObject;
     }
   }
}
```

We instantiate a new ball every `fireInterval` seconds from a `startHeight` position above the current head position and a small amount in front (`0.2f`) so that it doesn't land directly at the top of our head. No rotation is applied to the ball (`Quaternion.identity`).

Populate the public variables in Unity editor, as follows:

1. With `GameController` selected, drag the `BouncyBall` from **Project Assets** onto the **Ball** field of the **Ball Game** panel in **Inspector**.

2. Try it in VR.

When you hear the ball, look up and aim the angle of your face to direct the bounce of the ball. *COOOL!*

Now, we need the target. Perform the following steps:

1. Create a flat cylinder for the target, navigate to **Game Object | 3D Object | Cylinder**, and name it `Target`.

2. Set its **Scale** to (`3, 0.1, 3`) and **Position** to (`1, 0.2, 2.5`) so that it's out in front of you on the ground.

3. Drag the `Blue` material from the `Project Assets/Materials` folder (created in *Chapter 2, Objects and Scale*) onto it.

4. Note that its default Capsule Collider is domed, and it really won't do. On the Capsule Collider, select its *gear* icon | **Remove Component**.

5. Then, navigate to **Add Component | Physics | Mesh Collider**.

6. In the new **Mesh Collider**, check off the **Convex** checkbox and the **Is Trigger** checkbox.

7. Add an audio source by navigating to **Add Component | Audio | Audio Source**.

8. With the `Target` selected, click on the small *circle* icon on the far right of the **AudioClip** field to open the **Select AudioClip** dialog box, and choose the clip named `Land`.

9. And a new script, navigate to **Add Component | New Script**, name it `TriggerSound`, and open it in MonoDevelop.

The following `TriggerSound.cs` script will play a sound clip when you hit the target:

```
using UnityEngine;
using System.Collections;

public class TriggerSound : MonoBehaviour {
  public AudioClip hitSound;

  void Start() {
    audio = GetComponent<AudioSource> ();
  }

  void OnTriggerEnter(Collider other) {
    audio.Play ();
  }
}
```

The script uses the `OnTriggerEnter()` message handler to know when to play the audio clip. We're repurposing the `Land` clip that was provided with the **Characters** package under Unity's **Standard Assets**.

Try it in VR. It's a VR game! The following image shows the scene with the first-person's colliders and a ball bouncing off the cube collider towards the target:

 Extra challenge: Keep score. Provide an aiming reticle. Add a backboard. Add other features to make the game more challenging. For instance, you can vary the fire interval or increase the initial ball velocity.

Up to this point, we assigned **Bounciness** through a Physic Material attached to a sphere object. When the ball collides with another object, the Unity physics engine considers this bounciness to determine the ball's new velocity and direction. In the following section, we'll look at how one can transfer a bounce force from one object to another.

Trampoline and brick

A trampoline differs from a bouncy ball because the former makes things that collide with it bounce instead of itself bouncing. Unity doesn't do this automatically for us, So, we need to use scripting.

Feature: *When a brick drops from mid-air onto a trampoline, it bounces up, diminished by gravity.*

Build the scene and turn the target into a trampoline, as follows:

1. Navigate to **File | Save Scene As** and name it `BrickTrampoline`.
2. Delete the `BallGame` script component from `GameController` using *gear* icon | **Remove Component**. We won't need it.
3. Rename the `Target` object to `Trampoline`.
4. Set its **Position** to (`0`, `0.2`, `0`).
5. To create the brick, navigate to **GameObject | 3D Object | Cube** and rename it to `Brick`.
6. Set its **Scale** to (`0.25`, `0.5`, `1`) and **Position** to (`0`, `5`, `0`).
7. Drag the `Red` material onto it.
8. Add a Rigidbody by navigating to **Add Component | Physics | Rigidbody**.

When you play now, the brick drops to a dead stop. Make a new script on trampoline, as follows:

1. With `Trampoline` selected in **Hierarchy**, create the script by navigating to **Add Component | New Script**.
2. Name the `Trampoline` script, and open it for editing.

And the `Trampoline.cs` script as follows:

```
Using UnityEngine;
using System.Collections;

public class Trampoline : MonoBehaviour {
  public float bounceForce = 1000.0f;

  void OnTriggerEnter ( Collider other ) {
    Rigidbody rb = other.GetComponent<Rigidbody> ();
    if (rb != null) {
      rb.AddForce (Vector3.up * bounceForce);
    }
  }
}
```

When a rigid object collides with the trampoline, the `OnTriggerEnter()` function adds a `bounceForce` to its Rigidbody.

Save the scene. Run it in VR. The brick now bounces on the trampoline. You may need to adjust the **Bounce Force** value by either increasing or decreasing it.

In summary, we have a brick with a Rigidbody, a trampoline without, and upon collision, the trampoline adds an upward force on the brick.

A human trampoline

Now, you'll get to jump on the trampoline yourself.

Feature: *When a first-person character hits a trampoline, it bounces up, diminished by gravity.*

Like a brick

One approach towards implementing this feature could be to treat the MeMyselfEye first-person character like Brick and give it a Rigidbody and a Capsule Collider so that it can respond using physics. We'll try this first just to see whether it works. For this to work, we need to disable its Character Controller component and start at the brick's position above the trampoline so that we can just drop, as follows:

1. Navigate to **File | Save Scene As** and name it HumanTrampoline.
2. Delete Brick in **Hierarchy**; we won't need it.
3. With MeMyselfEye selected in **Hierarchy**, set **Position** to (0, 5, 0).
4. Navigate to **Add Component | Physics | Rigidbody**.
5. Navigate to **Add Component | Physics | Capsule Collider** and set its **Height** to 2.
6. In the **Rigidbody** panel, under **Constraints**, check off the **Freeze Rotation X, Y, Z** checkboxes so that we don't get sick.

Play the scene. *Wheeee!* We're jumping up and down. You may need to adjust the **Bounce Force** value.

The Trampoline script is calling the Rigidbody's AddForce() function with a bounceForce. However, the character has no locomotion of its own. We can continue down this path, but we won't.

Like a character

In the last chapter, we gave the first-person MeMyselfEye a Character Controller component because it gives us many nice features that are needed for a first-person character (including a collider and player-friendly physics). We want to use it again.

Start with a fresh copy of MeMyselfEye as follows:

1. In **Hierarchy**, delete the existing MeMyselfEye object.
2. From the Project Assets/Prefabs folder, drag the MeMyselfEye prefab into the scene.
3. Set its **Position** to (0, 1, -4).
4. Navigate to **Add Component | Physics | Character Controller**.
5. Add the HeadLookWalkBounce script by navigating to **Add Component | New Script**.

The script will be similar but slightly different from the HeadLookWalk script that we developed in *Chapter 6, First-person Character*. This time, we have to implement most of the physics ourselves. This means that instead of using CharacterController. SimpleMove(), we're going to use the more flexible CharacterController.Move() instead. SimpleMove ignores the *y*-axis in the move direction, but we need to apply this for the bounce.

Open the HeadLookWalkBounce.cs script and edit as follows:

```
using UnityEngine;
using System.Collections;

public class HeadLookWalkBounce : MonoBehaviour {
  public float velocity = 0.7f;
  public bool walking = false;

  public float gravity = 9.8f;
  public float bounceForce = 0.0f;

  private CharacterController controller;
  private Clicker clicker = new Clicker();
```

```
    private float verticalVelocity = 0.0f;
    private Vector3 moveDirection = Vector3.zero;

    void Start() {
      controller = GetComponent<CharacterController> ();
    }

    void Update () {
      if (clicker.clicked()) {
        walking = !walking;
      }
      if (walking) {
        moveDirection = Camera.main.transform.forward * velocity;
      } else {
        moveDirection = Vector3.zero;
      }
      if (controller.isGrounded) {
        verticalVelocity = 0.0f;
      }
      if (bounceForce != 0.0f) {
        verticalVelocity = bounceForce * 0.02f;
        bounceForce = 0.0f;
      }
      moveDirection.y = verticalVelocity;
      verticalVelocity -= gravity * Time.deltaTime;
      controller.Move (moveDirection * Time.deltaTime);
    }
}
```

The script manages not just the horizontal velocity, but also verticalVelocity, which is calculated from bounceForce and gravity. If you're standing on any solid object (isGrounded), verticalVelocity is zeroed. If you're airborne, you're no longer grounded and gravity will be applied.

Modify the Trampoline.cs script to send the bounceForce to the character's HeadLookWalk script component, as follows:

```
using UnityEngine;
using System.Collections;

public class Trampoline : MonoBehaviour {
```

```
        public float bounceForce = 300f;

        void OnTriggerEnter( Collider other ) {
          Rigidbody rb = other.GetComponent<Rigidbody> ();
          if (rb != null) {
            rb.AddForce (Vector3.up * bounceForce);
          } else {
            HeadLookWalkBounce locomotor =
              other.GetComponent<HeadLookWalkBounce> ();
            if (locomotor != null) {
              locomotor.bounceForce = bounceForce;
            }
          }
        }
      }
    }
```

The trampoline can now handle collision from characters or non-character objects. Bricks and characters respond differently to `bounceForce`. So, the magic `forceFactor` equalizes them (try adjusting this value and/or `bounceForce` in the trampoline).

Play it in VR. Walk forward onto the trampoline when a collision is detected. You'll go flying vertically and then descend back down.

This isn't a true trampoline mechanic, since you get pushed into the air just by touching it rather than having to jump on it first. However, it works for our purposes.

Just for fun, create a pillar next to the trampoline and try to land on it by performing the following steps:

1. Navigate to **GameObject | 3D Object | Cylinder** and rename it to `Pillar`.
2. Set its **Position** to (`-2`, `5`, `2.2`) and **Scale** to (`1`, `5`, `1`).
3. Drag the material named `Red` onto it.

Save the scene and play it in VR. *Whee!* Note how tall we get to jump. When in the air, look towards the pillar to land on it. If you keep walking off it, you drop back down to the ground. Here's what it will look like:

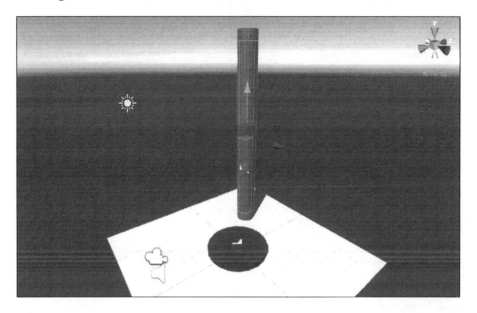

Summing up we did the following:

- At first, we had `BouncyBall` with a Physic Material, which Unity automatically applied upon collision, without scripting
- Then, we had a brick that received an upward force directly from the `Trampoline` script using `Rigidbody.AddForce()`
- Finally, in the preceding section, the first-person character script had its public `bounceForce` variable set by trampoline, which was manually applied as a vertical velocity along with gravity using `CharacterController.Move()`

The `BouncyBall` object with a Physic Material was moved automatically by the Unity physics engine, without scripting. The brick was moved by the trampoline, directly adding a force to the brick's Rigidbody. The first-person character was moved by calculating its own move direction based on gravity and a `bounceForce` variable set by trampoline.

Interlude – environment and things

Let's spice up the scene with some more interesting environment and geometry. This section is optional. You can follow along or even do your own thing.

I've provided assets in the download files associated with this book. Where mentioned in the following section, some of these may be a part of the free packages found in the Unity **Asset Store** and included with permission from the creators:

1. Start a new version of the scene, save it navigating to **File | Save Scene As...,** and name it `PhysicsWorld`.

2. Select the ground plane and change its **Scale** to (5, 1, 5).

Now, we'll add some sky and earth.

Wispy Sky

We will add a nicer skybox named `Wispy Sky`. To add the skybox, perform the following steps:

1. Import the assets package provided with this book named `WispySky.package`.

2. From the main menu bar, navigate to **Window | Lighting**.

3. In the **Lighting** panel, select the **Scene** tab.

4. In the **Skybox** field, click on the *circle* icon on the far right to open the **Select Material** dialog box.

5. Select the material named `WispySkyboxMat`.

You can also grab the entirely free `Wispy Skybox` package published by *Mundus Limited* at the **Asset Store**.

The planet Earth

Add an Earth globe. We can do this with the following steps:

1. Import the assets package provided with this book named `PlanetEarth.package`.

2. In the **Project** panel, drill down to find the `Earth3968Tris` prefab and drag it into the **Scene** view.

3. Set its **Position** to (100, 0, 300).

4. Set its **Scale** to (10, 10, 10).

5. Drag the EarthOrbit animation clip onto it.

6. Unfold the Earth3968Tris in **Hierarchy** and select its child with the same name, and on this object, set its **Rotation** to (0, 90, 340).

You can also grab the entirely free Planet Earth Free package that was published by *Close Quarter Games* at the **Asset Store**. The source of the textures is http://www.shadedrelief.com/natural3/pages/textures.html.

The corporate logo

Next, why don't we personalize the scene with something meaningful to you? We'll make it really big and jump on it. Maybe a guitar, a *My Little Pony* toy, or just a stack of some primitive 3D objects in Unity. I'm going to use the *Packt* logo because they're publishing this book. We'll use Blender for this.

Blender

As we need a vector graphic version of a logo image, I started with a PNG image file, cropped it in Gimp, uploaded it to Vector Magic (http://vectormagic.com/), and got back an SVG file. The source files are included with this book. Then, I converted the 2D art into a 3D model in Blender, simply extruding it once, by performing the following steps:

1. Open the Blender app and select **New** file.

2. Delete the default cube (right-click + *X* key).

3. Navigate to **File** | **Import** | **Scalable Vector Graphics** (.svg) and load Packt_Logo1.svg.

4. Change the view as **Top Ortho** (keypad *1* + *5*).

5. VectorMagic includes an object for the background. Select the object and then delete it (right-click + *X*).

6. Select all (*A* key).

7. For each letter, select it (right-click). In the **Properties** panel (the rightmost panel), select the *Data* icon tab. Under the **Geometry** pane, change the **Extrude** value to 0.01.

8. Save it as logo.blend file.

Unity

In Unity we perform the following steps:

1. Drag the `logo.blend` file into the `Project Assets/Models` folder.

2. Configure the **Import Settings** with **Scale Factor**: `10`, **Mesh Compression**: **High**, **Generate Colliders**: check, **Import Materials**: uncheck.

3. Scale and position it to your liking. I set **Position** to (`18`, `11`, `24`), **Rotation** to (`90`, `270`, `0`), and **Scale** to (`20`, `20`, `20`).

4. I polished it up with a metallic material. Create a new material, name it `ShinyMetalic`, set its **Metalic** value to `1`, and **Smoothness** to `0.8`. Drag it onto each of the letters in the logo.

The following image shows my scene:

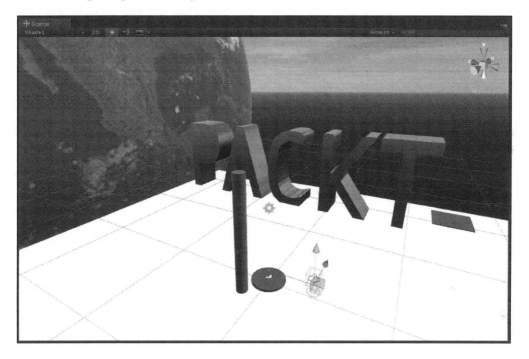

An elevator

Want to see the view from the top of the logo? Let's make a Mario-style elevator to get there.

Feature: *Provide an elevator platform, which moves up and down, that I can walk onto and ride to the top of my logo.*

Build it into the scene by performing the following steps:

1. Create the elevator platform by navigating to **GameObject | 3D Object | Cube**. Name it `Elevator`.

2. Set its so that it's aligned with the logo. By doing this, you can ride the platform and walk off it onto the top of the logo. I set **Position** to (`17`, `1.4`, `-8.8`) and **Scale** to (`4`, `0.1`, `4`).

3. Drag the `Blue` material onto it.

4. Create the script by navigating to **Add Component | New Script**. Name it `Elevate` and open it for editing.

Here's the `Elevate.cs` code:

```
using UnityEngine;
using System.Collections;

public class Elevator : MonoBehaviour {
  public float minHeight = 1.2f;
  public float maxHeight = 8.0f;
  public float velocity = 1;

  void Update () {
    float y = transform.position.y;
    y += velocity * Time.deltaTime;
    if (y > maxHeight) {
    y = maxHeight;
      velocity = -velocity;
    }
    if (y < minHeight) {
      y = minHeight;
      velocity = -velocity;
    }
    transform.position = new Vector3 (transform.position.x, y,
      transform.position.z);
  }
}
```

The script simply moves the platform up or down each frame. No physics, just simple animation. However, it's a rigid object, and we can stand on it.

Run this in VR. Try to walk onto the elevator, ride to the top, and then move onto the top of the object structures. The following image shows my view from the top:

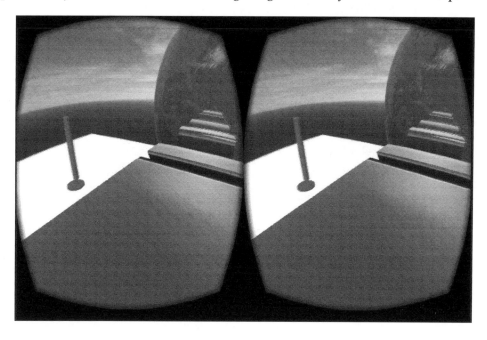

Jumping

When we created the trampoline, I mentioned that our implementation doesn't require you to jump to start bouncing. However, jumping is a fun idea, whether on a trampoline or not. Some games use the keyboard spacebar or a controller button to make your avatar jump. We'll now implement a simple jump gesture from the VR headset, which applies a vertical velocity to our movement.

 Note that this will not work with headsets that lack positional tracking, such as Google Cardboard and GearVR.

Feature: *When I jump, my character in VR jumps.*

To implement a jump gesture, we'll look for a rapid change in the **Y** position of the headset, which is very similar to the head nod gesture that we did in *Chapter 5, World Space UI*, (which checked for a rapid change in the *x*-axis angle). When a jump gesture is detected, we'll apply a vertical force to the first-person , as follows:

1. With MeMyselfEye selected in **Hierarchy**, create the script by navigating to **Add Component | New Script**.

2. Name it JumpGesture and open it for editing.

Edit the JumpGesture.cs script, as follows:

```
using UnityEngine;
using System.Collections;

public class JumpGesture : MonoBehaviour {
  public bool isJump = false;
  public float jumpForce = 1000.0f;

  private float jumpRate = 1.0f;
  private float previousHeight;
  private HeadLookWalkBounce walkBounce;

  void Start () {
    previousHeight = Camera.main.transform.position.y;
    walkBounce = GetComponent<HeadLookWalkBounce> ();
  }

  void Update () {
    if (DetectJump ()) {
      walkBounce.bounceForce = jumpForce;
    }
  }

  private bool DetectJump() {
    float height = Camera.main.transform.localPosition.y;
    float deltaHeight = height - previousHeight;
    float rate = deltaHeight / Time.deltaTime;
    previousHeight = height;
    return (rate >= jumpRate);
  }
}
```

The `Update()` function calls `DetectJump`, which determines whether the player has actually jumped in real life by detecting a quick change in the camera's **Y** position. If the player did jump, then it sets `bounceForce` in the `HeadLookWalkBounce` script, like the trampoline did. If you want, you can modify `jumpForce` to be different from the value used by the trampoline.

Try it in VR. *Ha! See, you don't need no stinkin' game controller to jump! Use your quads.*

This is a simple approximation for illustration purposes. It only looks at the motion changes from the previous frame. I encourage you to explore new and better ways to use your head and body as VR input.

> **Extra challenge**: For mobile VR devices with no positional tracking, try something else to invoke a jump.

Summary

In this chapter, we took a grand tour of Unity's physics engine. First, I explained in layman's terms the relationship between Rigidbody, Colliders, and Physic Materials, and how the physics engine uses these to determine the velocity and collision of objects in the scene.

Then, we went through a variety of examples that showed how one can use the physics engine directly, indirectly, and not at all. The bouncy balls used the engine without scripting, but then we wrote scripts on top of it to implement a headshot game and a shower of balls. The trampoline examples use the physics engine to detect collisions, and we scripted the transfer force to another object. Lastly, we implemented our own gravity and bounce forces on a first-person character, including a jump gesture. We did all of this while orbiting the Earth! Wonders never cease!

Physics mechanics are very important in game design as well as virtual reality. Unity's robust physics API gives developers the tools that are required to build pretty accurate and believable scenes as well as transcend reality and invent your own physics and oddities.

In the next chapter, we'll set aside much of the interactive features that we did in the past few chapters and look at some more canned or passive, animated VR experiences, such as rides and walkthroughs, which are commonly referred to as *riding on rails*.

Walk-throughs and Rendering

8

Living room simulation scene by Krystian Babilinsky, used with permission

In this chapter, we'll dig a bit into level design, modeling, and rendering, and implement an animated walk-through that you can experience in VR. The scene is a photo gallery, where you design a simple floor plan and use Blender to extrude it vertically into the walls. Use your own photos. Then, we will take a simple tour of it. At the end, we'll have a technical conversation about optimization, performance, and comfort.

In this chapter, we are going to discuss the following topics:

- Using Blender and Unity to build a simplistic art gallery
- Creating an animated walkthrough of the gallery scene
- Techniques that can be used to squeeze performance from complex scenes

Note that the projects in this chapter are separate and not directly required by the other chapters in this book. If you decide to skip any of it or not save your work, that's OK.

Building in Blender

Creating realistic models with convincing materials and lighting is an art and a science that extends beyond the scope of this book. Many people just find models online that are built by experts, including the Unity Asset Store. There is, of course, a wide range of design applications available, from the most advanced, such as 3D Studio Max (http://www.autodesk.com/products/3ds-max/) and Blender, to the most user-friendly, such as Home Styler (http://www.homestyler.com/) and SketchUp (http://www.sketchup.com/).

For this project, we just need something simple. We need a small art gallery exhibit room, about 24 by 36 feet. Keeping it minimal and instructive, I want to show how you can get started with building it in Blender.

Walls

To start, draw a simple floor plan on a piece of paper or use a drawing app. Mine is just an open space with two entrances and interior walls to display artwork (Gallery-floorplan.jpg), which looks like the following image:

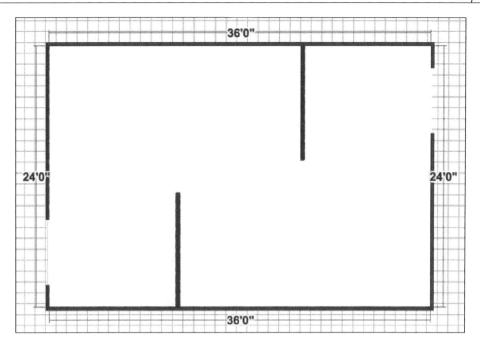

Now, open Blender. We'll use a common technique of starting with a simple object (a plane) and then extruding it to make each of the wall segments. To accomplish this, perform the following steps:

1. Start with an empty scene, press the *A* key to select all, and then press the *X* key to delete.

2. Add the floorplan image for reference and press the *N* key to open the properties panel. In the **Background Images** pane, select **Add Image**, click on **Open**, and select your image (`Gallery-floorplan.jpg`).

    Depending on the size and scale of your floor plan reference image, you'll want to choose a scale factor so that it's correct in the Blender world coordinate space. A scale of `6.25` works for me. Actually, the most important thing is the relative scale of the features in the diagram, since we can always adjust the scale in Unity in the **Import** settings, or even in the **Scene** view itself.

3. In the **Background Images** pane, set **Size** to 6.25. This pane, with the **Size** field highlighted, is shown in the following screenshot:

4. Go to the top view by pressing *7* on the numpad (or navigating to **View | Top**) and the orthographic view by pressing *5* (or navigating to **View | Persp/Ortho**). Note that the background image only gets drawn when it's in the **top-ortho** view.

5. Add a pane by pressing *Shift + A*. With these keys being selected, press *Tab* to go into the **Edit** mode. Press *Z* to toggle from the solid to the **wireframe** view. Press *G* to drag it into a corner and click *Enter* to confirm. Press *S* to scale it to fit the width of the wall, as shown in the following screenshot (You may recall that you can use the mouse scroll wheel to zoom and *Shift* and click on the middle mouse button to pan):

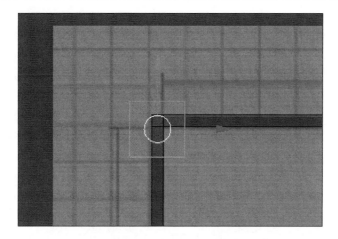

6. Now, we'll extrude to make the outer walls. Go into the **Edge Select** mode (via the icon shown in the following screenshot), press *A* to unselect all, and then right-click on the edge that you want to extrude. Press *E* to begin extruding, press *X* or *Y* to constrain it to that axis, and then press *Enter* to complete the extrusion where you want it:

7. Repeat the previous steps for each outer wall. Create a square at the corners so that you can extrude in the perpendicular direction. Leave gaps for the doorways. You may recall that if you need to modify the existing edges, select it with a right-click, *Shift* and right-click to select multiple, and move with *G*. You can also duplicate the selected items:

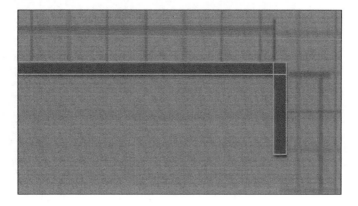

8. To extrude a face from the middle, we need to add an edge loop. With the mouse over the face, press *Ctrl + R* and left-click to create the cut. Slide the mouse to position it and left-click again to confirm. Repeat these steps for the width of the wall (making a square cut in the outer wall). Select the edge segment and press *E* to extrude it into the room:

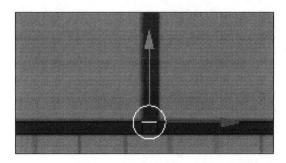

9. Once the floor plan is done, we can extrude it along the *z* axis to create the walls. Change the view from **Ortho** to **Persp** by pressing 5. Tilt it back using the middle mouse click and move. Select all by pressing *A*. Extrude with *E*. Begin to extrude with the mouse, press *Z* to constrain, and left-click to confirm.

10. Save the model to a file named `gallery.blend`:

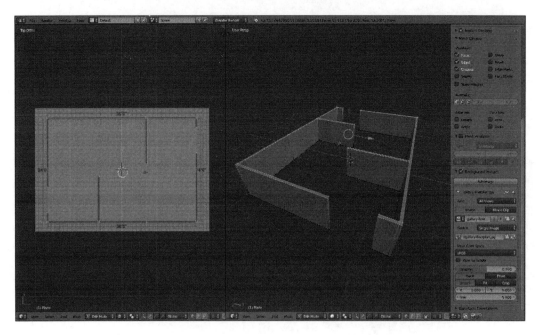

Ceiling

Now, add a ceiling with two skylights. The ceiling will just be a flat slab built from a single cube. Let's look at the steps to add a ceiling:

1. Return to **Object** mode using *Tab*.
2. Create a cube using *Shift + A*.
3. Position it at the center using *G*.
4. Scale it along *x* and *y* so that its size is the same as that of the room using *S + X* and *S + Y*.
5. Switch to the **Front** view using *1*, scale it so that it is flattened using *S + Z*, and move it to the top of the walls using *G + Z*, as shown in the following screenshot.

The skylights will be holes cut out of the ceiling, using another cube.

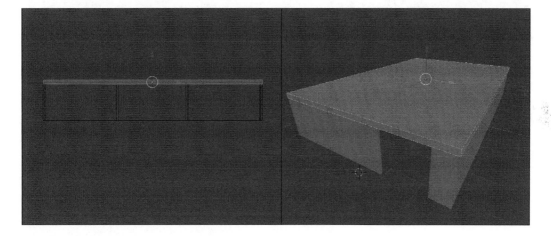

1. Add a cube, using *Shift + A*, scale it to the size, and move it to the position where you want the skylight.
2. Position the cube's *z* axis so that it cuts through the ceiling slab.

3. Duplicate the cube by pressing *Shift + D* and move it to the other skylight's position, as shown in the following screenshot:

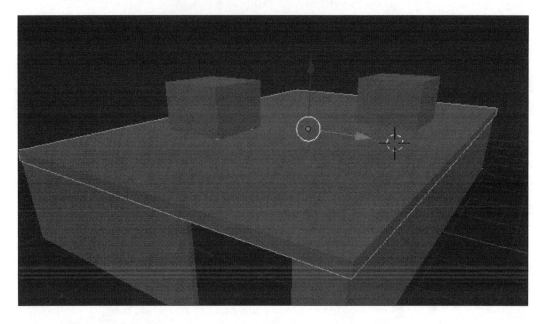

4. Select the ceiling slab with a right-click.

5. In the far right **Properties Editor** panel, select the wrench icon.

6. Then, navigate to **Add Modifier | Boolean** and for the **Operation** option, select **Difference**. For the **Object** option, select the first cube (Cube.001):

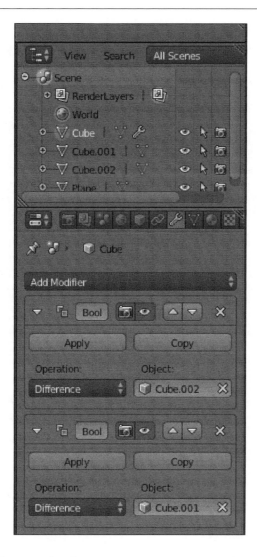

7. Click on **Apply** to make the operation permanent. Then, delete the cube (select it and press *X*).

8. Repeat the process, adding another Boolean modifier for the second cube.

If you get stuck, I've included a copy of the finished model with the files for this book. Alternatively, this model is simple enough to build using Unity's cubes. So much more can of course be done to make this a more realistic architectural model, but we're going to move ahead as is:

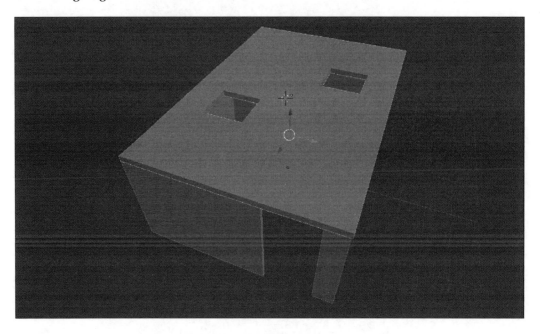

Assemble the scene in Unity

Now, we can use the gallery room model in Unity and add a floor and a ceiling with skylights. We will apply textures to the walls and add lighting.

The gallery room

First, we'll build the art gallery's room structure by performing the following steps:

1. Create a new scene by navigating to **File | New Scene**.

2. Create a floor plane by navigating to **GameObject | 3D Object | Plane**. Reset its **Transform** option and rename it to Floor.

3. Create the material for the floor and color it beige.

4. Our room is sized 24 by 36 feet, which in meters is 7.3 by 11. A Unity plane is 10 units square. So **Scale** it to (`0.73`, `1`, `1.1`).

5. Import the gallery model (for instance, `Gallery.blend`). Drag a copy from **Project Assets** into the **Scene**. Reset its **Transform** option.

6. Manually rotate and/or scale it to fit the floor, as needed (mine fits, but its **Rotate Y** value needed to be set to `90`). It may help if you first change the **Scene** view to **Top Iso**.

7. It is a good idea to add a collider to the walls so that a character doesn't just walk through them. To accomplish this, navigate to **Add Component | Physics | Mesh Collider**.

Note that when imported, as we defined in Blender, the **Gallery** has separate objects for the walls and the ceiling. A material is created (perhaps named `unnamed`) that has a neutral gray **Albedo** (204, 204, 204). I like this color for the walls, but I made a new material, all **White** (255, 255, 255) for the ceiling.

Next, add some sky and sunlight, as follows:

1. If a **Lighting** tab is not visible in your Unity editor, navigate to **Window | Lighting**.

2. In the **Lighting** pane, select the **Scene** tab.

3. For sunlight, in the **Lighting Scene** pane, at the **Sun** input, select the circle icon on the far right to open the **Select Light** dialog box and choose `Directional Light`.

4. For the sky, you can use Wispy Skybox like we did in *Chapter 7, Physics and the Environment*. Import the `WispySky.package` file.

5. Navigate to **Window | Lighting** in the **Lighting** panel and select the **Scene** tab.

6. In the **Skybox** field, click on the circle icon on the far right to open the **Select Material** dialog box and select the material named `WispySkyboxMat`.

The artwork rig

Now, we can plan the art exhibition. You are undoubtedly familiar with the photo galleries that are used on conventional websites, which let you swipe through a collection of images or view them as an animated slideshow. The widget code, the picture frame divs, and the CSS styling are defined once. Then the list of images is defined separately. We will do something similar here.

First, we'll create an artwork rig with a picture frame, lighting, and positioning. Then, we'll hang the art on the walls of the gallery. Later, we'll apply the actual images. The artwork rig will consist of a picture frame (a cube), a photo plane (a quad), and a spotlight, all relative to the artwork's placement on the wall. We will create the first one inside our **Scene**, save it as a `Prefab`, and then place duplicates on the walls throughout the gallery. I suggest doing this in the **Scene** view. Let's get started:

1. Create a container object by navigating to **GameObject | Create Empty**. Name it `ArtworkRig`.

2. Create the frame. With `ArtworkRig` selected, right-click and navigate to **GameObject | 3D Object | Cube**. Name it `ArtFrame`. In **Inspector**, set its **Scale Z** to `0.05`. Also, let's assume a `3:4` aspect ratio. So, set its **Scale Y** value to `0.75`.

3. Position the rig on a wall (the one facing the entrance on the upper right of the original floor plan). It may help to hide the ceiling child of the `Gallery` object (uncheck its **Enable** checkbox option). Then, change the **Scene** view to **Top and Iso** using **Scene View Gizmo** on the upper right of the **Scene** panel. Click on the green **Y** icon for the **Top** view and the middle square icon for the **Iso** view.

4. Select `ArtworkRig`, ensure that the **Translate** tool is active (the second icon in the top left icon toolbar), and use the *x* and *z* axis arrows to position it. Be sure to select and move the `ArtworkRig`. Leave the frame position at (0,0,0). Set the height at eye level (`Y=1.4`). The **Transform Position** value that works for me is (2, `1.4`, `-1.82`) and no **Rotation** at (0,0,0), as shown in the following step 7.

5. Make the frame black. Navigate to **Assets | Create | Material**, name it `FrameMaterial`, and set its Albedo color to black. Then in **Hierarchy**, select the **Frame** option and drag the `FrameMaterial` material onto it in **Inspector**.

6. Make the image placeholder. With `ArtFrame` selected in **Hierarchy**, right-click and navigate to **3D Object | Quad**. Name it `Image`. Position it just in front of the frame so that it's visible; set its **Position** to (0, 0, `-0.03`) and scale it so that it's slightly smaller than the frame by setting **Scale** to (`0.9`, `0.65`, 1).

7. To better appreciate the current scale and eye level, try inserting a copy of **Ethan** into the scene:

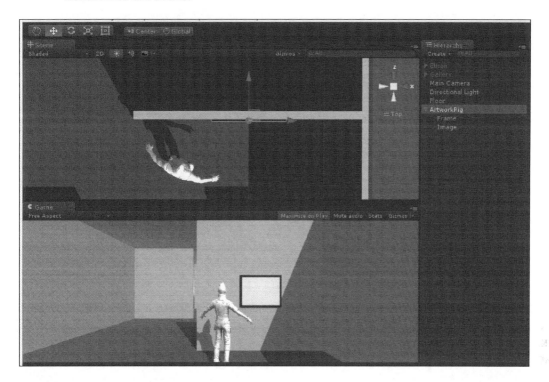

Next, we'll add a spotlight to the rig, as follows:

1. First, put the ceiling back in by checking off the **Enable** checkbox option for the child object of **Gallery**.

2. With `ArtworkRig` selected in **Hierarchy**, right-click, navigate to **Light | Spotlight**, and position it one meter away from the wall (z=-1.5) and up near the ceiling. The exact height doesn't matter much since we don't actually have a light fixture. We just have a Vector3 location for the source. I set **Position** to (1, 2, -1.5).

3. Now, adjust the `Spotlight` value so that it appropriately illuminates the artwork. I set **Rotation X** to `51`, **Spot Angle** to `30`, **Intensity** to `6`, and **Range** to `4`. The results are shown in the following screenshot. Also, set **Render Mode** to `Important` if you see the light fulcrum become washed out at varying angles from the camera:

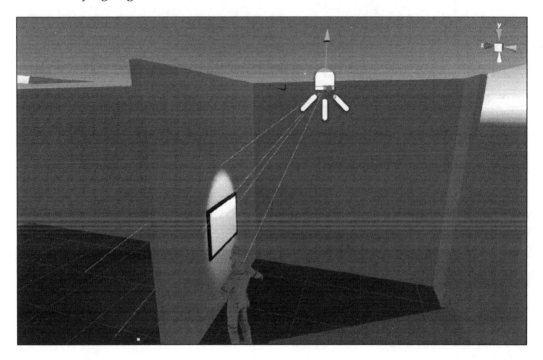

4. To preserve the rig as a `Prefab`, select `ArtworkRig` in **Hierarchy** and drag it into the **Project Assets** folder.

The exhibition plan

The next step is to duplicate `ArtworkRig` on each wall where we want to display the images. Position it and rotate as needed. If you follow the plan shown in the following diagram, your exhibition will display ten images, indicated by the stars:

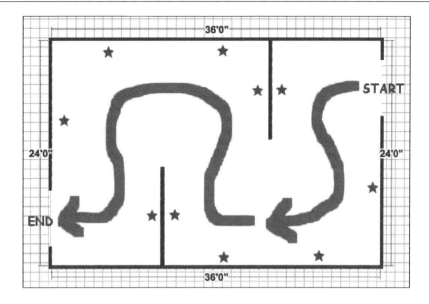

The following are the steps to duplicate `ArtworkRig` on each wall:

1. As before, it may be easier to hide the ceiling and change the **Scene View** panel to **Top and Iso**.

2. On the top left of the **Scene View** panel, change **Transform Gizmo Toggles** so that the tool handle is placed at the **Pivot** point rather than **Center**.

For each location, place an artwork in the gallery, as follows:

1. Select an existing `ArtworkRig` in the **Hierarchy**.

2. Duplicate `ArtworkRig` with right-click on **Duplicate**, or press *Ctrl + D*.

3. Rotate the rig so that it faces the correct direction by setting **Rotation Y** to `0`, `90`, `180`, or `-90`.

4. Position the rig on the wall.

The settings that work for my gallery are provided in the following table:

	Position X	Position Z	Rotation Y
0	2	-1.8	0
1	-1.25	-5.28	-180
2	-3.45	-3.5	-90
3	-3.45	0	-90
4	-2	1.6	0

	Position X	Position Z	Rotation Y
5	2	-1.7	180
6	3.5	0	90
7	3.5	3.5	90
8	1.25	5.15	0
9	-2	1.7	180

Note that the objects are listed in the same order that we'll use in the animated walk-through of the scene. Place them, as children of `Artworks`, in this order in **Hierarchy**.

Adding photos to the gallery

Please find 10 of your favorite photos from your photo library to use and add them to a new **Project Assets** folder named `Photos`. Follow the following steps to add photos to the gallery:

1. To create the photos folder, navigate to **Assets | Create | Folder** and name it `Photos`.

2. Import 10 photos by dragging and dropping them from your **File Explorer** into the `Photos` folder that you just created (or navigate to **Assets | Import New Asset...**).

3. Now, we'll write a script to populate **Artworks Images**. In **Hierarchy**, select `Artworks`. Then, in **Inspector**, navigate to **Add Component | New Script** and name it `PopulateArtFrames`.

4. Open the new script in **MonoDevelop**.

   Edit the code for `PopulateArtFrames.cs`, as follows (I've written the code in more lines than it was probably necessary so that I could provide explanations):

```
using UnityEngine;
using System.Collections;
public class PopulateArtFrames : MonoBehaviour {
  public Texture[] images;
  void Start () {
    int imageIndex = 0;
    foreach (Transform artwork in transform) {
      GameObject art = artwork.FindChild("Image").gameObject;
      Renderer rend = art.GetComponent<Renderer>();
      Shader shader = Shader.Find("Standard");
```

```
        Material mat = new Material( shader );
        mat.mainTexture = images[imageIndex];
        rend.material = mat;
        imageIndex++;
        if (imageIndex == images.Length) imageIndex = 0;
      }
    }
  }
```

How does the script work? As you know, as shown in the following screenshot, each `ArtworkRig` contains a child image quad. We'll create a new material for each quad (replacing its **Default-Material**) and assign it a particular texture image:

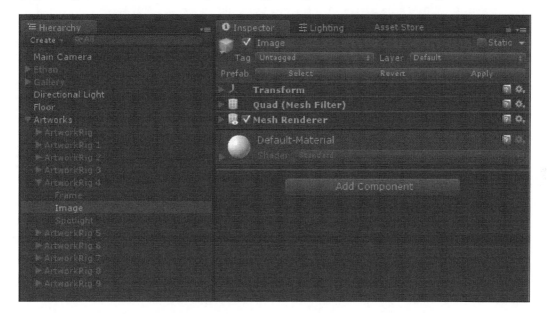

In the script, the first thing we do is declare an array of **Texture** named `images`. We will fill this parameter with the actual images using Unity editor. Then, we define a `Start()` function, which puts these images into each `ArtworkRig`.

The `foreach (Transform artwork in transform)` line loops through each child `ArtworkRig` of **Artworks**, assigning the `artwork` loop variable.

For each `artwork`, we find its child `Image` quad object, assign it to a local variable named `art`, and get its `Renderer` component (assigned to `rend`).

Next, we create a new material named `mat`, which uses `Standard Shader`. It receives an image texture from the images array (`mat.mainTexture = images[imageIndex]`).

We increment `imageIndex` so that each `ArtworkRig` gets a different image from the images array in order. Note that if there are more `ArtworkRigs` than images, it'll start from the beginning instead of causing an error.

To finish this up, let's perform the following steps:

1. Save the script and return to the Unity editor.
2. With `Artworks` selected in **Hierarchy**, unfold the **Populate Art Frames** script component in **Inspector** and unfold the **Images** parameter.
3. Set the **Images Size** value to `10`.
4. Find the images you imported in the `Photos` folder under the `Project/Assets/` directory and drag them, one at a time, into the **Images** slots as **Element 0** through **Element 9**.

When you click on **Play mode**, the artwork in the scene will get populated with the images in the order that you specified:

 Extra challenge: Since we manage the list of images as a separate array, the images can come from anywhere. We manually imported them into Unity to build the array, but you can extend this application to find images from an external source, such as your hard drive, a website, your Facebook album, or a camera gallery.

An animated walk-through

Next, we'll implement an automated walk-through of the scene. In conventional games, this is often used for a cut-scene, that is, a canned fly-through animation as a transition from one level to another. In VR, it's somewhat different. Walk-throughs can really be the VR experience itself. Head tracking is still active. So, it's not simply a pre-recorded video. You can look around and experience it, and it is more like an amusement park ride. This is often called an *on-the-rails* VR experience.

Unity's animation system

Unity's animation system is a powerful multipart system that lets you build advanced and intricate animation behaviors. The animation system has different but similar sounding parts:

- An **Animation Curve** defines a spline curve for a specific property that changes its value over time.

- An **Animation Clip** is a named set of curves that can be applied to an object and played (it animates the object). It can be edited in the **Animation View** panel.

- An **Animator Controller** keeps track of the clips that should be playing and when these clips should be changed or blended together. It can be edited with the **Animator** panel visual editor.

- An object can be given an **Animator Component**, which is then assigned one (or more) **Animator Controller**.

Prior to Unity 5, there were separate legacy and Mecanim humanoid animation systems, which have since been combined into a single main animation system of Unity. The legacy system included an **Animation Component**, which is no longer used.

The Unity animation system is largely oriented towards humanoid animations, or at least, building complex animations from multiple clips that may be blended together and can respond to other events. Details of **Animator Controller** and animating humanoid character movements are outside the scope of this book, but it is a fascinating specialty.

I've introduced this topic because we're not going to use it. Say what? Well, the animation that we require for this project is just a simple **Transform** update. So, using the animation system would be overkill, but the context is important. Given an **Animation Component** on an object, it references an **Animator Controller** that orchestrates one or more named **Animation Clips**. **Animation Clips** consist of key-frame curves for the properties that you want to animate. We will just make and use our own **Animation Curves** without all the other stuff.

Scripted animation

For this project, we will add a script to the first-person character (MeMyselfEye) to change its **Transform** position and rotation over time. It works by defining the key-frame transforms. As the name suggests, for key-frame animation, we define the camera's location at specific key times in the ride. The in-between frames are calculated automatically.

Our first job is to decide where the key nodes on the track should be placed and which way the camera should be facing. We will set three parameters for the first-person character — position X, position Z, and rotation Y. You can do this manually by using the built-in **Animation View** panel. Instead, we'll do it with a script.

In our gallery's fun ride, I want to make sure that the visitor gets to see each of the photos on the walls. So for each key frame, the user should be directly in front of one of the artworks as the ride progresses through the exhibition. For this to work properly, ensure that ArtworkRigs under **Artworks** are in the exact order in which you want to ride through the scene. We'll place each key position one meter away from the middle of the frame, using the following steps:

1. If necessary, drag MeMyselfEye from the Prefabs folder under the Project Assets/ directory into **Hierarchy**, position it at the entrance, like $X = 2.6$, $Z = -4.7$, and delete the default **Main Camera** option.

2. In **Hierarchy**, select MeMyselfEye. Then in **Inspector**, navigate to **Add Component | New Script** and name it ExhibitionRide.

3. Open the new script in **MonoDevelop**.

4. Edit the ExhibitionRide.cs script, as follows:

```
using UnityEngine;
using System.Collections;
public class ExhibitionRide : MonoBehaviour {
  public GameObject artworks;
  public float startDelay = 3f;
  public float transitionTime = 5f;
```

```
private AnimationCurve xCurve, zCurve, rCurve;
void Start () {
    int count = artworks.transform.childCount + 1;
    Keyframe[] xKeys = new Keyframe[count];
    Keyframe[] zKeys = new Keyframe[count];
    Keyframe[] rKeys = new Keyframe[count];
    int i = 0;
    float time = startDelay;
    xKeys [0] = new Keyframe (time, transform.position.x);
    zKeys [0] = new Keyframe (time, transform.position.z);
    rKeys [0] = new Keyframe (time, transform.rotation.y);
    foreach (Transform artwork in artworks.transform) {
        i++;
        time += transitionTime;
        Vector3 pos = artwork.position - artwork.forward;
        xKeys[i] = new Keyframe( time, pos.x );
        zKeys[i] = new Keyframe( time, pos.z );
        rKeys[i] = new Keyframe( time, artwork.rotation.y );
    }
    xCurve = new AnimationCurve (xKeys);
    zCurve = new AnimationCurve (zKeys);
    rCurve = new AnimationCurve (rKeys);
}
void Update () {
    transform.position = new Vector3 (xCurve.Evaluate
(Time.time), transform.position.y, zCurve.Evaluate
(Time.time));
    Quaternion rot = transform.rotation;
    rot.y = rCurve.Evaluate (Time.time);
    transform.rotation = rot;
}
}
```

In the script, we declare three public parameters. The GameObject artworks
variable should get initialized to the parent (Artworks), which contains the
ArtworkRig objects in the order in which they will get visited in the animation.
The startDelay variable is the number of seconds before the ride begins, and the
transitionTime variable is the time taken to travel from one viewing position (key
frame) to the next.

We also define three private AnimationCurve variables named xCurve, zCurve,
and rCurve for the X and Z position and the y-axis rotation at each viewing position.
The Start() function initializes these curves.

An `AnimationCurve` object is defined as an array of `Keyframes`. We will have one Keyframe for each viewing position plus the initial start point. Therefore, the first element of the Keyframe arrays is set to the initial `MeMyselfEye transform. position.x`, `transform.position.z`, and `transform.rotation.y` values. For each subsequent Keyframe, we use the artwork **Transform** to find a point in the space one meter in front of the frame (`Vector3 pos = artwork.position - artwork.forward`).

Then in `Update()`, we update the `transform.position` and `transform.rotation` properties to the interpolated values for the current `Time.time` property.

Save the script and then perform the following step:

1. From **Hierarchy**, select `MeMyselfEye`.
2. Drag the `Artworks` object (which contains all `ArtworkRigs`) onto the **Exhibition Ride (Script) Artworks** parameter field.

When you play the scene, you get a nice easy ride through the art gallery, with a slight pause to view each photo. That's real nice! Hopefully, you picked images that you can show to all your friends and family!

In this script, I used the `transform.rotation` Quaternion y value directly. It's usually not recommended to manipulate Quaternion's value directly, but since we're consistently changing only a single axis, it is safe.

Extra challenge: There are many things that you can add to enhance and complete the VR experience. Add an introductory splash screen and a "Click to Start" button. Add audio to the `ArtworkRig` that plays appropriate sounds, or a narration explaining each art piece. You can modify the size of images and/or frames for variety. You can also adjust the viewing distance, velocity per image, and so on. As mentioned earlier, you can load images at runtime from external sources, such as the Web, phone, or, hmm, Facebook!

Optimizing for performance and comfort

Admittedly, this chapter has been mostly about level design and is not specifically about virtual reality. However, I didn't want to just give you a pre-built Unity package and say, "Hey, import this so that we can do a walk-through!"

It should be abundantly clear by now that developing for VR has many facets (pun intended). Once you have a "fancy schmancy" scene created with models, textures, and lighting and you provide a thrilling ride-through for your visitors, you'll inevitably need to start thinking about rendering performance, frames per second, latency, and motion sickness.

> *We developers rapidly become immune to all but the most obvious rendering errors, and as a result we are the worst people at testing our own code. It introduces a new and exciting variation of the coder's defense that "it works on my machine" – in this case, "it works for my brain".*

> –*Tom Forsyth, Oculus*

There are some very good articles that are written by experts and which outline the strategies and techniques that are used to optimize games for performant VR experiences. At the time of writing this book, here are some good references:

- *Squeezing Performance out of Your Unity Gear VR Game*, by Chris Pruett, Oculus, May 12, 2015, `https://developer.oculus.com/blog/squeezing-performance-out-of-your-unity-gear-vr-game/`

- *12 Performance Tricks for Optimizing VR Apps in Unity*, by Darshan Shankar, VR developer, May 12, 2015, `http://dshankar.svbtle.com/performance-optimization-for-vr-apps`

- *Unity VR Optimisation Hints and Tips*, Nick Pittom, VR developer "Crystal Rift", October 31, 2014, `http://gamasutra.com/blogs/NickPittom/20141031/229074/Unity_VR_optimisation_hints_and_tips.php`

- *Optimizing Graphics Performance*, Unity Manual, `http://docs.unity3d.com/460/Documentation/Manual/OptimizingGraphicsPerformance.html`

- *Practical Guide to Optimization for Mobiles*, Unity Manual, `http://docs.unity3d.com/Manual/MobileOptimizationPracticalGuide.html`

Many of the lessons and techniques that are applicable to mobile game development can be applied to VR as well.

Developing for VR is a moving target—the platform hardware, software SDK, and the Unity 3D engine itself are all changing and improving relatively rapidly. Blog posts and web-based articles can be readily updated or superseded as product improvements and new developer insights emerge. Like the other parts of this book, I need to ask myself whether we can break this down into basic principles that will stay relevant even as the details change.

In general, there are optimization techniques that focus on the design and/or limitations of each of the following:

- Your game implementation and content
- The Unity engine rendering pipeline
- The target platform hardware and drivers

The following discussion is a survey of things that you can do and an introduction for further reading and research.

Optimizing your implementation and content

The one thing that you have the most control over is the content that you're building. Some decisions that impact performance are the conscious, intentional, and creative ones. Maybe you want hyper-realistic graphics with high-fidelity sound because it must be so awesome! Changes may constitute a difficult design compromise. However, it is very likely that with a little creative outside-the-box thinking and experimentation, you can achieve (nearly) identical visual results with a much better performance. Quality is not only how it looks, but also how it feels. So, optimizing for user experience is a fundamental decision.

Simplify your models

Minimize the number of vertices and faces in your model meshes. Avoid complex meshes. Remove faces that will never be seen, such as the ones inside solid objects. Clean up duplicate vertices and remove doubles. This will most likely be done in the same application that you used to create them in the first place. For example, Blender has the tools for this. Also, there are third-party tools that you can purchase to simplify model meshes. Less than 300 vertices for (nonstatic) meshes are required for dynamic batching (see the following section).

Using texture maps instead of complex meshes

If you didn't care about the polygon count, you could model surface detail and texture bumps with complex meshes that have many vertices. Of course, that's computationally impractical. Texture maps to the rescue! Consider normal maps versus height maps.

Normal maps are simple texture maps that are used to fake the lighting of bumps and dents on a model's surface. In some 3D renderings, you can succeed quite well with normal maps, but in VR, it looks just too flat. When you move your head, it appears like a wallpaper.

Height maps use a texture image to produce a very convincing representation of 3D surface geometry. Height maps are better than a normal map as they not only define the bumpiness of a surface, but also provide parallax. However, as a shader, they're computationally expensive. Nevertheless, it's not as costly as doing it with meshes. See `http://docs.unity3d.com/Manual/StandardShaderMaterialParameters.html`.

Limiting the objects to be drawn

Occlusion culling disables the rendering of objects when they are not seen by the camera because they are obscured (occluded) by other objects. Read the Unity page, `http://docs.unity3d.com/Manual/OcclusionCulling.html`, to learn how to set up occlusion culling in your projects.

Another way to reduce the details in a scene is by using Global Fog, which is based on distance. Objects further away than the fog limits will not be drawn. See the *Project Graphics Settings*, `http://docs.unity3d.com/Manual/class-GraphicsSettings.html`.

Level of detail, or LOD groups, are a great way of simplifying geometry in such a way that things close up are detailed, while those further away are rendered with simpler models. Unity can automatically switch between each LOD geometry as the camera moves closer. See `http://docs.unity3d.com/Manual/class-LODGroup.html`.

 The one thing that you have the most control over is the content that you're building. Minimize the number of vertices and faces in your model meshes. Height maps can be an effective substitute for complex geometry. The more you try to reduce the number of objects that need to be rendered, the better.

Lighting and shadow performance

You also have a great deal of control over the number of lights, types of lights, their placement, and settings. Use baked lightmaps whenever possible, which pre-calculates the lighting effects into a separate image rather than at runtime.

Use real-time shadows sparingly. When an object casts shadows, a shadow map is generated, which will be used to render the other objects that might receive shadows. Shadows have a high rendering overhead and generally require high-end GPU hardware. Read up on it in the Unity manual, which can be found at `http://docs.unity3d.com/Manual/LightPerformance.html`.

Other techniques, such as light probes (either real-time or baked) and the choice of shaders (and the shader options), can make your scene look really amazing. However, they can also have a significant effect on the performance. Balancing aesthetics and graphics performance is an art and a science that I would love to master some day.

Optimizing your scripts

Every `Update()` callback function that you write is called for each frame. Remove unused updates. Use a state variable (and an `if` statement) to turn off the calculations when they are not needed.

At some point, you may have to use a profiling tool to see how your code is performing under the hood. The Unity **Profiler** (see the following section) will run while your game is in the **Play Mode** and provide details about where exactly it's spending its time and the duration for the same. If the **Profiler** indicates that a large amount of time is spent on the scripts that you've written, you should consider another way to refactor the code so that it's more efficient. Often, this is related to memory management, but it could be math or physics. See `http://docs.unity3d.com/Manual/MobileOptimizationPracticalScriptingOptimizations.html`.

Optimizing for the Unity rendering pipeline

There are a number of important performance considerations that are specific to how Unity does its rendering. Some of these may be common for any graphics engine. Alternatively, they can change in the newer versions of Unity itself, since rendering is a competitive business; algorithms can be replaced and implementations reworked.

> A 50-minute presentation from Unity – The Unity Rendering Pipeline (January, 2014) can be seen at `https://unity3d.com/learn/resources/unity-rendering-pipeline`.

Life's a batch

Perhaps, the biggest bang for the buck is a feature in Unity that groups different meshes into a single batch, which is then shoveled into the graphics hardware all at once. This is much faster than sending the meshes separately. Meshes are actually first compiled into an OpenGL vertex buffer object, or a VBO (for more information, visit `http://en.wikipedia.org/wiki/Vertex_Buffer_Object`), but that's a low-level detail of the rendering pipeline.

Each batch takes one draw call. Reducing the number of draw calls in a scene is more significant than the actual number of vertices or triangles.

There are two types of batching—static batching and dynamic batching.

First, be sure to enable **Static Batching** and **Dynamic Batching** in **Player Settings**.

For static batching, simply mark the objects as static by checking off the **Static** checkbox in the Unity **Inspector** for each object in the scene. Marking an object static tells Unity that it will never move, animate, or scale. Unity will automatically batch together the meshes that share the same material into a single, large mesh.

The key here is the caveat—meshes that share the same material. All the meshes in a batch must have the same material settings—the same texture, shader, shader parameters, and the material pointer object.

How can this be? They're different objects! This can be done by combining multiple textures into a single macro-texture file or TextureAtlas and then UV-mapping as many models as will fit. It's a lot like a sprite image used for 2D and web graphics. Sound difficult? There are third-party tools, such as Pro Draw Call Optimize, that help you build these.

When managing textures in scripts, use `Renderer.sharedMaterial` rather than `Renderer.material` to avoid creating duplicate materials. Objects receiving a duplicate material will opt out of the batch.

You may recall that in the **Gallery** project earlier in this chapter, we created separate materials for each `ArtworkRig Image` in a script. If tagged **Static**, they will not be batched. However, it turns out that it's fine because the texture is a full-resolution photographic image—too big to merge with other textures anyway. The point is that sometimes, it's appropriate to worry about batching, and sometimes, it's not.

 Marking an object **Static** tells Unity that it will never move, animate, or scale. Unity will automatically batch together meshes that share the same material into a single large VBO, which is then shoveled into the graphics hardware all at once.

Dynamic batching is similar to static batching. For objects that are not marked **Static**, Unity will still try to batch them, albeit it will be a slower process since it needs to think about it frame by frame (the CPU cost). The shared material requirement still holds, as well as other restrictions such as vertex count (less than 300 vertices) and uniform **Transform Scale** rules. See `http://docs.unity3d.com/Manual/DrawCallBatching.html`.

Currently, only **Mesh Renderers** and **Particle Systems** are batched. This means that skinned meshes, cloth, trail renderers, and other types of rendering components are not.

Multipass pixel filling

Another concern in the rendering pipeline is sometimes referred to as the pixel fillrate. If you think about it, the ultimate goal of rendering is to fill each pixel on the display device with the correct color value. If it has to paint any pixels more than once, that's more costly. For example, watch out for transparent particle effects such as smoke that touch many pixels with mostly transparent quads.

Actually for VR, Unity paints into a frame buffer memory that is larger than the physical display dimensions, which is then post-processed for ocular distortion correction – barrel effect and chromatic aberration correction – color separation, before getting tossed onto the HMD display. In fact, there may be multiple overlay buffers that get composited before the post-processing.

This multipass pixel filling is how some advanced renderers work. Lighting and material effects such as multiple lights, dynamic shadows, and transparency (**Transparent** and **Fade Render** modes) are implemented in this way. Unity 5 Specular Shader as well. Basically, all the good stuff!

VBO batches with materials that require multipass pixel filling get submitted multiple times, thus increasing the net number of draw calls. Depending on your project, you may choose to either optimize the heck out of it and avoid multipass pixel filling altogether, or carefully curate the scenes with an understanding of what should have a high performance and what should have a high fidelity.

 Depending on your project, you may choose to optimize the heck out of it and avoid multi-pass pixel filling altogether, or carefully curate the scenes with an understanding of which objects should have a high performance versus high fidelity.

Multipass can be avoided if you precalculate the lighting and shadows using baked lightmaps. It's the Unity 4.X way. Just use **Legacy Shaders/Lightmapped/Diffuse** (see `http://docs.unity3d.com/Manual/LightmapParameters.html`). However, if you bake, you lose Unity 5 software's awesome new physically-based shaders (`http://blogs.unity3d.com/2015/02/18/working-with-physically-based-shading-a-practical-approach/`).

Nevertheless, you can use **Light Probes** to inexpensively simulate dynamic lighting of your dynamic objects. As the Unity manual states, "**Light Probes** are baked cubemaps that store information about direct, indirect, and even emissive light at various points in your scene. As a dynamic object moves, it interpolates samples of the nearby light probes to approximate the lighting at that specific position. This is a cheap way of simulating realistic lighting on dynamic objects without using expensive real-time lights". Visit `http://docs.unity3d.com/Manual/LightProbes.html` for more information.

Set the total number of simultaneous lights in **Quality Settings** to one. "*The closest light will be rendered per-pixel, and surrounding lights will be calculated using spherical harmonics*", Chris Pruett of Oculus explains. Alternatively, you can even drop all the pixel lights and rely on Light Probes.

Other rendering tips

Nick Pittom recommends that you should create textures at a 2048 resolution and import to the default setting of 1,024. This speeds up the renderer.

Another tip from Darshan Shankar when discussing GearVR is that when you are rendering to Android with quality settings for no shadows, you need to switch targets to the PC, bake the lighting with high resolution and the hard and soft shadows enabled, and then switch back to Android. See `http://dshankar.svbtle.com/developing-crossplatform-vr-apps-for-oculus-rift-and-gearvr` for more information.

What tips can you find or recommend? Maybe someone should start a forum or something! Visit `http://forum.unity3d.com/` for more information.

Optimizing for the target hardware and drivers

Hardware architectures are evolving towards performance that benefits graphics pipelines of virtual reality (and augmented reality). VR introduces requirements that weren't so important for traditional video gaming. For example, latency and dropped frames (where rendering a frame takes longer than the refresh rate) took a back seat to high-fidelity triple-AAA rendering capabilities. VR needs to render each frame in time and do it twice—once for each eye. Driven by the requirements of this emerging industry, semiconductor and hardware manufacturers are building new and improved architectures, which will inevitably impact how content developers think about optimization.

That said, you should develop and optimize for the lower spec machine or device that you want to target. If such optimizations necessitate undesirable compromises, consider separate versions of the game for high- versus low-end platforms. VR device manufacturers have started publishing minimum/recommended hardware specifications, which take much of the guesswork out of it.

Learn the Unity **Quality** settings (by navigating to **Edit | Project Settings | Quality**) that can be configured on a per-target-platform basis. Start with the recommendations of your device manufacturer (such as Oculus) as regards the suggested values, and adjust as needed. For example, you can adjust parameters such as **Pixel Light Count**, **Anti Aliasing**, and **Soft Particles**.

For instance, for mobile VR, it is recommended that you tune for CPU-bound versus GPU-bound usage. Some games will make the CPU work harder, others will impact the GPU. Normally, you should favor CPU over GPU. The Oculus Mobile SDK (GearVR) has an API that is used to throttle the CPU and GPU to control heat and battery drain.

Unity Profiler

Optimizing can be a lot of work, and a steep learning curve is required to get to grips with it. The good news is that it can be accomplished incrementally. Tackle the more obvious, bigger bang-for-the-buck things first, especially the ones that cause little or no visual degradation.

The Unity editor includes two built-in tools to assess performance—the **Stats** pane and the **Profiler** pane.

 While profiling and optimizing, write down (or take a screenshot of) the stats and label them, perhaps in a spreadsheet, so that you can keep a log of your progress and measure the effectiveness of each technique that you try.

In the **Game** panel, you can enable the **Stats** pane, as shown in the following screenshot, which displays (among other things) the number of batches, triangles, vertices, and runtime frames per second. (See `http://docs.unity3d.com/Manual/RenderingStatistics.html`):

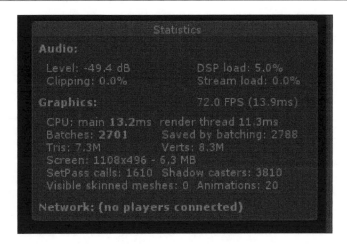

The Unity **Profiler** option is a performance instrumentation tool that reports how much time is spent in various areas of your game, including rendering and scripts. It records the statistics over time during gameplay and shows them in a timeline graph. Clicking lets you drill down into the details. See `http://docs.unity3d.com/Manual/Profiler.html`. Pictured in the following screenshot is a profile of the classic Oculus Tuscany demo scene:

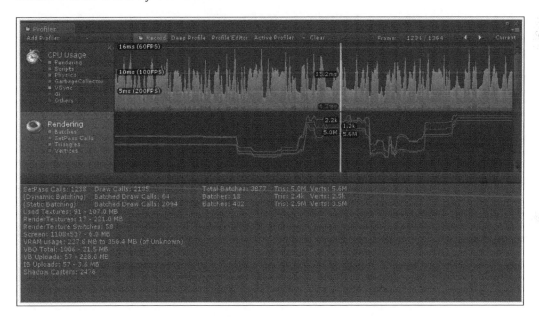

Before you start optimizing, get a handle on your performance of various camera locations in the scene for various animation and action sequences and different scenes. Write down (or take a screenshot of) the stats and label them, perhaps in a spreadsheet, so that you can keep a log of your progress and measure the effectiveness of each optimization technique that you try.

Summary

In this chapter, we built an art gallery scene from scratch, starting with a plan drawing and going into Blender to construct an architectural structure. We imported the model into Unity and added some environmental lighting. Then, we built an artwork rig consisting of an image quad, a picture frame, and a spotlight, and placed instances of the rig on various walls throughout the gallery. Next, we imported a bunch of personal photos and wrote a script that populates the art frames at runtime. Finally, we wrote a script that takes the first-person camera on a walk-through of the scene, pausing to look at each picture one at a time for a nice, simple VR-on-rails experience.

Then, we had a detailed discussion about optimizing projects for performance and VR comfort, which means that you have to be mindful of your content and model complexity, the rendering pipeline, and the capabilities of your target platform.

In the next chapter, we will take a look at a different kind of VR experience using pre-recorded 360-degree media. You will build and learn about photospheres, equirectangular projections, and infographics.

9
Using All 360 Degrees

Statue of Atlas holding the celestial sphere, 2nd Cent BCE.
(source http://ancientrome.ru/art/artworken/img.htm?id=4657).

360-degree photos and videos are different ways of using virtual reality that are accessible to consumers today, both in terms of experiencing them as well as producing and publishing them. Viewing prerecorded images requires much less compute power than rendering full 3D scenes, and this works very well on mobile VR devices. In this chapter, we will explore the following topics:

- Using textures to view globes, panoramas, and photo spheres
- Understanding what 360-degree media is?

- Adding a photosphere and a 360-degree video to your Unity projects
- What a field of view is and how one can record a 360-degree video?

Note that the projects in this chapter are separate and not directly required by the other chapters in this book. If you decide to skip any of it or not save your work, that's okay.

360-degree media

The "360-degree" and "virtual reality" terms have been tossed around a lot lately, often in the same sentence. Consumers may be led to believe that it's all the same thing, it's all figured out, and it's all very easy to produce, when in fact, it is not so simple.

Generally, the "360-degree" term refers to the viewing of prerecorded photos or videos in a manner that allows you to rotate your view's direction to reveal content that was just outside your field of view.

Non-VR 360-degree media has become relatively common. For example, many real-estate listing sites provide panoramic walkthroughs with a web-based player that lets you interactively pan around to view the space. Similarly, YouTube supports the uploading and playback of 360-degree videos and provides a player with interactive controls to look around during the playback. Google Maps lets you upload 360-degree still **photosphere** images, much like their Street View tool, that you can create with an Android or iOS app or a consumer camera (for more information, visit `https://www.google.com/maps/about/contribute/photosphere/`). The Internet is teaming with 360-degree media!

With a VR headset, viewing 360-degree media is surprisingly immersive, even just for still photos. You're standing at the center of a sphere with an image projected onto the inside surface, but you feel like you're really there in the captured scene. Simply turn your head to look around. It's one of those things that gets people interested in VR the first time they see it, and it is a popular application for Google Cardboard and GearVR.

In this chapter, we will explore a variety of uses of media that take advantage of Unity and VR's ability to use all 360 degrees.

Crystal balls

To begin, let's have a little fun while we apply a regular rectangular image as a texture to a sphere, just to see what it does and how bad it looks.

First, set up a new scene for this chapter by performing the following steps:

1. Create a new scene by navigating to **File | New Scene**. Then, navigate to **File | Save Scene As...** and name it 360Degrees.

2. Create a new plane by navigating to **GameObject | 3D Object | Plane** and reset its transformation using the **Transform** component's *gear* icon | **Reset**.

3. Insert an instance of MeMyselfEye from the project prefab, set its **Position** to (0, 1, -1), and delete the default Main Camera.

Now, create the first sphere and write a rotator script while you're at it. I'm using the EthanSkull.png image that was provided with this book (drag and drop it into the **Project Assets/Textures** folder). Then, perform the following steps:

1. Create a new sphere by navigating to **GameObject | 3D Object | Sphere**, reset its transformation using the **Transform** component's *gear* icon | **Reset**, and name it Sphere 1.

2. Set its **Position** to (0, 1.5, 0).

3. Drag and drop the texture named EthanSkull (you can use any photo that you want) onto the sphere.

4. Create a new script by navigating to **Add Component | New Script** and name it Rotator.

Open the rotator.cs script and edit it, as follows:

```
using UnityEngine;
using System.Collections;

public class Rotator : MonoBehaviour {
  public float xRate = 0f; // degrees per second
  public float yRate = 0f;
  public float zRate = 0f;

  void Update () {
    transform.Rotate (new Vector3 (xRate, yRate, zRate) *
  Time.deltaTime);
  }
}
```

Then, set the rotation rate so that it spins around the *y* axis at 20 degrees per second, as follows:

1. On the **Rotator Script** component, set **Rates** for **X, Y, Z** as (0, 20, 0).
2. Save the scene. Try it in VR.

Is that scary or what? No worries. The projected image may be distorted, but it looks wicked cool. For some applications, a little distortion is the artistic intent, and you don't need to worry about it.

 Extra challenge: Try making the sphere look more like crystal glass using physically-based shaders and reflection probes in Unity 5 (for more information, visit http://blogs.unity3d.com/2014/10/29/physically-based-shading-in-unity-5-a-primer/).

Magic orbs

For the next example, we'll look at the sphere from the inside, mapping an ordinary image onto its inside surface. Then, we'll put a solid colored *shell* around the outside. So, you have to actually walk up to the sphere and stick your head into it to see what's there!

Follow these steps to build it (I'm using the `GrandCanyon.png` image that we introduced back in *Chapter 2*, *Objects and Scale*, but you can use any image—preferably a landscape with big sky):

1. Move `Sphere 1` out of the way and set its **Position** to (`-3, 1.5, -1.5`).

2. Create a new sphere by navigating to **GameObject | 3D Object | Sphere**, set its **Position** to (`0, 1.5, 0`), and name it `Sphere 2`.

3. Disable its **Sphere Collider** component by unchecking the checkbox.

4. Create a new material by navigating to **Assets | Create | Material** and name it `GrandCanyonInward`.

5. Drag the `GrandCanyonInward` material onto `Sphere 2`.

6. Locate the `GrandCanyon` texture image and drag it onto the `GrandCanyonInward` component's **Albedo** texture (onto the square towards the far left of the **Albedo** field).

At this point, we have a sphere with an image wrapped around its outside, as in the previous example. Now, we'll reverse it so that the texture is rendered on the inside surface. We do this by using a custom shader, as follows:

1. Create a new custom shader by navigating to **Assets | Create | Shader** and name it `InwardShader`.

2. In the **Project Assets**, double-click on the new `InwardShader` to open it in MonoDevelop.

Edit the shader's definition file, as follows:

```
Shader "Custom/InwardShader" {
  Properties {
    _MainTex ("Albedo (RGB)", 2D) = "white" {}
  }
  SubShader {
    Tags { "RenderType"="Opaque" }
    LOD 200

    Cull Front

    CGPROGRAM
    #pragma surface surf Standard vertex:vert

    void vert(inout appdata_full v) {
      v.normal.xyz = v.normal * -1;
```

```
    }

    sampler2D _MainTex;

    struct Input {
      float2 uv_MainTex;
    };

    void surf (Input IN, inout SurfaceOutputStandard o) {
      fixed4 c = tex2D (_MainTex, IN.uv_MainTex);
      o.Albedo = c.rgb;
    }
    ENDCG
  }
  FallBack "Diffuse"
}
```

A Unity shader is a text script file with directives on how Unity's rendering pipeline does its magic. Reading through the preceding shader code, our custom shader is named InwardShader. It has one **Properties** panel—the **Albedo** texture that you can set from the Unity editor. We set the Cull mode to Front (the possible values are Back, Front, and Off); the word **cull** in this context means "to remove or ignore". Thus, it'll ignore the front faces but render the back ones. We also invert the normal vectors of each face (v.normal.xyz = v.normal * -1) for lighting calculations. The surf() sampler function, called by the Unity renderer, applies the properties defined in the shader, which is only the main texture image in this case.

To be honest, I actually found this code from a Web search, studied it, and then simplified it for this example. You can learn more about Unity's ShaderLab from http://docs.unity3d.com/Manual/ShadersOverview.html.

Now, apply the shader and ensure that the Sphere 2 object is selected. On its GrandCanyonInsider material component in **Inspector**, navigate to **Shader | Custom | InwardShader**.

Try it in VR. From the outside, it looks especially weird, but walk into the sphere and look around. *Well? I think it's cool.*

For locomotion, you may need to add the HeadLookWalk script (written in *Chapter 6, First-person Character*) to MeMyselfEye, or just use Unity's standard FPSController prefab in place of MeMyselfEye.

Finally, we'll encase it in a solid colored orb by performing the following steps:

1. Select the `Sphere 2` object in **Hierarchy**, right-click, and navigate to **3D Object | Sphere** so that the new sphere is a child of `Sphere 2`.

2. Disable its **Sphere Collider** component by unchecking it.

3. Find a solid material, such as the one we made in a previous chapter, named `Red` and drag it onto the new sphere.

Try it in VR. The following image is a capture of what I see. It's like peering into an egg shell!

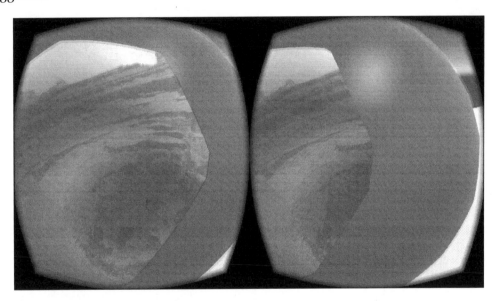

We created two concentric spheres—same size and position. We disabled their colliders so that we can penetrate through their surfaces. One sphere has a default shader, which renders the outward facing surface (in red). The other sphere uses a custom shader named `InwardShader`.

As a first-person character, you can go into the sphere and look around. If you're using a headset that supports positional tracking such as Oculus Rift, then you don't have to actually walk into the sphere. You can stop in front of it and lean in to stick your head into it! *It's like magic!*

Panoramas

What if the image was really wide, such as a panoramic photo that you can take with your phone? Let's try this and map it onto a cylinder.

I was in Los Angeles last year. I hiked to the top of the Hollywood sign, where I took two 180-degree panoramic images with my phone, and later I quickly stitched them together in Gimp. The `Hollywood.png` image is included with this book, or you can use your own panorama:

Putting it together, using the following steps:

1. Move `Sphere 2` out of the way and set its **Position** to (-3, 1.5, 0).

2. Create a new cylinder by navigating to **GameObject | 3D Object | Cylinder**, set its **Position** to (0, 1.5, 0), and name it `Cylinder 3`.

3. Set the **Scale** to (2, 0.5, 2).

4. Disable its **Capsule Collider** component by unchecking the checkbox.

5. Drag the `Hollywood` texture onto the cylinder.

6. Ensure that the `Cylinder 3` object is selected. On its `Hollywood` material component in **Inspector**, navigate to **Shader | Custom | InwardShader**.

A default cylinder in Unity is 2 units tall and 1 unit wide (a radius of 0.5 units). My image has a resolution of 5242 x 780, which is an aspect ratio of about 6.75:1. How big should the cylinder be to respect this aspect ratio and not distort the image? If you set **Y** to 0.5 to normalize the height to 1.0 unit, then we need a circumference of 6.75 units. Given *circumference* = $2 \prod r$, then *r* should be 1.0 units. So, we set the **Transform** component's **Scale** to (2, 0.5, 2). The result looks like this:

Try it in VR. Walk inside the cylinder and look around.

Undesirably, the texture image is also mapped onto the top and bottom circle planes at either end of the cylinder. If you're interested, you can use Blender to build a proper cylinder with no faces on the ends.

However, while panoramas are fun in a "Year 2009" kind of way, the real answer is that panoramic cylinders are pretty lame for VR. Nevertheless, there may be other practical applications of cylindrical projections in VR, especially for the display of two-dimensional quantitative information, which we will explore next.

Infographics

An **infographic** is a visual chart or diagram used to represent information or data. To find examples, just do a Google Image search for "infographics". Infographics can get quite large, which makes them difficult to view on a desktop computer screen, let alone a mobile phone. However, we have virtually infinite space to work with in VR. Let's take a look.

I came across this awesome Histomap chart depicting the history of the world, produced in 1931 by John B. Sparks for Rand McNally. The original is 158 cm tall by 31 cm wide, with an aspect ratio of about 1:5. We'll map it onto a half of the cylinder. That's 180 degrees, twice:

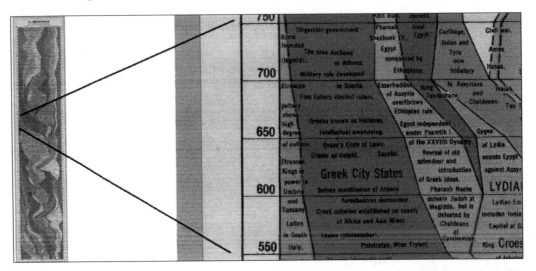

Histomap by John B. Sparks, Rand McNally, 1931 (source http://www.davidrumsey.com/luna/servlet/detail/RUMSEY~8~1~200375~3001080:The-Histomap-)

Let's VR it, as follows:

1. Move `Cylinder 3` out of the way and set its **Position** to (3, 1.5, -3.5).

2. Create a new cylinder by navigating to **GameObject | 3D Object | Cylinder**, set its **Position** to (0, 11.5, 0), and name it `Cylinder 4`.

3. Set the **Scale** to (2, 10, 2).

4. Disable its **Capsule Collider** component by unchecking the checkbox.

5. Import the `Histomap.jpg` image (if it's not already present).

6. Select the `Histomap` texture in **Project Assets**. In the **Inspector** panel's **Import** settings, set **Max Size** to the largest, 8192, so that the text will remain readable. Then, click on **Apply**.

7. Drag the `Histomap` texture onto the cylinder.

8. With `Cylinder 4` selected, in **Inspector**, on the **Histomap** material component, set **Tiling X = -1**.

9. On the **Histomap** material component, navigate to **Shader | Custom | InwardShader**.

Like in the previous example, we can use the aspect ratio of the chart to calculate the correct scale, accounting for the fact that we're tiling it twice (180 degrees) and the default radius is 0.5 units. A **Scale** of (2, 10, 2) works nicely.

We need the largest pixel resolution that we can get (8192) so that the text will be readable. We also need to reverse the texture for the text to be readable on the inside by setting the X-tiling to negative.

The following image is a view inside the infographic tube, looking up towards the top:

To complete this project, we need to give the user a way to move up and down through the infographic tube. For simplicity, we'll move first-person MeMyselfEye to the center of the tube and write a simple head look up down script, as follows:

1. Select MeMyselfEye in **Hierarchy** and reset its transform by selecting its **Transform** component's *gear* icon | **Reset**.
2. Create a new script by navigating to **Add Component** | **New Script** and name it HeadLookUpDown.

Edit the HeadLookUpDown.cs script, as follows:

```
using UnityEngine;
using System.Collections;

public class HeadLookUpDown : MonoBehaviour {
  public float velocity = 0.7f;
```

```
    public float maxHeight = 20f;

  void Update () {
    float moveY = Camera.main.transform.forward.y * velocity *
    Time.deltaTime;
    float newY = transform.position.y + moveY;
    if (newY >= 0f && newY < maxHeight) {
      transform.position = new Vector3 (transform.position.x,
      newY, transform.position.z);
    }
  }
}
```

The script uses the direction of your gaze (`Camera.main.transform.forward`) to determine a vertical offset, which is applied to the current transform position (clipped by the minimum and maximum values).

Try it in VR. *Now that is really interesting!*

For further enhancement, we can add a **Spotlight** as a child of the `Head` object of `MeMyselfEye`. So, as you move your head, it illuminates what you're reading, like a miner's headlamp.

1. In **Hierarchy**, find the `Main Camera` child of `MeMyselfEye`.

2. Right-click and navigate to **Light | Spotlight**.

3. Adjust the **Light** parameters as follows: **Range**: 4, **Spot Angle**: 140, and **Intensity**: 0.6.

4. For a more dramatic effect, if the ambient light and shadows from outside the tube are interfering, you may want to uncheck the **Receive Shadows** checkbox in the **Mesh Renderer** component and disable **Directional Light**.

Try it in VR. *We have a reading lamp!*

Equirectangular projections

Ever since it was discovered that the Earth is round, cartographers and mariners have struggled with how to project the spherical globe onto a two-dimensional chart. The variations are plentiful and the history is fascinating (if you're fascinated by that sort of thing!) The result is an inevitable distortion of some areas of the globe.

 To learn more about map projections and spherical distortions, visit http://en.wikipedia.org/wiki/Map_projection.

As a computer graphics designer, it's perhaps a little less mysterious than it was to ancient mariners because we know about *UV Texture mapping*.

3D computer models in Unity are defined by *meshes*—a set of Vector3 points connected with edges, forming triangular shaped facets. You can unwrap a mesh (in Blender, for instance) into a flattened 2D configuration to define the mapping of texture pixels to the corresponding areas on the mesh surface (the UV coordinates). A globe of the Earth, when unwrapped, will be distorted, as defined by the unwrapped mesh. The resulting image is called a UV Texture image.

In computer graphic modeling, this UV mapping can be arbitrary and depends on the artistic requirements at hand. However, for 360-degree media, this is typically done using an **equirectangular** (or a Meridian) projection (for more information, visit `http://en.wikipedia.org/wiki/Equirectangular_projection`), where the sphere is unraveled into a cylindrical projection, stretching the texture as you progress towards the north and south poles while keeping the meridians as equidistant vertical straight lines. The following *Tissot's Indicatrix* (visit `http://en.wikipedia.org/wiki/Tissot%27s_indicatrix` for more information) shows a globe with strategically arranged identical circles (illustration by Stefan Kühn):

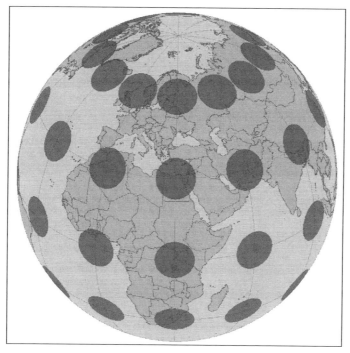

Tissot's indicatrix illustration by Stefan Kuhn, Creative Commons license
(source `https://en.wikipedia.org/wiki/Tissot%27s_indicatrix`)

The following image shows the globe unwrapped with an equirectangular projection:

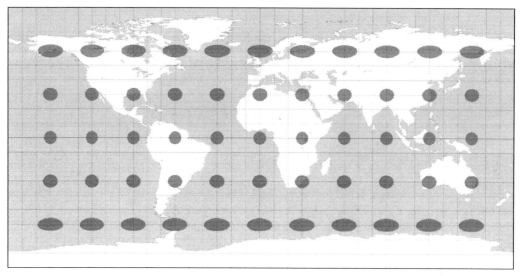

Equirectangular projection illustration by Eric Gaba (Sting), Wikimedia Commons license
(source https://en.wikipedia.org/wiki/Equirectangular_projection)

We will use an equirectangular mesh for our photo spheres and an appropriately projected (warped) image for its texture map.

Globes

First, let's use a standard Unity sphere, such as the one that we used in the earlier *Crystal Ball* example with the Earth texture image. Import this `Tissot_euirectangular.png` image, which is included with this book and perform the following steps:

1. Move `Cylinder 4` out of the way and set its **Position** to (-3, 0, -3.5).

2. Create a new sphere by navigating to **GameObject | 3D Object | Sphere**, set its **Position** to (0, 1.5, 0), and name it `Sphere 5`. Add the Rotator script if you want.

3. Drag the texture named `Tissot_equirectangular` onto the sphere.

4. Try it in VR. Take a close look at the globe, as shown in the following image:

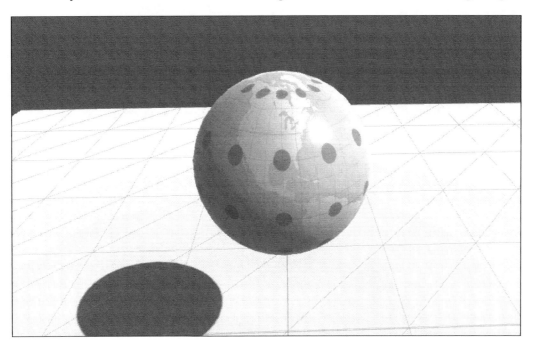

Note that unfortunately, the Tissot circles are oval, not circular, except along the equator. It turns out that the default sphere provided in Unity does not mesh well for equirectangular texture maps. Instead, I have provided one designed specifically for this purpose, `PhotoSphere.fbx` (which happens to be the default sphere model in 3D Studio Max). Let's try it:

1. Move `Sphere 5` out of the way and set its **Position** to (`3`, `1.5`, `1.5`).
2. Import the file. From the **Project** panel (perhaps while the `Assets/Models` folder is selected, if you have created one), right-click and select **Import New Asset...**, and find the `PhotoSphere.fbx` file to import it.
3. Create a new equirectangular sphere by dragging the `PhotoSphere` prefab from **Project Assets** into **Scene**.
4. Set its **Position** to (`0`, `1.5`, `0`) and name it `Sphere 6`. Add the `Rotator` script if you want.
5. Drag the texture named `Tissot_equirectangular` onto the sphere.

Try it in VR. *Much better.* You can see the texture is correctly mapped now; the circles are round:

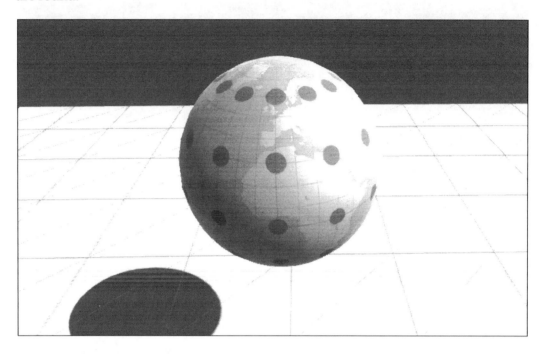

Photospheres

Yes sir, it's all the rage these days. It's better than panoramas. It's better than selfies. It's maybe even better than Snapchat! We're finally getting to the moment that you've been waiting for! It's 360-degree photospheres!

We have covered a lot of topics in this chapter, which will now make it fairly easy to talk about 360-degree photospheres. Now, all we need is a 360-degree photo. You can try searching on Google Images for a 360-degree photo. Alternatively, you can check out the Flickr pool (`https://www.flickr.com/groups/equirectangular/pool/`). You can also make your own using a Ricoh Theta camera, or Google's Photo Sphere app that is available for Android and iOS. For this example, I'll use one named `FarmHouse.jpg`, which is provided with this book:

Let's build it. Here are the complete steps to set up a photo sphere in Unity, starting with a new empty scene:

1. Create a new scene by navigating to **File | New Scene**. Then, navigate to **File | Save Scene** and name it PhotoSphere.

2. Create an equirectangular sphere by dragging the PhotoSphere model from **Project Assets/Models** into the Scene (as imported from PhotoSphere.fbx in the previous example).

3. Reset its **Transform** component's *gear* icon | **Reset**.

4. Set its **Scale** to (10, 10, 10).

5. Create a material by navigating to **Assets | Create | Material** and rename it to PhotoSphereMat.

6. With PhotoSphereMat selected, navigate to **Shader | Custom | InwardShader** (as created earlier in this chapter in the *Magic orbs* section).

7. If there will be other objects in the scene, you may need to disable shadows. In the **Mesh Renderer** component, uncheck the **Receive Shadows** checkbox.

8. Disable global **Directional Light** in the scene (uncheck it).

9. Illuminate the inside of the sphere. Add a point light by navigating to **GameObject | Light | Point Light** and reset its **Transform** component's *gear* icon | **Reset**.

10. Delete Main Camera in the scene.

11. Drag an instance of `MeMyselfEye` from **Project Assets** into the Scene and set its **Position** to (`0, -0.4, 0`).

12. Import the photo that you want to use; ours is named `FarmHouse.jpg`. In its **Import** settings, choose the highest **Max Size** to `8192`.

13. With `PhotoSphere` selected (or the `PhotoSphereMat` itself), drag the `FarmHouse` texture onto the **Albedo** texture tile.

If you are using a device with positional tracking, such as the Oculus Rift, we need to disable it, as follows:

1. Select the `MemMyselfEye` object in **Hierarchy**.

2. Navigate to **Add Component | New Script** and name it `DisablePositionalTracking`.

Edit the `DisablePositionalTracking.cs` script, as follows:

```
using UnityEngine;
using System.Collections;

public class DisablePositionalTracking : MonoBehaviour {
  private Vector3 position;

  void Start () {
    position = Camera.main.transform.position;
  }

  void Update () {
    Camera.main.transform.position = position;
  }
}
```

This script just resets the camera position to its starting position on each update. Save the script and try it in VR.

A few notes about what we did. The creation of the sphere, material, and the custom shader was covered earlier in the chapter.

The `MeMyselfEye` prefab that was set up in *Chapter 3, VR Build & Run* has the camera positioned 0.4 units above its center. We want the camera at the origin, (0,0,0). The correct way to experience a photo sphere in VR is the dead center, and while you can turn your head in all directions to look around, positional tracking should be disabled. (Another technique for making the head position stationary is to scale `MeMyselfEye` to a very large size.)

Including a point light dead center is also a good idea. Although, if your image has obvious light sources, it can be effective to position one or more lights at other locations within the sphere.

Perhaps, there's a way to improve the custom shader so that it does not receive shadows or light sources from the outside. However, we made these adjustments manually.

To switch images, repeat the last two steps—import the asset and assign it to the **Albedo** texture of the `PhotoSphereMat` material. If you want to do this in game, you can do this in a script (for example, by using `Material.mainTexture()`).

Playing 360-degree videos is similar to this; you use `MovieTexture` instead of an image texture. There are limitations with movie textures on mobile devices. Please read the Unity documentation for details (`http://docs.unity3d.com/Manual/class-MovieTexture.html`). Or consider using a third-party solutions in the Unity Assets Store.

Field of view – FOV

OK, we looked at spheres, cylinders, balls, and orbs. That was fun! Now, let's talk some more about 360-degree media and virtual reality and why it seems so compelling. There's a huge difference in the experience of viewing a 360-degree video on a flat screen versus inside a VR headset. Why?

In a theater, on a computer screen, or in VR, the angle from one edge of the view area to the opposite is commonly referred to as the angle of view or **field of view** (FOV). For example, an IMAX cinema theater with larger screens than that of the conventional cinema encompasses more of your peripheral vision and has a wider field of view. The following table compares the horizontal field of view of various viewing experiences. A wider field of view is important to provide immersive experiences.

These FOV values pertain to looking in one direction without moving your head or eyes:

Viewing experience	Horizontal field of view (FOV)
A 27" computer monitor	26 degrees
A movie theater	54 degrees
An IMAX theater	70 degrees
Google Cardboard	90 degrees
Oculus Rift DK2	100 degrees

Viewing experience	Horizontal field of view (FOV)
GoPro camera	74 - 140 degrees
Human vision	180 degrees

In Unity, the **Camera** component that is used to render a scene has a configurable FOV angle. This setting adjusts the size of the viewport rectangle, or *frustum*, that is used to peer into the scene. It's like adjusting a real camera lens' focal length (for instance, normal versus wide angle). This viewport is mapped to the physical display, be it a TV, monitor, or a mobile device screen.

 For more information about FOV adjustments in conventional video games, read this excellent article, *All about Field of View (FOV)*, (July 18, 2014) by visiting http://steamcommunity.com/sharedfiles/filedetails/?id=287241027.

Similarly, inside a VR head-mounted display is a physical mobile phone-sized screen with physical width and height. However, through the headset lenses, the apparent width of the screen is much bigger (and further away).

In VR, you're not so obviously limited by the FOV and physical dimensions of the screen, because you can easily move your head to change your view direction at any time. This provides a fully immersive view, horizontal 360 degrees, as you look side to side and up and down by 180 degrees. In VR, the field of view is only significant with regard to the outer reaches of your peripheral vision and eyeball movement.

To recap, this is how viewing a 360-degree photosphere works:

- Say we have an equirectangular sphere defined by a mesh of small triangular faces
- An equirectangular-projected texture is mapped onto the inside of a sphere
- We have a VR camera rig at the center of the sphere with left and right eye cameras
- The cameras see a section of the inside of the sphere, limited by the field of view
- As you move your head in VR, the area that the cameras see changes in unison with your movement
- You will have an uninterrupted view of the 360-degree image

It may not be real-time 3D computer graphics, but that, my friend, is still cool.

Capturing a 360-degree media

So far, we've been talking about monoscopic media—a 360-degree photo or video shot with a single lens point of view, albeit from all directions. When viewed in VR, yes, there are left and right eyes, but this is a stereo view of the same flat image that was projected onto a sphere. It doesn't provide any real parallax or illusion of depth through occlusion. You can rotate your head, but you should not move its position from the center of the sphere. Otherwise, the immersive illusion may be broken.

What about true 360-degree stereo? What if each eye has its own photo sphere offset from the other eye's position? Stereoscopic 360-degree recording and playback is a very difficult problem.

To capture non-stereo 360-degree media, you can use a rig such as GoPro Kolor, pictured in the following image on the left. It records all six directions at once with six separate GoPro cameras. The synchronized videos are then stitched together with special, advanced imaging software, much like the Photo Sphere app mentioned at the beginning of this chapter, but for videos.

To capture stereo 360-degree media, you'd need a rig such as Google Jump, which arranges 16 separate GoPro cameras in a cylindrical array, pictured at the center of the following image. Advanced image processing software then constructs stereographic views using batch cloud processing power that may take hours to complete.

 For a more detailed explanation of how rigs such as the Google Jump 16-camera array work, read the article, *Stereographic 3D Panoramic Images*, by Paul Bourke (May, 2002) by visiting `http://paulbourke.net/stereographics/stereopanoramic/`.

To capture fully immersive 360-degree media, new technologies such as the JauntVR NEO light field camera, pictured in the following image, on the right-hand side, are being invented from the ground up, specifically for cinematic VR content:

| GoPro Kolor | Google Jump | JauntVR NEO |

Time will tell how these media technologies will develop and become a part of our creative toolbox.

Want In-game 360 Degree Image Captures?

You can capture a 360-degree equirectangular panorama of the player's in-game surroundings and save/upload it for later viewing using a Unity plugin created by eVRydayVR. See `https://www.assetstore.unity3d.com/en/#!/content/38755`.

Summary

In this chapter, we started simply by mapping a regular image on to the outside of a sphere. Then, we inverted it with a custom shader, mapping the image inside the sphere. We explored cylindrical projections of panoramas and large infographics. Then, we took several sections to understand equirectangular spherical projections and photospheres and how they're used for 360-degree immersive media in virtual reality. Lastly, we explored some of the technology behind viewing and capturing 360-degree media.

In the next chapter, we go social as we look at ways to add multi-user networking to Unity VR projects and how to add scenes to the emerging metaverse. Multiplayer games are familiar to most of us, but when combined with virtual reality, this provides a social experience that is unparalleled by any other technology. We will learn about networking technology and the new Unity Networking features that were introduced in Unity 5.1.

10
Social VR Metaverse

That's me, Linojon, the guy with a baseball cap in front, to the left! Momentously, the preceding photo was captured during the eve of the metaverse on December 21, 2014 in a live VRChat session. I had built a seasonally-themed world named GingerLand and invited my chat room friends to visit during one of the weekly meetups. Then, someone suggested, "Hey, let's take a group picture!" So, we all assembled on the front porch of my wintery cabin and said, "Cheese!" The rest is history.

For many people, the visceral experience of socially interacting live with other people in VR is at least as dramatic as the difference between using Facebook versus browsing a static website, or sharing Snapchats versus viewing an online photo album. It's very personal and alive. If you've tried it out yourself, you know exactly what I mean. We're now going to look at how social VR experiences can be implemented using Unity. There are many approaches, from building it from scratch to plugging into an existing VR world. In this chapter, we will discuss the following topics:

- An introduction to how multiplayer networking works
- Implementing a multiplayer scene that runs in VR using the Unity networking engine
- Building and sharing a custom VRChat room

Note that the projects in this chapter are separate and not directly required by the other chapters in this book. If you decide to skip any of it or not save your work, that's OK.

Multiplayer networking

Before we begin implementation, let's take a look at what multiplayer networking is all about and define some terms.

Networking services

Consider a situation where you are running a VR application that is connected to a server, and several of your friends are running the same application on their own VR rigs at the same time. When you move your first-person view within the game, shoot things, or otherwise interact with the virtual environment, you expect the other players to see that, too. Their version of the game stays in sync with yours and vice versa. How does this work?

Your game creates a connection to a server. Other players are simultaneously connected to the same service. When you move, your character's new position is broadcast to each of the other connections, which then updates your avatar's position in their own views. Similarly, when your game receives the changed position of another character, it is updated in your view. The faster, the better. That is, the less delay (latency) between the *send* and *receive* messages and the corresponding screen updates, the more live, or real time, the interaction feels.

Multiplayer services should help you manage the sharing of the game's state between all active clients, the spawning of new players and objects, security considerations, as well as the management of low-level network connections, protocols, and the quality of service (such as data rate and performance).

Networking is built as a series of layers, where the low-level layers deal with details of the data transport and are agnostic to the content of the data. Middle and higher layers provide increasingly aggregated features that also may be more directly helpful for the networking application—in our case, multiplayer gaming and social VR. Ideally, the high-level layer will provide all you need to implement multiplayer features into your games with minimal custom scripting, while offering access to other layers through a clean API in case you have special requirements.

There are a number of multiplayer services available, including Photon from Exit Games, and other services from Google, Apple, Microsoft, Amazon, and more.

The popular Photon Cloud service can be easily added using their free **Photon Unity Networking (PUN)** package from the Unity Asset Store (for more information, visit `https://www.assetstore.unity3d.com/#/content/1786`). If you are interested in trying Photon with VR, take a look at `http://www.convrge.co/multiplayer-oculus-rift-games-in-unity-tutorial`, a blog post from Convrge.

Unity 5 has its own built-in Unity networking system, which was recently rewritten from scratch and greatly improved from what it was in Unity 4. Unity networking reduces the need for custom scripting and provides a feature-rich set of components and API that tightly integrate with Unity.

The network architecture

The key to networking is the client-server system architecture. We see this all around us in today's world—your web browser is a client and websites are hosted on a server. Your favorite music listening app is a client, and its streaming service is a server. Similarly, each instance of your game, when connected to a network, is a client. It talks to a server, which communicates the status and control information between all the other game clients.

I say *server*, but it doesn't necessarily need to be a separate physical computer somewhere. It could be, but it's probably not. It's best to think of a client and server as *processes*—instances of a program or an application running somewhere. A **cloud server** is a virtual process that is accessible via the Internet as a service.

A single app can sometimes act as both a client and a server at the same time. This latter case, where the server and client are one, is said to be running as a host. With Unity networking, games can be run as a client, a server, and/or as a host.

Even so, a public **IP (Internet Protocol)** address is needed for game instances to talk to one another. A lightweight relay server can provide this service with minimal resources.

Local versus server

In Unity, you can use scripting to create, or instantiate, new objects during gameplay. In a multiplayer situation, these objects need to be activated, or spawned, locally as well as on the network so that all the clients will know about it. A *spawning system* manages objects across all the clients.

 It is important to make a distinction between objects that are *local player objects* versus the network ones. Local player objects are owned by you on your client.

For example, in a first-person experience, your player's avatar will be spawned with a Camera component, whereas the other players' avatars will not. It is also an important security consideration to prevent users from hacking a game and changing other player's characters.

Local player objects have *local authority*, that is, the player object is responsible for controlling itself, such as its own movement. Otherwise, when the creation, movement, and destruction of objects are not controlled by a player, the authority should reside on the server.

On the other hand, *server authority* is needed. For example, when a game creates enemies at random locations, you'd want all the clients to get the same random locations. When a new player joins an ongoing game, the server helps create and set up objects that are active in the current gameplay. You wouldn't want an object to show up in its default position and then jump to a different current position as it's syncing with the other clients.

The following image from Unity documentation shows ways in which actions are performed across the network. The server makes **remote procedure calls (RPC)** to the client to spawn or update objects.

The client sends commands to the server to affect actions, which then are communicated to all the remote clients:

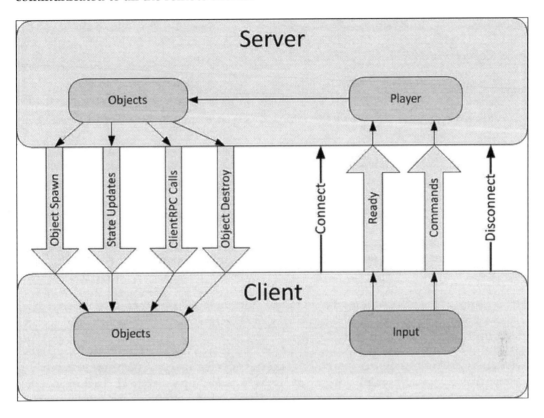

Real-time networking is a deep engineering discipline. Layered network architectures aim to simplify and shield you from brutally arcane details.

 It all comes down to performance, security, and reliability. If you need to debug or optimize any of these in your multiplayer game, you may need to dig in your heels and work to gain a better understanding of what's going on under the hood.

The Unity networking system

The Unity networking engine includes a robust set of high-level components (scripts) that make it easy to add multiplayer capabilities to your games. Some of the more important components include *Network Identity, Network Behavior, Network Transform,* and *Network Manager.*

The *Network Identity* component is required on each game object prefab that may be spawned (created) on clients. Internally, it provides a unique asset ID and other parameters so that objects can be unambiguously identified and spawned across the network.

The *Network Behavior* class is derived from `MonoBehavior` and provides network functionality to scripts. Details of the same are documented at `http://docs.unity3d.com/Manual/class-NetworkBehaviour.html`.

When you want to synchronize the movement and physics of objects, add a *Network Transform* component. It's like a shortcut for the more general `SyncVar` variable synchronization with additional intelligent interpolation for smoother movement between updates.

The *Network Manager* component is the glue that puts it all together. It handles the managing of connections, the spawning of objects across the network, and configuration.

When new player objects are spawned, you can specify a spawn position in the *Network Manager* component. Alternatively, you can add game objects to your scene and give them a *Network Start Position* component, which can be used by the spawning system.

Nonplayer objects that can get spawned can also be set in the *Network Manager* spawn list. Additionally, the *Network Manager* component handles scene changes and provides debugging information.

Related to the *Network Manager* component is the matchmaking functionality, which can be configured to match up players, making them come together and start a game at the same time—a multiplayer *lobby manager*, where players can set themselves as ready for the game to start, is among the other useful features.

Setting up a simple scene

Let's jump right in and make our own multiplayer demo project.

For instructional purposes, we'll start out with a very simple scene with a standard first-person camera to get the networking implemented. Then, we'll adapt it to VR.

Creating a scene environment

To get set up, we will make a new scene with a ground plane and a cube, then we'll create a basic first-person character.

Create a new scene by navigating to **File | New Scene**. Then, **File | Save Scene As...** and name the scene `MultiPlayer`.

Create a new plane by navigating to **GameObject | 3D Object | Plane**, rename it `GroundPlane`, and reset its **Transform** using the **Transform** component's *gear* icon | **Reset**. Make the plane bigger by setting **Scale** to (`10, 1, 10`). Perform the following steps:

1. Make `GroundPlane` easier on the eyes with a gray material. Navigate to **Assets | Create | Material**, name it `Gray`, click on its **Albedo** color chip, and select a neutral gray, such as RGB (150, 150, 150). Drag the `Gray` material onto `GroundPlane`.

2. To provide some context and orientation, we'll just add a cube. Navigate to **GameObject | 3D Object | Cube**, reset its **Transform** using the **Transform** component's *gear* icon | **Reset**. Set its **Position** a bit to the side to something like (`-2, 0.75, 1`).

3. Give the cube some color. Navigate to **Assets | Create | Material**, name it `Red`, click on its **Albedo** color chip, and select a nice red, such as RGB (`240, 115, 115`). Drag the `Red` material onto the cube.

Next, we'll add a standard first-person character, `FPSController`, as follows:

1. If you do not have the standard **Characters** assets package loaded, navigate to **Assets | Import Package | Characters** and choose **Import**.

2. Find the `FPSController` in **Project Assets / Standard Assets / Characters / FirstPersonCharacter / Prefabs / FPSController** and drag it into the scene.

3. Reset its **Transform** using the **Transform** component's *gear* icon | **Reset**. Set it looking at the front of objects. Set **Position** to (5, 1.4, 3) and **Rotation** to (0, 225, 0).

4. With FPSController selected, in the **Inspector**, on the **First Person Controller** component, check off the **Is Walking** checkbox and set **Walk Speed** to 1.

If you're currently using a project with VR enabled in **Player Settings**, please disable it for the time being:

1. Navigate to **File** | **Build Settings....** In the **Build Settings** dialog box, select **Player Settings...** and then, under **Other Settings**, uncheck the **Virtual Reality Supported** checkbox.

2. Save the scene. Click on the *Play* mode and verify that you can move and look around as usual using a keyboard (*WASD*), arrows, and a mouse.

Creating an avatar head

Next, you'll need an avatar to represent yourself and your friends. Again, I'm going to keep this super simple so that we can focus on the fundamentals. Forget about a body for now. Just make a floating head with a face. Here's what I did. Your mileage may vary. Just be sure that it's facing forward (the positive Z direction):

1. Create an avatar container. Navigate to **GameObject** | **Create Empty**, rename it Avatar, reset its transformation using the **Transform** component's *gear* icon | Reset. Set its Position to eye level, such as (0, 1.4, 0).

2. Create a sphere under the Avatar for the head. Navigate to **GameObject** | **3D Object** | **Sphere**, rename it Head, reset its transformation using the **Transform** component's *gear* icon | **Reset**, and set **Scale** to (0.5, 0.5, 0.5).

3. Give the head some color. Navigate to **Assets** | **Create** | **Material**, name it Blue, click on its **Albedo** color chip, and select a nice blue, such as RGB (115, 115, 240). Drag the Blue material onto the Head.

4. The dude has got to be cool (albeit bald headed). We'll borrow a pair of Ethan's glasses and put them on the head. Navigate to **GameObject** | **Create Empty**, rename it Glasses, reset its transformation using the **Transform** component's *gear* icon | **Reset**, and set its **Position** to (0, -5.6, 0.1) and **Scale** to (4, 4, 4).

5. Then, while Glasses is selected, go to the Project pane, find Assets / Standard Assets / Characters / ThirdPersonCharacter / Models / Ethan / EthanGlasses.fbx (the mesh file), and drag it into the **Inspector** panel. *Be sure to select the fbx* version of EthanGlasses, not the prefab.

6. It has a mesh, but it needs a material. While Glasses is selected, go to the **Project** pane, find Assets / Standard Assets / Characters / ThirdPersonCharacter / Materials / EthanWhite, and drag it into the **Inspector** panel.

The following screenshot shows a version of mine (which also includes a mouth):

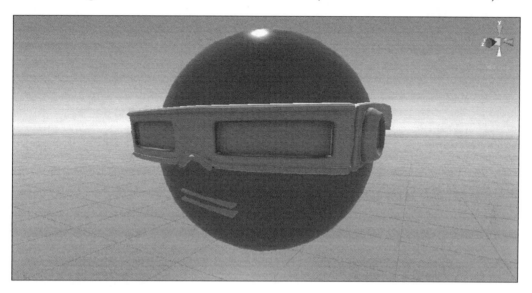

When running as multiplayer, an instance of the avatar will get spawned for each connected player. So, we must first save the object as a prefab and remove it from the scene, as follows:

1. With Avatar selected in the **Hierarchy** panel, drag it into **Project Assets**.

2. Select Avatar again from the **Hierarchy** panel and delete it.

3. Save the scene.

OK. Now, we should be ready to add multiplayer networking.

Adding multiplayer networking

To make the scene run as multiplayer we need, at a minimum, a Network Manager component, and we need to identify any objects that will get spawned using the Network Identity component.

Network Manager and HUD

First, we'll add the Network Manager component, as follows:

1. Navigate to **GameObject** | **Create Empty** and rename it `NetworkController`.
2. Navigate to **Add Component** | **Network** | **Network Manager**.
3. Navigate to **Add Component** | **Network** | **Network Manager HUD**.

We also added a **Network Controller HUD** menu, a crude default menu that Unity offers to select the runtime networking options (you can see it in the images that follow). It's for development. In a real project, you'll probably replace the default HUD with something more appropriate.

Network Identity and Transform

Next, add a Network Identity to the `Avatar` prefab. We will also add a Network Transform, which instructs the networking system to synchronize the player's **Transform** values to the avatar instances on each client, as follows:

1. In **Project Assets**, select the `Avatar` prefab.
2. Navigate to **Add Component** | **Network** | **Network Identity**.
3. Check off the **Local Player Authority** checkbox.
4. Navigate to **Add Component** | **Network** | **Network Transform**.
5. Ensure that **Transform Sync Mode** is set to **Sync Transform** and **Rotation Axis** is set to **XYZ (full 3D)**.
6. Now, tell the Network Manager that our `Avatar` prefab represents players.
7. In **Hierarchy**, select `NetworkController`.
8. In **Inspector**, unfold the **Network Manager Spawn Info** parameters so that you can see the **Player Prefab** slot.
9. In **Project Assets**, find the `Avatar` prefab and drag it onto the **Player Prefab** slot.
10. Save the scene.

Running as a host

Click on the *Play* mode. As shown in the following screenshot, the screen comes up with the HUD start menu, which lets you select whether you wish to run and connect this game:

Choose **LAN Host**. This will initiate a server (default port 7777 on localhost) and spawn an Avatar. The avatar is positioned at a default location, (0, 0, 0). Also, it's not connected to the camera. So, it is more like a third-person view.

The next thing to do is run a second instance of the game and see two spawned avatars in the scene. However, we wouldn't want them to overlap as both are positioned at the origin, So first, define a couple of spawn positions.

Adding spawn positions

To add a spawn position, you just need a game object with a Network Start Position component:

1. Navigate to **GameObject | Create Empty**, rename it Spawn1, and set its **Position** to (0, 1.4, 1).

2. Navigate to **Add Component | Network | Network Start Position**.

3. Navigate to **GameObject | Create Empty**, rename it Spawn2, and set its **Position** to (0, 1.4, -1).

4. Navigate to **Add Component | Network | Network Start Position**.

5. In **Hierarchy**, select NetworkController. In **Inspector > Network Manager > Spawn Info, Player Spawn Method**, select **Round Robin**.

We now have two different spawn locations. The Network Manager will choose one or the other when a new player joins the game.

Running two instances of the game

A reasonable way to run two copies of the game on the same machine is to build and run one instance as a separate executable and the other instance from the Unity editor (the *Play* mode). Build the executable as usual:

1. Navigate to **File | Build Settings...**.

2. In the **Build Settings** dialog box, ensure that the **Platform** is set to **PC, Mac & Linux Standalone** and the **Target Platform** is set to your current development OS.

3. Click on **Player Settings...** and in the **Inspector**, under **Resolution and Presentation**, check off the **Run In Background** checkbox.

4. Ensure that the current scene is the only one checked off in **Scenes In Build**. If it's not present, click on **Add Current**.

5. Select **Build and Run**, give it a name, and then launch the game by double-clicking after it's been built.

Enabling the **Run In Background** will permit the user input controls (keyboard and mouse) in each window when running the executables.

In the Unity editor, click on the *Play* mode and select **LAN Host**, like we did previously. Double-click on the executable app and check off the **Windowed** checkbox so that it's not fullscreen. Then, in the executable window, select **LAN Client**. In each game, you should now see two instances of the avatar, one for each player, as shown in the following screenshot:

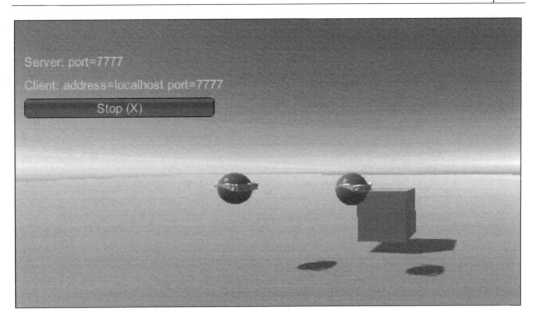

If you want to run an instance of the game on a separate machine, enter the IP address of the host machine into the **Client** input field (for instance, 10.0.1.14 on my LAN) instead of localhost.

A few keyboard shortcuts can also come in handy. On the HUD, use **H** for select Host, **C** to select Client, and use *Alt + Tab* (or *Command + Tab* on Mac) to switch between windows without using the mouse.

Associating avatar with the first-person character

It's not very interesting if the avatars don't move. That's the last piece of the puzzle.

You might think that we should have parented the avatar object under the first-person controller, FPSController, renamed and saved it as a Prefab, and then told the Network Manager to use that for spawns. But then, you'd end up with multiple FPSControllers in the scene, each with active cameras and controller scripts listening to user input. Not good.

We must have only one active FPSController, one camera, one instance of the input controller, and so on. Other players' avatars get spawned but are not controlled here. In other words, when the local player (and only the local player) gets spawned, that avatar should become a child of the camera. To achieve this, we will write a script:

1. In **Project Assets**, select Avatar, navigate to **Add Component | New Script**, name it AvatarMultiplayer.cs, and open it in MonoDevelop.

2. Edit the AvatarMultiplayer.cs script, as follows:

```
using UnityEngine;
using UnityEngine.Networking;

public class AvatarMultiplayer : NetworkBehaviour {

    public override void OnStartLocalPlayer () {
        GameObject camera = GameObject.FindWithTag ("MainCamera");
        transform.parent = camera.transform;
        transform.localPosition = Vector3.zero;
    }
}
```

The first thing you'll notice is that we need to include the UnityEngine.Networking library to access the networking API. Then, the class AvatarMultiplayer is a type of NetworkBehaviour, which internally is derived from MonoBehavior.

NetworkBehaviour provides a lot of new callback functions. We are going to use OnStartLocalPlayer, which gets called whenever the local player object is spawned. However, it is not called when the remote player objects are spawned. Its declaration requires the override keyword.

OnStartLocalPlayer is exactly what we want because only when a local player is spawned do we want to parent it to the camera. We got the current MainCamera object (GameObject.FindWithTag ("MainCamera")) and made it the avatar's parent (transform.parent = camera.transform). We also reset the avatar's transform so that it's centered at the camera's position.

Run two instances of the game—**Build** and **Run** to execute one, and *Play* mode for the other. Now when you control the player in one window, it moves the avatar in the other. Wow! You can even launch more executables and have a party!

Adding multiplayer virtual reality

So far, we've learned about implementing multiplayer networking in Unity, but not specifically for VR. Now, we're ready for this. The way I've set things up, we do not need to change anything in our scene for it to work in VR.

Our avatar is just a head for a reason. In VR, the camera transform is controlled by the head pose from the **HMD (Head-mounted Display)** sensors. When the avatar is parented by the camera, it'll move in sync. While wearing the HMD, when you move your head and look around, the corresponding avatar in all the clients will move accordingly.

The Oculus Rift players

The scene presently has an instance of the standard FPSController, which includes a Camera component. We can use Unity 5's built-in VR support.

Navigate to **File | Build Settings...**. In the **Build Settings** dialog box, select **Player Settings...**. Then, under **Other Settings**, check off the **Virtual Reality Supported** checkbox.

The built-in Network Manager HUD is implemented in screen space. So, it will not appear if you play the scene now. One solution is to write your own HUD in world space to connect the game to the network. Another solution is to start in non-VR mode and then switch on the headset after connecting to the network. We will take the latter approach here, which will require two small scripts:

1. With NetworkController selected in **Hierarchy**, navigate to **Add Component | New Script**, name it NetworkStart, and open it in MonoDevelop.

2. Edit the NetworkStart.cs script, as follows:

```
using UnityEngine;
using UnityEngine.VR;

public class NetworkStart : MonoBehaviour {

  void Awake() {
    VRSettings.enabled = false;
  }
}
```

Note that we're using the `UnityEngine.VR` library. When the game first initializes, `Awake()` is called, where we disable VR. Now, it will start in non-VR mode. The user can see the screen space UI and choose their runtime network options. Then, we enable VR when the player is spawned.

Next, open the `AvatarMultiplayer.cs` script and modify it, as follows:

```
using UnityEngine;
using UnityEngine.Networking;
using UnityEngine.VR;

public class AvatarMultiplayer : NetworkBehaviour {

  public override void OnStartLocalPlayer () {

    VRSettings.enabled = true;

    GameObject camera = GameObject.FindWithTag ("MainCamera");
    transform.parent = camera.transform;
    transform.localPosition = Vector3.zero;
  }
}
```

Save the scene.

Run two instances of the game—**Build** and **Run** to execute one, and *Play* mode for the other. Wow, it's a VR party! When your headset moves, the avatar head moves in each of the clients.

During testing, if you're like me and only have one Oculus Rift (!), you may want to run VR in only one instance. Naturally, providing a **Start** menu with the option to choose a device is one way to go. For the purpose of this example, let's say you can only run VR on the Host instance; other clients are not VR. Modify the `AvatarMultiplayer.cs` script, as follows:

```
  public override void OnStartLocalPlayer () {

    if (isServer) {
      VRSettings.enabled = true;
    }
    . . .
```

We check whether the current instance is running as a server (Host is both a client and a server) using `isServer`. With this *hack*, Host instances can use the Rift, non-Host clients will not.

The Google Cardboard players

For Cardboard, we can use Cardboard's own main camera prefab, `CardboardMain`, instead of the `FPSController`. We'll attempt to add this without affecting anything that is already working so that the same project can build and run on multiple platforms without extra modification.

Add the Cardboard main camera and disable the `FPSController` that is already in the scene, as follows:

1. If you do not have the Google Cardboard SDK package loaded, navigate to **Assets | Import Package | Custom Package...**, find your downloaded copy of `CardboardSDKForUnity.package`, click on **Open** and select **Import**.

2. Find the `CardboardMain` in `Project Assets / Cardboard / Prefabs / CardboardMain` and drag it into the scene.

3. Copy the **Transform** values from `FPSController` or reset its **Transform** using the **Transform** component's *gear* icon | **Reset** and set **Position** to (`5, 1.4, 3`) and **Rotation** to (`0, 225, 0`).

4. Select the `FPSController` in **Hierarchy** and disable it by unchecking the **Enable** checkbox.

Open the script file that we created before, `NetworkStart.cs`, in MonoDevelop and edit it, as follows:

```
using UnityEngine;
using UnityEngine.Networking;
using UnityEngine.VR;

public class NetworkStart : MonoBehaviour {
  public GameObject oculusMain;
  public GameObject cardboardMain;
  public string hostIP = "10.0.1.14";

  void Awake() {
    VRSettings.enabled = false;

#if (UNITY_ANDROID || UNITY_IPHONE)
    oculusMain.SetActive (false);
    cardboardMain.SetActive (true);
```

```
      NetworkManager net = GetComponent<NetworkManager> ();
      net.networkAddress = hostIP;
      net.StartClient ();
#else
      oculusMain.SetActive (true);
      cardboardMain.SetActive (false);
#endif
   }
}
```

The script declares the `public GameObject` variables for `oculusMain` and `cardboardMain`, which we'll set in the Editor.

I don't know about you, but the Network Manager HUD menu is too small on my phone to interact with, especially to enter a custom IP address. So, I've added a built-in IP address into the script instead. My development machine running as host is at `10.0.1.14`.

> This is for the simplicity and development of this example. In a real project, you will provide UI in the game or use the Unity cloud services.

You can now build for Android and install the app on your phone. (Instructions for Cardboard on iOS are similar). As explained in *Chapter 3, VR Build and Run*, ensure that your system is set up for Android development. Then, switch your project build platform to Android, as follows:

1. Navigate to **File | Build Settings...**. In the **Build Settings** dialog box **Platform** area, select **Android** and select **Switch Platform**.

2. Select **Player Settings...**. In the **Inspector** panel, ensure that you've set **Default Orientation: Landscape Left** and set **Bundle Identifier** in **Other Settings**.

3. Save the scene and project. Build an `.apk` file for Android.

4. Switch platforms and build executables for Windows and/or Mac.

5. Fire up the apps on each platform! Party!

The following image is a screenshot of the scene from my Android phone. I have three player games running multiplayer—a Windows build running as Host and using an Oculus Rift, a Mac build running as a client on the Mac, and an Android build running as a client with Cardboard:

Three separate builds of the same project running multiplayer on separate platforms with different VR devices!

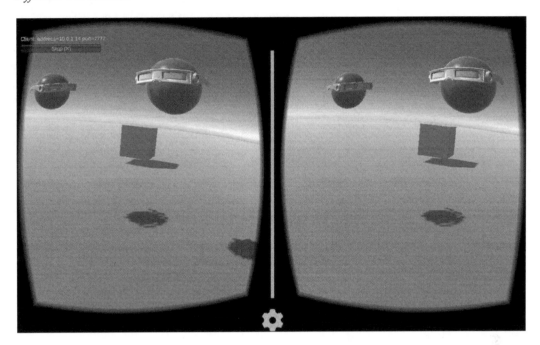

Next steps

This was an introduction to Unity networking with VR. A whole book can be dedicated to this topic. Some areas for further exploration include the following:

- Building a custom world space HUD start menu for network connections and device options.
- Connecting clients via the Unity Multiplayer cloud service.
- Letting users customize their avatar, such as enabling them to choose their own color.
- Showing usernames in an **Info Bubble** above their heads.
- Providing a full-bodied avatar with animation.

- Optimizing data rates for smoother movement.

- Adding chat and/or audio voice communications. For example, take a look at Mumble (`http://www.mumble.com/`) and TeamSpeak (`http://www.teamspeak.com/`).

- Spawning nonplayer objects, such as a bouncy ball and playing a game of headshot volleyball! (See `http://docs.unity3d.com/Manual/UNetSpawning.html` and *Chapter 7, Physics and the Environment* under the *Headshots* section).

Building and sharing a custom VRChat room

If your goal is simpler—to build a virtual reality world and share it with others as a shared social experience—you can use one of the number of existing social VR applications that provide the infrastructure and allow customization. At the time of writing this book, these include VRChat, JanusVR, AltSpaceVR, ConVRge, VRoom, and others.

One of my favorites is VRChat, which we will use in the next project. VRChat is built with Unity, and you can use Unity to make custom worlds and avatars. If you haven't tried it, download a copy of the client from `http://www.vrchat.net/download` and play around with it. (At the time of writing this book, you can enter VRChat using the Oculus Rift, but not on your mobile. However, it can also run in non-VR desktop mode.)

Choose a scene to play in VRChat. Pick any Unity scene you want. It could be the `Diorama` playground that we used earlier in this book, the PhotoGallery from *Chapter 8, Walk-throughs and Rendering*, or something else. Open the scene in Unity that you want to export.

Preparing and building the world

To begin, download the VRChat SDK from `http://www.vrchat.net/download` and check the documentation at `http://www.vrchat.net/docs/sdk/guide` for the latest instructions:

1. Import the VRChat SDK package. Navigate to **Assets | Import Package | Custom Package...**, find your downloaded copy of `VRCSDK-*.package`, click on **Open**, and select **Import**.

2. The object hierarchy required for a VRChat world may be organized in a way that is different from your current scene. So, I recommend that you first save a new copy by navigating to **File | Save Scene As...** and give it a new name, such as VRChatRoom.

3. Create a root object and parent your room objects under it. Navigate to **GameObject | Create Empty**, rename it Room. Select all the objects in the **Hierarchy** panel that belong to it and drag them as the children of Room. Do not include any cameras or anything else that you do not want to export.

4. Add the VRC_SceneDescriptor script to Room. In **Hierarchy**, select Room and then navigate to **Add Component | Scripts | VRCSDK2 | VRC_Scene Descriptor**.

5. Create a position. Navigate to **GameObject | Create Empty**, rename it Spawn, and move as a child of Room. In the **Scene** view, drag into position.

6. With Room selected in **Hierarchy**, unfold the Spawns list in **Inspector**, set **Size** to 1, and then drag the Spawn object into the **Element 0** slot.

7. Export the world. Select Room in the **Hierarchy** and then, navigate to **VRChat | Build and Run Custom Scene from Selection**.

You can preview this in VRChat.

Host the world

When you're ready to share your room with the world, you need to copy the built .vrcs file to a web-accessible location, such as a public Dropbox folder or a web server. You'll need to paste the URL of the file. So, grab a copy of that, and perform the following steps:

1. Launch the VRChat client.

2. Click on the **Create a Room** button.

3. Click on the **Level Name** dropdown and select **Custom**.

4. Paste or enter the URL of your world (such as http://mywebsite.com/myWorld.vrcs).

5. Click on **Hide Room** if you don't want your room to appear in the room list. Click on **Persistent** if you don't want your room to disappear from the list after everybody has left your room.

6. Click on **Create Room**.

The following image shows the dialog box inside VRChat:

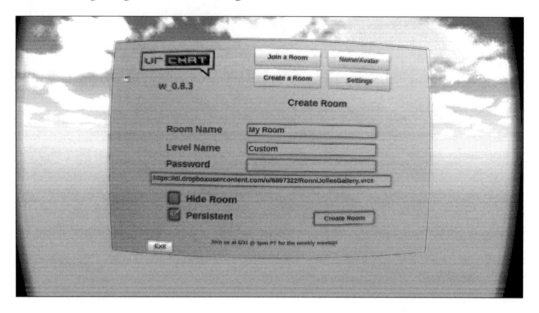

There you have it. It's immediately accessible to every friend and foe. Press *V* to speak (*Esc* for other options). Now you and others can join your room, play, and *partttteeee!*

Summary

In this chapter, we learned about networking concepts and architecture, and used some of the many features of Unity's own multiplayer networking system. We built a simple scene and an avatar, keeping in mind that the intent was to allow the avatar's head movement to be synchronized with the player's head-mounted display.

We then converted the scene to multiplayer, adding the Unity Network components, which simplified the multiplayer implementation to just a handful of clicks.

Next, we added virtual reality to the multiplayer experience, first by using Unity's built-in support for the Oculus Rift and then by adding Google Cardboard support for Android.

Finally, I showed you how easy it is to create a virtual room in the VRChat metaverse by exporting a scene that you can share almost instantly.

11
What's Next?

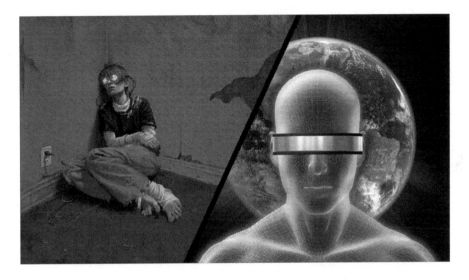

Composite, Getty Images (book cover image) and VR addict Public Domain
(source http://www.wallpapershome.com/art/graphics/wallpaper-cyberpunk-virtual-
reality-glass-addict-room-395.html)

Whether you read this book from the beginning to the end or jumped around picking and choosing what you wanted to try, I hope you learned a thing or two about virtual reality, Unity, and how to build your own VR experiences. This is just the beginning for all of us. We are pioneers, and you have an opportunity to help invent the future.

I have a few more parting thoughts that are more philosophical than you might expect in a technical book like this.

Humans are especially good at navigating 3D spaces and remembering where they've been. Having visited a place in person, you're much more likely to retain its memory than if you were just told about it. There are proven memorization techniques, such as the *memory palace*, where you remember names at a dinner party or lines of Shakespeare by building an imaginary castle in your mind with hallways and rooms representing places to "store" things. It works because it draws upon our innate abilities to remember spaces.

With this instinctive spatial memory, we form cognitive maps that help us solve problems, which might otherwise prove too abstract or complex. Such capacities have been attributed not only to physical navigation, but also to engineering, mathematics, music, literature, visual thinking, science, social models, and, in fact, most areas of human endeavor. We engage *mental models* to gain critical understanding of the problems at hand.

One reason behind why virtual reality is compelling is because it exploits our inherent capacity to experience and use three-dimensional spaces without being limited to the physical world. Applications of VR offer the promise of enhancing human memory and intelligence.

Photorealism is not necessarily required. It's now recognized that *almost-real* is often worse than cartoons in what's called the **uncanny valley**, where we experience virtuality, especially humanoid characters, as creepy and unnatural (for more information, visit http://en.wikipedia.org/wiki/Uncanny_valley). Realism can be good up to a point, but sometimes, abstraction or cartooning is more effective. Keep this in mind when designing your own VR experiences.

Still, many people are drawn to virtual reality with the expectation or at least the eventual promise of have realistic real-life experiences in cyberspace. I think that this is a mistake. Do not assume that for VR to succeed, we must experience a full sensory simulation of life-like virtual environments. Are you going to just jack yourself into the metaverse with feeding tubes, like *The Matrix* or *Ready Player One*?

More likely, as VR goes mainstream, it will develop into its own medium for expression, communications, education, problem solving, and storytelling. Your grandparents needed to learn to type and read. Your parents needed to learn PowerPoint and browse the web. Your children will build castles and teleport between virtual spaces. VR will not replace the real world and our humanity; it will enhance it.

Index

making 125
moving, in direction 126
moving, starting 130, 131
moving, stopping 130, 131
passing through solid objects,
    avoiding 127-129
small objects, stepping over 130
uneven terrain, handling 130
Flickr pool
  URL 222
frames per second (FPS) 55
functions 65

G

gallery exhibit room, building in Blender
  about 176
  ceiling 181-183
  walls 176-180
gallery room model, assembling in Unity
  about 184
  artwork rig, creating 185-188
  exhibition plan 188-190
  gallery room structure 184, 185
game element UI
  about 82
  defining 93-96
game mechanics 6
games
  versus applications 6-9
Gizmo 20
GLAM
  URL 44
globes 220, 221
glTF
  URL 44
Google Cardboard
  URL 5
Google Cardboard players 245, 246
Google play, for Cardboard app
  URL 6
Google Project Tango
  URL 8
GoPro® 11
Graphical user interface (GUI) 81
graphics processing unit (GPU) 4

H

Hand tool 22
head-mounted display (HMD)
  about 4
  desktop VR 4
  mobile VR 5
  types 4
headshots
  implementing 156-160
High Fidelity
  URL 44
HoloLens 5
Home Styler
  URL 176
HTC/Valve Vive 4
human trampoline
  about 162
  like brick 162
  like character 163-166

I

implementation and content, optimization
  about 198
  lighting effects 199
  models, simplifying 198
  objects to be drawn, limiting 199
  scripts, optimizing 200
  shadow performance 199
  texture maps, using 198, 199
Indicatrix, Tissot
  URL 219
info bubble
  about 82
  defining 96-99
infographics
  defining 215-217
in-game dashboard 82
in-game dashboard, with input events
  button, highlighting 106-108
  buttons, activating from script 104, 105
  Clicker class, using 108, 109
  clicking, to select 108, 109
  dashboard, creating with buttons 100-102
  defining 99, 100

Thank you for buying
Unity Virtual Reality Projects

About Packt Publishing

Packt, pronounced 'packed', published its first book, *Mastering phpMyAdmin for Effective MySQL Management*, in April 2004, and subsequently continued to specialize in publishing highly focused books on specific technologies and solutions.

Our books and publications share the experiences of your fellow IT professionals in adapting and customizing today's systems, applications, and frameworks. Our solution-based books give you the knowledge and power to customize the software and technologies you're using to get the job done. Packt books are more specific and less general than the IT books you have seen in the past. Our unique business model allows us to bring you more focused information, giving you more of what you need to know, and less of what you don't.

Packt is a modern yet unique publishing company that focuses on producing quality, cutting-edge books for communities of developers, administrators, and newbies alike. For more information, please visit our website at www.packtpub.com.

About Packt Open Source

In 2010, Packt launched two new brands, Packt Open Source and Packt Enterprise, in order to continue its focus on specialization. This book is part of the Packt Open Source brand, home to books published on software built around open source licenses, and offering information to anybody from advanced developers to budding web designers. The Open Source brand also runs Packt's Open Source Royalty Scheme, by which Packt gives a royalty to each open source project about whose software a book is sold.

Writing for Packt

We welcome all inquiries from people who are interested in authoring. Book proposals should be sent to author@packtpub.com. If your book idea is still at an early stage and you would like to discuss it first before writing a formal book proposal, then please contact us; one of our commissioning editors will get in touch with you.

We're not just looking for published authors; if you have strong technical skills but no writing experience, our experienced editors can help you develop a writing career, or simply get some additional reward for your expertise.

Unity 4.x Cookbook

ISBN: 978-1-84969-042-3   Paperback: 386 pages

Over 100 recipes to spice up your Unity skills

1. A wide range of topics are covered, ranging in complexity, offering something for every Unity 4 game developer.

2. Every recipe provides step-by-step instructions, followed by an explanation of how it all works, and alternative approaches or refinements.

3. Book developed with the latest version of Unity (4.x).

Unity AI Programming Essentials

ISBN: 978-1-78355-355-6   Paperback: 162 pages

Use Unity3D, a popular game development ecosystem, to add realistic AI to your games quickly and effortlessly

1. Implement pathfinding, pathfollowing, and use navigation mesh generation to move your AI characters within the game environment.

2. Use behaviour trees to design logic for your game characters and make them "think".

3. A practical guide that will not only cover the basics of AI frameworks but also will teach how to customize them.

Learning Unity Physics

ISBN: 978-1-78355-369-3   Paperback: 128 pages

Learn to implement Physics in interactive development using the powerful components of Unity3D

1. Learn how to utilize the robust features of Unity3D to develop physics-based interactive applications and games.

2. Optimize your application performance while using physics in Unity3D.

3. An easy-to-follow guide accompanied by examples, which will help developers to learn and apply physics to games.

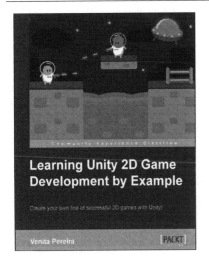

Learning Unity 2D Game Development by Example

ISBN: 978-1-78355-904-6   Paperback: 266 pages

Create your own line of successful 2D games with Unity!

1. Dive into 2D game development with no previous experience.

2. Learn how to use the new Unity 2D toolset.

3. Create and deploy your very own 2D game with confidence.

Please check **www.PacktPub.com** for information on our titles

Made in the USA
Middletown, DE
10 September 2016